W0114436

TOUCH ME, I'M SICK

TOUCH ME, I'M SICK

A MEMOIR *in* ESSAYS

MARGEAUX FELDMAN

BEACON PRESS, BOSTON

BEACON PRESS
Boston, Massachusetts
www.beacon.org

Beacon Press books
are published under the auspices of
the Unitarian Universalist Association of Congregations.

28 27 26 25   8 7 6 5 4 3 2 1

This book is printed on acid-free paper that meets the uncoated paper
ANSI/NISO specifications for permanence as revised in 1992.

Text design and composition by Kim Arney

*Library of Congress Cataloging-in-Publication
Data is available for this title.*
ISBN: 978-0-8070-1975-7; e-book: 978-0-8070-1977-1;
audiobook: 978-0-8070-2232-0

The authorized representative in the EU for product safety and
compliance is Easy Access System Europe 16879218, Mustamäe tee 50,
10621 Tallinn, Estonia: http://beacon.org/eu-contact

CONTENTS

PRELUDE

You're sixteen when you lose your voice. For weeks at a time, you're unable to speak. The only sound that leaves your mouth is a cough that is unrelenting. You're haunted by a scene at the lake. You've taken a walk with a family friend, a man who could be your surrogate father. Suddenly, he's pulled you close to him and is trying to kiss you. You resist. And, eventually, you manage to push him away.

You try telling your parents what happened, but no one believes you and this man continues to visit your home. When he leaves, so too does your voice. But your parents fail to notice this correlation. As you cough and cough and cough, they become concerned. A psychoanalyst is called to come and see you. He's a family friend. Before he can figure out what's wrong with you, your voice returns and the cough disappears.

The lake scene continues to haunt you. A year later, when your symptoms return, and you lose consciousness, the psychoanalyst is called once again. You'll be diagnosed as a hysteric. He will eventually realize that this scene at the lake was a site of trauma for you (that, in fact, this isn't the first time this man has attempted to kiss you; trauma upon trauma). But the psychoanalyst can't wrap his head around your psychosomatic response: *You should want this man's advances. You should be flattered by his attention.* After only a few sessions, you tell him that you won't be returning. You refuse to be gaslit by him any further.

Except this isn't your story. This is Dora's story. Or, more accurately, Ida Bauer's story (Dora is the name that Freud gives her). But it could be yours, if you replace a few details.

Fast forward from 1896 to 1999. In your story, the lake becomes a forest. Instead of the old family friend, it's a seventeen-year-old boy. You're fourteen. You've gone to the park by your childhood home, where your former babysitter's son hangs out with some boys a few years older than you. They get you high. Then one of them takes you into the forest. He's not interested in kissing you. Instead, he pulls down your pants and pulls you onto his lap. The pain so sharp it takes your breath away. That is not the only thing it takes away from you that night.

Instead of a cough, a rash spreads like wildfire over your legs. Eczema. The etymology of eczema means something thrown out by heat. Trauma as heat. Eczema as that which is thrown out of the body, externalizing that which is internal.

Like Dora, you also cannot speak. You don't yet understand that there's a word for what happened to you in the woods that night. Four letters haunt you and take up residence in your body. The body, it turns out, always knows before the mind is able to reckon. Even if you did have the language, you know that you cannot tell your father. There will be punishment. He will blame you for what happened and keep you under lock and key. You're poor, and so there is no psychoanalyst to call. You remain silent. While your body continues to speak for you.

TOUCH ME, I'M SICK

In many ways, I've known sickness my whole life. Born with eczema that covered my arms and legs in red, rashy welts, peaking as a teenager and returning, uninvited, throughout my adulthood. As a teen, I had regular tonsil infections, two strains of mononucleosis at the same time—"I've never seen this before," remarked my doctor—and the norovirus. In my thirties, a friend who'd known me since undergrad told me, "I'm not sure I've ever seen you not sick for more than a couple of weeks."

Sickness didn't just take up residence in my body. It inhabited my home too. When I was ten, my dad and mom sat my brother and me down to inform us that my mom had cervical cancer. Radiation hadn't worked. Now, they'd start chemo, and my mom's illness would become visible to us all. Over that year, we'd visit her in hospital rooms, and I'd tell her all about my dance recitals and the boys I had crushes on. One day, we sat in a hospital room with her oncologist, as he told us that my mom had just a few months left to live. She moved home and we turned our living room into her sick room, and it is here that she will die. One night I'm sitting with her on the couch watching television when she turns to me and asks for more strawberries. "Mom, we ate all of the strawberries last week." "Oh." She paused. "Right. Of course." I watched her deteriorate in front of me as the pain meds and the cancer left her confused. Time all out of joint.

About a month before her death, my aunt, uncle, and cousin drove up and across the border from Connecticut, and my other aunt and

3

uncle drove down from Barrie for one last night together as a family. We looked at old slides of my mom and her sisters living abroad in Europe when they were kids. And then we all paused on one slide: a photo of my mother when she was twelve or thirteen, head cocked slightly to the side, a defiant but playful look on her face. It could have been me—the resemblance was uncanny. After my mother died, my aunt sent me a print of that photo. I keep it at my altar.

That same night, my cousin and I performed a few dances we'd made up to songs from *A Chorus Line*, including "Dance 10, Looks 3," also called "Tits and Ass." We wore bicycle helmets in lieu of top hats, and our family members are pictured laughing to the point of tears. In one of my favorite photos from that night, my mom is sitting on the couch in a lavender T-shirt, blanket wrapped around her, my brother and dad on each side. The bones in her face protrude, making her already tiny body all the more skeletal. But she's smiling as she looks at me. I can see her joy through the sickness.

The next day we walked to the park near my house, and my mom and her two sisters sat down on a bench for a photograph. Years later, on the twentieth anniversary of her death, I decided to make a shrine. As I went through old photographs, I discovered that picture—and also, an earlier photo, taken on that same bench maybe three years before. I placed these two photos together, like in a flip-book, and glued them to the cardboard box that is my shrine. The earlier photo feels like a premonition.

Not long after her death, my father started to drop things. A cup slipping out of his hand and shattering on the kitchen floor. He'd go to see his doctor and then a neurologist. No one could tell him what was wrong. The muscles in his arms started to atrophy from disuse. By the time I was seventeen, I had to help him drive: my hands on the steering wheel when we had to make a sharp turn. At my high school graduation, he attempted to jump down into what we called "the pit" in our gymnasium. Without the weight of his upper arms, he fell and landed face down on the floor. As the people around us gasped and ran over to help him up, I stood there mortified while he smiled and tried to shrug it off. By age eighteen, I was feeding, bathing, and clothing him.

Eventually, he'd get a diagnosis: a rare form of Lou Gehrig's disease. Also known as amyotrophic lateral sclerosis, ALS is a motor neuron disease in which your brain stops sending signals to different parts of your body that it's time to move. Eventually, due to lack of movement, muscle tissue deteriorates, and parts of your body stop functioning permanently. ALS usually starts in the arms or legs, what doctors call limb onset. Once those parts of your body have atrophied, the disease moves inward to your diaphragm, making it hard to expand the lungs fully with each breath; it impacts your ability to swallow and eat, and eventually even your eyes become stagnant. No ability to move, speak, or communicate. There is no cure for ALS. You get it, and within two to four years you are dead. Only 10 percent of cases live longer than ten years. My dad was one of those cases: He lived with ALS for twenty years.

The year before his death, in 2016, sickness entered my life like a wrecking ball. First it was a spike in my anxiety that struck me, making it difficult to get out of bed in the morning. Then it was a UTI, which led to a kidney infection. And then a viral sinus infection that lasted three months. After that I had the stomach flu accompanied by a herpes outbreak—the first since I had contracted the virus in 2008. Six months later, when the string of viruses had finished with me, I was utterly exhausted. I got winded making dinner. I slept for fourteen hours a night and napped throughout the day. Then, after two glorious weeks of passable good health, my body started to ache. The kind of aches you get when you're sick, except there was no sneezing, coughing, or other classic cold symptoms. It felt like I'd decided to do the most intense gym workout of my life after a yearlong hiatus, while also coming down with the season's worst flu virus.

My doctor and naturopath didn't have much of a sense of what was wrong, but we had some suspects. First was anemia. But then, when a second round of blood work came back negative, the next suspect was diabetes. That too was ruled out. It's hard to adequately describe my ambivalence at this news: One part of me was happy that I wouldn't be dependent on insulin for the rest of my life. And the other part of me was sad that it wasn't diabetes. Because if it wasn't that, then we still didn't have a culprit. Whatever was making me sick was a fugitive evading capture. We decided that the next step was to see a rheumatologist. I remember opening the letter from the hospital with my appointment date inside. A deep swell of despair moved through my body when I saw that it would be eight months before my appointment: eight more months before any possibility of an answer. While I was grateful for Canada's universal healthcare system, that stretch of time felt interminable. And so, like any good graduate student, I took things into my own hands.

I began to look for books about autoimmune diseases and chronic illness. I'm a literature student critical of the medical-industrial complex, so the books I gravitated toward weren't written by medical health professionals or other experts. I read poems about being sick, essays about the links between chronic pain and trauma, novels about autoimmune diseases with characters that are trying to solve the mystery of a body that has turned against itself. I devoured Porochista Khakpour's *Sick*, picked up Esmé Weuijun Wang's *The Collected Schizophrenias*, read Catherine Lacey's *The Answers,* found my way to Amy Berkowitz's *Tender Points,* and Sarah Manguso's *The Two Kinds of Decay*. I read every essay published in Roxane Gay's Unruly Bodies series. Like Anne Elizabeth Moore, the author of *Body Horror*, I was diagnosing myself by way of literature. It wasn't just that I wanted to solve the mystery of my body. I wanted to feel less alone. *Who else is sick?* I wondered. *Who else feels trapped by their body?* Given that illness is kept out of sight, relegated to the home or the hospital, I knew that it might be hard to find such stories. But I was determined to build a genealogy, to find the many sick mothers of my heart.

This phrase is inspired by Maggie Nelson's reference to "the many gendered mothers of my heart" in her book *The Argonauts*. But this phrasing doesn't belong to Nelson. She notes how she is borrowing it from Dana Ward's poem "A Kentucky of Mothers": "O god save all the many gendered-mothers of my heart, & all the other mothers, who do not need god or savior." Nelson, like Ward, wants us to read the word *mother* capaciously. It is not just the familial mother that they're talking about; nor is the mother necessarily a woman. For Nelson, "the many-gendered mothers" of her heart include the artists and theorists and philosophers and educators who have, whether intentionally or unintentionally, taught her something. Among all the mothers I found while reading, I found myself returning to Freud's Dora. The originary sick mother, if there ever was one.

In the introduction to *Dora*, editor Philip Rieff describes Dora's case history as follows: "The sick daughter has a sick father, who has a sick mistress, who has a sick husband, who proposes himself to the sick daughter as her lover." The sickness referenced here is both literal and metaphorical: The father is sick with tuberculosis and syphilis and the mother suffers from abdominal pains. But Rieff also invokes sickness in another sense, denoting that which is morally repugnant. Mistresses and lovers corrupt the scene just as much as physical ailments do. Sickness is never neutral.

In Freud's case study, we're taken back to 1898, the year in which a family friend, Herr K., propositions the sixteen-year-old Dora in front of the lake near her family's summer resort. Shortly after, Dora can't stop coughing and loses her voice. Additionally, Dora has been "a source of heavy trials for her parents," Freud remarks, with her "low spirits and an alteration in her character." Dora's father calls upon Freud to determine the source of her illness. Freud believes that Dora needs psychological treatment for these physical symptoms, but the attack passes, and Dora's family believes that all is well again. The following year, however, Dora's sick again, this time with a "feverish disorder which was diagnosed at the time as appendicitis." It's not until the following year that Dora's symptoms return, she loses consciousness, and she becomes Freud's patient.

Dora displays all the characteristics of hysteria: a psychic trauma, a conflict of affects, and a disturbance in the sphere of sexuality. At first Freud assumes that the scene at the lake might be the site of the psychic trauma. But he'll soon learn of an earlier encounter between Herr K. and Dora. We're told that at the age of fourteen, Dora found herself alone with Herr K. while watching a church festival. Herr K. pulled Dora toward him and kissed her. Instead of reading this as a scene of sexual assault, Freud is confused by Dora's response. "This was surely just the situation to call up a distinct feeling of sexual excitement in a girl of fourteen who had never before been approached. But Dora had at that moment a violent feeling of disgust, tore herself free from the man, and hurried past him to the staircase and from there to the street door."

For Freud, Dora's feelings of disgust and revulsion are the markers of desire gone wrong, and so it is not surprising that Freud pathologizes

Dora's response. For Freud, Herr K.'s kiss should produce sexual excitement, but instead Dora feels it as "preponderantly or exclusively unpleasant." This reversal of affect, with its excessive intensity, marks Dora as a hysteric. Hysterics are girls and women with a range of undiagnosable symptoms, yes.* But they are also marked by having all of the wrong feelings: feelings that are either excessive or totally absent.

Despite Dora's response to the kiss, Freud will go on to claim that Dora is in love with her assailant. Upon interpreting her aphonia, or loss of voice, Freud argues that Dora gave up speaking when Herr K. was gone because she could not speak to him. In a footnote, Freud describes this translation of affect (the feeling of missing Herr K.) to somatic response as a "flight into illness." Freud's turn of phrase highlights precisely how, when in danger, our fight or flight response is activated. For most people, the fight or flight response—or the sympathetic nervous system—comes into action when we're faced with a real danger and we need to determine how best to respond. Swerving to avoid a car accident? That's the flight response. Shooting when shot at? That's the fight response. If fight or flight aren't options, our parasympathetic nervous system is activated, and we freeze or submit. In other words, we shut down, play dead.

The flight into illness is, as Freud explains, "economically the most convenient solution when there is a mental conflict." Authors and social critics Barbara Ehrenreich and Deirdre English make a similar claim in their 1970s manifesto, *Complaints and Disorders: The Sexual Politics of Sickness*: "In the epidemic of hysteria, women were both accepting their inherent 'sickness' *and* finding a way to rebel against an intolerable social role." In a world in which women are meant to feel desire when any man kisses them, there's no way to

---

*As a nonbinary femme currently in their "boy with cleavage era," I want to make it clear that throughout this book I will be using the terms *girl* and *woman* capaciously. I speak of these gendered identities along the same lines as Johanna Hedva in their essay "Sick Woman Theory": "Though the identity of 'woman' has erased and excluded many (especially women of color and trans/nonbinary/genderfluid people), I choose to use it because it still represents the uncared for, the secondary, the oppressed, the non-, the un-, the less-than."

resolve this conflict. Sickness becomes a means of escape. The desire to avoid nonconsensual touch can, in other words, make one sick.

I can't help but wonder if there's another reading of Dora's aphonia. It would be much too dangerous to speak of these assaults while Herr K. is present to refute them. His leaving, then, would provide the ideal opportunity for Dora to tell her parents what happened. Her loss of voice would appear to be inconveniently timed: a cruel joke that makes it impossible for Dora to speak her trauma. This inability to speak is actually a protective mechanism, the work of Dora's parasympathetic nervous system, or the freeze response. For even if she could speak of her trauma, Dora will not be believed. And so this loss of voice is her body's way of protecting her from the double trauma of having her family disbelieve her.

As someone who couldn't speak of my own trauma, more than one hundred years later, I understand the impulse. I told no one about the rape in the woods. In part because it would take me another decade to realize that it was rape. But I also knew that I wouldn't receive the support I needed from my father. It's possible he might have believed me. I carry that hope inside me, like one shields a candle flame from the wind. But even if he had, he wouldn't have known what to do with the information. It was better to remain silent than to burden him.

There's another way to read this loss of voice: as an act of resistance. In *Disquieting: Essays on Silence*, poet and academic Cynthia Cruz argues that silence is a form of resistance. Cruz explains she's been haunted by a question: "How does one speak when one is weighed down with the incomprehensibility of the world?" For Cruz, systemic oppression "added to experiences of trauma on top of trauma makes for a kind of inability to speak." This speechlessness is "often driven into the body as illness." Silence becomes a mode of resistance, "the refusal to conform." Dora's loss of voice, then, is a mode of resistance and an acknowledgment that any attempt to speak her trauma will result in silence anyway.

Remembering that Dora's symptoms began at a much earlier age, I believe that Freud and Breuer were right when they proposed in their preliminary statement in *Studies on Hysteria* that neuroses emerge when it's not possible for the subject to adequately respond to the psychical trauma they've experienced. Breuer and Freud explain that "the nature of the trauma precluded a reaction, as in the seemingly irreplaceable loss of a loved one, or because social circumstances made a reaction impossible, or because things were involved that the patient wanted to forget." Dora's loss of voice is the somatic response to the fact that "social circumstances made a reaction impossible." And so it is best that we try to forget.

If only Freud had reached this hypothesis. Unfortunately, the psychoanalyst moves away from the recognition that Dora was sexually assaulted to claim that Dora's hysteria is caused by her desire "to touch her father's heart and to detach him from Frau K." Here, real sexual abuse becomes a sexual fantasy. But Freud will also dismiss this hypothesis in favor of another, one that removes all men from the equation: Dora is actually in love with Frau K., and her queer desire is the source of her illness. Freud is never able to fully prove these claims, however, as Dora terminates her work with the psychoanalyst without warning at the start of their third session together. In a move that feels like Freud's only avenue to punishing the disobedient Dora, he will conclude, in "An Autobiographical Study," that he was "at last obliged to recognize that these scenes of seduction had never taken place, and that they were only fantasies which my patients had made up."

This conclusion not only saves Freud from the embarrassment of being undermined by Dora; it also protects him from the fallout that would surely come from his hypothesis in *The Aetiology of Hysteria* that "at the bottom of every case of hysteria there are *one or more occurrences of premature sexual experience*, occurrences which belong to the earliest years of childhood." Trauma specialist Judith Herman explains that Freud was "increasingly troubled by the radical social implications of his hypothesis." She writes: "Hysteria was so common among women that if his patients' stories were true, and if his theory were correct, he would be forced to conclude that what he called 'perverted acts against children' were endemic, not only among the proletariat of Paris, where he had first studied hysteria, but also among the respectable bourgeois families of Vienna, where he had established this practice. This idea was simply unacceptable. It was beyond credibility." So how does Freud rescue himself from proclaiming that young women were living in rape culture? He'll propose that hysterics *imagined* these scenes. The individual is thus the one to blame and the one in need of a cure. Years before the term *gaslighting* was coined, Freud was already putting it into practice: Rape is transformed into seduction. And it is Dora who is punished for rebelling.

I can't help but wonder: What would have happened if instead of labeling Dora's bodily response to this trauma as pathology, we returned to the original meaning of disease? Obsolete meaning: An absence of ease; to feel uneasiness or discomfort; but also, inconvenience, annoyance. Another obsolete meaning that cannot and should not be ignored: Molestation. To do disease to, to molest. What if we could see how, through the loss of her voice, Dora's body was manifesting the *dis-ease* of being a woman living under the patriarchy?

Tied to the history of rape culture—and one of its sustaining forces—is the pathologization of women's feelings. A woman feels afraid when a man walks behind her at night: That's irrational. A woman feels angry when being catcalled: She's a bitch. A woman refuses to smile when commanded by a stranger: There must be something wrong with her. Let's rewrite these examples of pathologization: A woman feels disease (discomfort) when a man walks behind her at night; a woman feels disease (molested) when being catcalled; a woman feels disease (annoyance) when being told to smile. How and why did these feelings of dis-ease become a disease? The short answer: #patriarchy.

The *DSM-V* will remove hysteria as an official diagnosis in 1980, the same year that it adds post-traumatic stress disorder. While the term *hysteria* can no longer be found in the pages of the *DSM*, the specter of hysteria can be found in the treatment of girls and women who live with trauma and/or chronic illness. Put another way: The story of chronic illness is also the story of hysteria and trauma. It is not the case that all stories of chronic illness are also stories of trauma, and, at the same time, the connection between trauma and chronic illness is becoming much more widely recognized by those specializing in trauma resolution.

Before I learned about the link between trauma and chronic illness from medical professionals, it was brought to my attention through literature. My return to Dora wasn't accidental. Another sick mother of my heart helped me get there. In her poetry collection *Tender Points*, Amy Berkowitz tells the reader, "As I read more about the history of invisible illness, I'm surprised and amused to diagnose myself with hysteria." But of course, hysteria isn't the official diagnosis. Berkowitz has fibromyalgia, an illness characterized by chronic pain, fatigue, and brain fog. The best hypothesis is that fibromyalgia is a chronic illness that begins with an overactive sympathetic nervous system that refuses to turn off when it is time to sleep.

When you live with trauma, the nervous system doesn't understand that the danger is over. And so it stays on alert in order to protect you, thereby inhibiting deep sleep. This lack of sleep sets off a chain reaction that prevents adequate growth hormone release, which interferes with muscle tissue repair, and leads to muscle pain. As a response to this pain, muscles and their surrounding connective tissues are chronically tightened to respond to danger and become painful. The nervous system becomes overwhelmed and hyperreactive to pain.

Berkowitz recalls her relief upon receiving this diagnosis, but she also notes: "I know the true name of this disease—My Body Is Haunted by a Certain Trauma—so I don't care what other name it has, so long as it has one. Something to point to. Something to call it." I read her words and am reminded of Freud's famous proclamation that "hysterics suffer for the most part from reminiscences." Hysterics, in other words, are haunted by a certain trauma.

Medea of Greek mythology, haunted by a man who used her and disposed of her in his pursuit of the Golden Fleece. The unnamed woman in Charlotte Perkins Gilman's infamous novella *The Yellow Wallpaper*, haunted by the trauma of living under the patriarchy and further traumatized by being confined by doctor and husband to a room until she is deemed rational again. *A Streetcar Named Desire*'s Blanche DuBois—haunted by a husband who died by suicide and her sister's husband, very much alive, who abuses her physically, psychologically, and sexually. Nancy in the 1990s cult classic *The Craft*, haunted by the boys who slept with her and then called her a slut afterward. Britney Spears, haunted by the trauma of being a child star, controlled by a manipulative father and the manipulative men that populate the music industry.

My search for the many sick mothers of my heart has led me back here, to the stories of the hysterics I love so dearly. I'm startled by the revelation that I never processed the uncanny similarities between their stories and my own. It might seem like a mere coincidence. In my attempt to make meaning out of what I refused to acknowledge each time I read the histories of Freud's hysterics, I may be guilty of over-reading. But then what do I make of the fact that Jean-Martin Charcot, the French neurologist who became famous for his work on hysteria at the Salpêtrière, was the one to discover amyotrophic lateral sclerosis—the disease that killed my father. In fact, Charcot would not have discovered it without dissecting the brains of his hysterics.

☾

There's another similarity between myself and the hysterics, one that has felt much harder to acknowledge: We've all been sexually assaulted. In the summer of 1999, when I was fourteen years old, I started going down to a park near my house where a group of older boys hung out, smoking cigarettes and joints. I knew one of them: He was the son of my old babysitter. I'd stand around with these boys, in a cropped tank top and extreme low-rise flared jeans, hips visible, and soak in their attention. While all adolescents are awkward, I was not deemed to be one of the pretty ones. Boys liked to hang out with me in private while publicly dating the popular girls. I learned early on to accept whatever slivers of attention I received. I was so thirsty for attention; I wanted to feel like I too could be desirable. Night after night, I'd let these boys get me high, blowing me supers so that our lips almost touched. One night, we must have walked into the woods adjacent to the park. All I can remember is that one minute I'm sitting on the lap of a boy I liked, and the next minute he's inside of me. The pain was so sharp—I was still a virgin—and after a couple of thrusts I asked him to stop. Thankfully, he did. But the damage was done.

I'll continue to see that boy, whom we'll call A.J., for the rest of the summer and into the fall of grade nine. Seventeen and beautiful, A.J. had blue eyes and blond hair. In the one photo of him I kept in my journal, he is wearing baggy jeans, boxers exposed, and a baseball cap with a wide rim. No shirt. Six-pack visible. In the photo he is looking directly at the camera, daring me to take his photo. Beside him, I've written the word *ASSHOLE*.

The fact that his photo remained in my journal is a testament to my inability to acknowledge the truth: that he'd raped me. He'll come to my house with his friends after midnight and I'll sneak out to get high and pool hop. A.J. tells me that he doesn't have a girlfriend. That the girl who stands across the street from his house, glaring at me, is an ex. In his darkened basement, I'll lay there, passively, while he enters me again. Too high and too sad to say no. Maybe I'm repeating the original trauma in an attempt to assert some sense of agency. If I let it happen again, it's as though the first time couldn't have been rape.

It didn't help that I had no language to describe what had happened. It would be years before I learned that rape happens when one is too high or drunk to consent. And it would still take many years after that, into my early twenties, before I'd use the word rape to describe what happened to me. I'd done a fabulous job of gaslighting myself.

In many ways, the rape wasn't the most traumatic part of what happened that summer. Right before I'm set to begin high school, a rumor spread throughout my suburban town: I had slept with A.J. I'm a slut. My two best friends abandon me after hearing the rumors. It turns out that they want to be popular, and you can't be popular with a friend like me. I will start high school totally alone and branded. Walking through the hallway to my next class, I will hear the loud booming voice of a teenager boy "SLUT! WHORE!" and watch as everyone turns to look at me.

But that isn't the worst of it. At the end of the day, I am stopped by a group of girls in the parking lot as I try to walk home. They surround me, their faces mere inches from my own, and ask if I like being a homewrecker and a slut. I'd stand there frozen, barely breathing, praying that they wouldn't become violent—and thankfully, they never did. (Later, I am surprised and not surprised to learn, upon reading Leora Tanenbaum's book *Slut!*, that the term *slut* "is typically applied by females to other females" and by those who are also likely sexually active. That summer, I would hear stories about the cool girls giving blow jobs to boys at parties. And yet they were exempt from being called sluts.)

Once these girls let me go, I would take refuge at home (though that space was another filled with trauma and a different bully: my father). I am so deeply grateful that I grew up without social media. I resonate with Melissa Febos's words in her book of essays *Girlhood*: "When I imagine there having been an internet, social media, or smartphones when I was an adolescent, the future—my present—goes hazy. It's tempting to believe in my own underlying integrity at that age, to believe that I would have prevailed even then to whatever extent I have, but in truth I suspect I might not have survived at all." In 2016, the Centers for Disease Control and Prevention (CDC) shared that, between 1999 and 2014, suicide rates rose 200 percent among girls aged ten to fourteen. While I felt so alone at the time, I now know that two out of five girls will be called a slut in junior high or high school. This information produces ambivalent feelings inside of me: relief that I wasn't the only one and grief at this kinship.

Of course, teen girls aren't the only ones subjected to slut-shaming in the wake of sexual assault. In my thirties, I'd read the news about the Jian Ghomeshi trial happening in Toronto. Ghomeshi was a famous radio host who'd been charged with four counts of sexual assault, and one count of overcoming resistance by choking. During the trial, his defense attorney, Marie Henein, interrogated actress Lucy DeCoutere, one of Ghomeshi's victims.

Henein torn apart DeCoutere's credibility when she presented the court with a series of emails written by DeCoutere in the hours following the assault. In one email she wrote: "You kicked my ass last night and that makes me want to fuck your brains out." This evidence not only called into question whether the sex was consensual; it framed DeCoutere as a slut, as someone who "wanted it." I am not surprised to learn that those who often receive the label of slut are those who have been raped or sexually assaulted. It didn't matter that DeCoutere's response was that she had blamed herself for what had happened and was afraid of Ghomeshi, so this was her attempt to placate him. DeCoutere's credibility shot, Ghomeshi went free.

It is all too common for women to bear the consequences of both sexual assault and slut-shaming. My experiences led me to believe that it was dangerous to talk about sex. In my early twenties, I'd sit with my two best friends as they talked about the very consensual sex they were having. While they shared their stories, I sat there frozen. Sometimes I'd have to get up and leave the room. It will take me until my late twenties before I am able to tell them about the amazing sex I'm having in the first non-abusive relationship I will experience in my adult life. I can tell that my best friends are shocked and amazed that I am talking about sex, but they don't say a word, as though I am a deer that will startle if they draw attention to this moment. Despite my interest in exploring kink, I can only do so with those who I know. As soon as I put kink on my dating profiles, I receive messages from strangers asking me what I am into, and I go mute. They unmatch from me. And the feeling of shame I have around being a feminist who can't talk about sex only increases.

There are so many layers of shame that I've had to peel back. Shame built up during all the years I didn't realize I had been raped. Shame from gaslighting myself: It couldn't have been rape because I continued to see A.J. Eventually, I'd come to understand why I did. In *Healing the Fragmented Selves of Trauma Survivors*, trauma specialist and therapist Janina Fisher explains, "Trauma survivors all too often develop other symptoms that represent neurobiologically regulating attempts to cope with the trauma," including reenactment. Other survivor strategies include self-injury (the dull razor in my bathroom when I am eighteen); suicidality (I told myself I wasn't suicidal because "I could never kill myself" and leave my family to lose another family member. Such thoughts, it turns out, are called suicidal ideation); risk-taking (stealing, hanging out with people in gangs, staying out all night, having unprotected sex); caretaking and self-sacrifice ("let me put your needs before mine, always"); revictimization (experiencing assault after assault, abusive relationship after abusive relationship); and addictive behavior (using substances every day from ages fourteen to twenty-three).

"All of these behaviors," writes Fisher, "represent different ways of modulating a dysregulated nervous system and preparing for the next threat." These attempts at self-regulation are all too often read as pathological and used to discredit survivors. Fisher notes, "It would be rare in the mental health treatment world to think of these symptoms as adaptive strategies made possible by the body's instinctive survival defenses. But from a neurobiologically informed perspective, they are 'survival resources,' ways that the body and mind adapted for optimal survival in a dangerous world." Fisher's non-pathologizing approach enables me to feel compassion for that fourteen-year-old who'd subject themselves again and again to the same acts of violence with A.J.: get high, have unprotected nonconsensual sex, be ghosted.

Fisher is not surprised that "trauma and self-destructive behavior go hand-in-hand." These acts are "congruent with past experiences of being treated as an object whose welfare doesn't matter, whose life has no purpose other than to be used." I wonder what might happen if we stopped viewing these behaviors as signs of pathology and see how they're valid responses to living under rape culture, which teaches cis men that it's not only okay, but expected, for them to use women and femmes. It has taken so many years of therapy to understand that I didn't deserve to be used—that, in fact, I deserved so much more than what was offered to me.

I wish I could say that I was sexually assaulted only once, but it was just the beginning. After the rape, I would have sex with any boy who wanted to: always high, drunk, or both. I have very few memories from these years of my life, thanks to dissociation and blacking out from different combinations of alcohol, ecstasy, speed, K, cocaine, or whatever mysterious substance was offered to me. Just fragments: a bathroom floor, pants down but the rest of our clothes on; Christmas lights in a bedroom, the room spiraling thanks to weed laced with PCP, and the sex that followed after I puked; group sex with two boys and a close friend one night when I was barely fifteen. The sloppy kisses of one of the boys, who I didn't want to have sex with but did anyway because I didn't want to kill the buzz; my friend's boyfriend fucking me doggystyle behind the roller-skating rink. There were a few boys who actually liked me, who were proud to be seen with me in public. But their interest in me was too overwhelming. It repulsed me. Our relationships never lasted long.

At the age of nineteen, I started a relationship with Ashley, and she would choke me and slap my face during sex without my consent. Even after I told her that I didn't want her to do that, it would happen again. Consequently, my desire for her waned. When she would start to kiss me with the hunger of wanting more, I would take on the position of the hysteric and tell her that I was tired or feeling unwell: *Do not touch me, I am sick.* This attempt to protect myself backfired. She would get out of bed, head downstairs, and ignore me for hours, often leaving me to spend the night alone. The belief that I couldn't have connection without sacrificing my safety only got stronger, until sex and danger became so intertwined that they were indistinguishable. Eventually, the assaults from Ashley stopped. I can't remember a timeline here, but I know that we remained together for some time after the abuse stopped and broke up amicably after three years of being together. More than a decade later, I see that Ashley has "Super Liked" me while swiping on Tinder. I freeze, horrified. There was never any apology for the harm she had caused me. No acknowledgment. No repair. After a decade of silence, a bright blue star beside a picture of her face. How could she do this? How did she not remember?

When chronic pain and dissociation disrupted my life, I'd just returned from a research trip in New Orleans. While there, I went on some dates with Nate, a man I'd matched with on the same dating app. We had the most incredible sex and intellectually engaging conversations, and we started to develop feelings. This was against the rules of Nate's open relationship, in which sex was allowed but feelings were forbidden. Before we had to reckon with the emotional bond that was forming, we met in a hotel room on his final night living in New Orleans. Sitting up with his back against the headboard, me riding on top of him, Nate asked if he could put his hand around my throat and I nodded. This was the first and only time I'd allowed someone to touch me that way since my ex had done so without my consent, almost a decade before. It felt so healing to reclaim this act. A hand around a throat didn't need to belong to the territory of trauma. Or so I thought.

We continued talking after that night and began to plan trips to visit each other. Then, one day, Nate told me that he couldn't talk to me anymore. He was developing feelings for me. This sudden break in our connection plummeted me into traumatic reliving. I remember waking up in the middle of the night, certain that I needed to book a flight to Chicago and find him, somehow, without knowing where he lived. I would show up and he would see that we had to be together. But I couldn't afford to travel. I had to let him go. In the days and weeks after this ending, I'd walk the streets of Toronto in a daze, feeling like I was on the verge of tears. I knew panic attacks and intrusive thoughts all too well, but I was unfamiliar with the disembodied feeling that I was floating above myself, disconnected from the world I lived in. Later, I'd learn that this was dissociation—and that it was actually a lot more familiar than I'd recognized at the time, for I'd been dissociating my whole life, and, in particular, whenever I had sex.

That these months of dissociation coincided with the emergence of chronic fatigue and pain no longer confuses me. My body was doing everything in its power to protect me from the trauma that had been triggered by what happened in New Orleans, all of the trauma that had come before it. I'd trusted someone to do something so intimate and terrifying to me, and then he ended things. It felt like an abandonment. As I went to doctor's appointment after doctor's appointment, peeling myself from my couch as my body screamed in pain from every joint, I found a somatic therapist who specialized in complex trauma. Together, we'd start to process two decades' worth of trauma and the sickness it had brought with it: all of the ways in which touch has made me sick.

When I started my PhD, I knew that I wanted to talk about teen girls and their ability to sit with ambivalence and revel in excess. This line of interest led, very quickly, to the hysterics. Excess and ambivalence, which were once read as symptoms of hysteria, have been reclaimed by fourth-wave feminists and artists such as Petra Collins. Collins's first big claim to fame came when she was asked to design a T-shirt for American Apparel. Entitled "Menstruation Power," Collins's T-shirt depicts a femme hand with long painted nails gently touching the clitoris, legs spread, pubic hair, menstrual blood, and all. Her T-shirt was called "vile" and "disturbing."

Continuing in this tradition, Collins launched an exhibit entitled *Discharge* in 2014. The exhibit uses a variety of mediums to discuss the sexuality of those assigned female at birth: from neon lights that say, again and again, "I love it, I love it, I love it when you eat it," to sculptures of beautiful panties stained with menstrual blood. Instead of feeling humiliated or disgusted, Collins revels in her secretions. And her pleasure is excessive. It's not just one pair of panties, but many. It's not just one iteration of "I love it when you eat it," but ten—with "I love it" repeated twenty-two times.

Collins's most explicit engagement with the legacy of hysteria came in her 2016 exhibition, *24 Hour Psycho,* in which she displayed ten large-scale portraits of her friends' faces while crying. In an interview with *Dazed Magazine,* Collins explains her motivations for the project: "Women's emotions are constantly labeled. Any slight deviation from 'pleasantness,' and we are labeled as hysterical. When we are angry, sad, depressed, or manic, we are immediately seen as unfeminine, or ugly, or weak."

Collins's decision to print these photos on such a large scale—a little over five and a half feet tall and three and a half feet wide—makes the images excessive both in form and in content—evoking the ways in which the feelings of girls and young women have always been "too much." In embracing the hysteric, these women have refused to be isolated, locked away, and silenced. Instead, they've put their trauma on display for all to see. When I see *24 Hour Psycho* in San Francisco, I get my friend to take a photo of me in front of a blue neon light, shaped like a teardrop, enclosing the words *24 HR PSYCHO.* I feel at home.

Reading through the pages of Freud's case study of Dora, you'll find that the word *excessive* and its synonyms come up again and again. There is Dora's "excessively repulsive fantasy"; her "excessive reinforcement"; the "surplusage of intensity" she experiences; and her "excessive overaccentuation." In *Three Essays on the Theory of Sexuality,* Freud categorizes hysterics as "excessively civilized persons," due to the strength of their restrictive forces: shame, morality, and most importantly, disgust. Within the hysteric exists an "exaggerated sexual craving," to borrow Freud's phrasing. He is not the only one to use the language of excess when talking about young girls. In his two-volume treatise published in 1904, American psychologist and educator G. Stanley Hall argues that there is an "excessive unfoldment" for the adolescent girl, in which, "every trait and faculty is liable to exaggeration and excess." Hall tethers excess to sexuality in discussing the excessive frustration or restrainment of sexuality and links excessive menstruation to hysteria. While Freud and Hall marked excess as a negative affective state that is pathological, the work being done by Collins to embrace excess demonstrates that the only thing that makes excess pathological is labeling it as such.

Excess isn't the only symptom of hysteria that's being reclaimed by feminists. Ambivalence has also found itself at the center of fourth-wave feminist art. Jean Laplanche and Jean-Bertrand Pontalis define ambivalence as the "simultaneous existence of contradictory tendencies, attitudes or feelings in relation to a single object, especially the co-existence of love and hate." Ambivalence is such a common experience that countless articles have been written about it—and yet we are deeply uncomfortable with this state of mixed feelings. Perhaps one reason is that we have done a great job of pathologizing ambivalence. In fact, the word was coined by the Swiss psychiatrist Eugen Bleuler in 1910 to denote what he and later psychoanalysts identified as a fundamental symptom or mechanism of schizophrenia. By definition, ambivalence is pathological.

Psychoanalysis has a long history of analyzing the psychic impact of ambivalent feelings upon the subject. Freud is perhaps the best example. In *Becoming Freud: The Making of a Psychoanalyst*, Adam Phillips claims that psychoanalysis brought about the invention of a deeply ambivalent person. In an article for the *London Review of Books*, "Against Self-Criticism," Phillips builds upon this comment, stating, "In Freud's vision we are, above all, ambivalent animals: wherever we hate we love, wherever we love we hate. If someone can satisfy us, they can frustrate us; and if someone can frustrate us we always believe they can satisfy us." But these ambivalent feelings aren't disruptive in and of themselves. Rather, it is the fact that we have somehow internalized a narrative that says: You must only feel positively toward the object of your desire. For Freud, "Thoughts in the unconscious live very comfortably side by side, and even contraries get on together without disputes." It is our inability to accept ambivalence that leads to pathology. There is something liberating, then, in accepting our ambivalent feelings.

Montreal artist Ambivalently Yours first began her project of reclaiming ambivalence on Tumblr in 2012. On her website, AY shares:

> I do not want to tell you how to feel, we are perpetually ambivalent.
> Every feeling has a counter-feeling, a feeling omitted for brevity, a
> feeling appended for homogeneity. We must express ourselves delib-
> erately, honesty only exists in our moments of hesitation.
>
> Every choice is a statement, every statement is an ending. If we
> choose not to choose, the ending keeps beginning. (I have decided not
> to choose, my choice is ambivalence.)

Using soft pastel hues, and pink as her predominant color of choice, AY
takes the teen girl as her subject in her art. I am taken by the intimacy
depicted in her work, which often features conjoined twins, meant to
represent the two sides of our ambivalent feelings, with their arms
wrapped around each other. With words around them declaring "I feel
nothing I feel everything," "I'm not afraid of your emotions," and "We
can heal together," AY's work captures how, when we acknowledge
our ambivalent desires and feelings, we make intimacy possible.

In a collaborative installation entitled *Friendship Is Magic*, Ambivalently Yours teamed up with Clea Felien and Damali Abrams the
Glitter Priestess to explore "how the enthusiasm, language and rituals of girl culture can be used to represent ideas of friendship as a
radical act of resistance in a political climate that is increasingly pro-
moting xenophobia and separatism." Pink balloons hang from the
ceiling and the walls are covered in different sections of floral print
wallpaper, like in a stereotypical girl's bedroom. Pinned to the walls
is art by each of the collaborators. Beside a photo of Abrams and
friends are AY's words that read, "We affectionately called each other
bitches, whores, and sluts so it hurt less when others labeled us that
way" and "softer together." There is barely a space left untouched on
the walls, as visitors are invited to make their own drawings and pin
them up, bringing together excess and ambivalence in all their glory.

I am, frankly, exhausted by the argument that trauma and sickness impede intimacy. What if the qualities that make the hysteric
pathological—a love of ambivalence and excess—can open up other

possibilities for care and interdependence that make life not just possible, but pleasurable? Intimacy is what happens when bodies come together in all of their messiness and ambivalence and are affirmed and cared for.

Intimacy does not have to be threatened by hysteria. In fact, all intimacy is hysterical because intimacy requires that we might be deemed "too much" for someone else. But if we willingly situate our relationships within a landscape of hysterical intimacies, ambivalence and excess and the full spectrum of emotions are welcome: Within this exchange, in which I expose myself before you and you choose to stick around, you celebrate my too muchness—it might even turn you on. When it comes to hysterical intimacies, there's no such thing as oversharing, no pathologization of affects. If what I share "exceeds" the boundaries of what is deemed "normal" or "healthy," you, my intimate person, do not feel that what I've shared is too much. In fact, you'll respond by asking for more and you'll offer yourself up to me, letting me into those dark depths, so that the closeness we foster is built upon a reciprocal exchange. Neither of us is forced to be more or less vulnerable than the other.

I can no longer be in relationships with humans who refuse to be vulnerable or who are so afraid of being "too much" that they cannot show up authentically for our connection. Of course, showing up authentically and vulnerably is easier said than done. In the wake of trauma, our sense of self has been shattered because trauma threatens and destroys our self-worth. To make sense of what happened to us, to regain a sense of control, we blame ourselves: "If [insert bad thing] happened to me, it must be because I'm bad." I get why we do this. Blaming ourselves enables us to feel a sense of control after our autonomy has been taken from us. And we also live in a victim-blaming world. It is a double hit.

We can, however, rebuild a sense of self and reclaim our dignity by sharing our story with others. For rape survivor Susan Brison, the act of telling one's story to another reveals the ways in which "the autonomous self and the relational self are shown to be interdependent, even constitutive of one another." I read her words and I'm reminded of philosopher Judith Butler's *Giving an Account of Oneself*: "When the 'I' seeks to give an account of itself, it can start with itself, but it will find that this self is already implicated in a social temporality that exceeds its own capacities for narration." We are hardwired for connection and are inextricably linked to one another—for better and for worse.

This view of the self as both autonomous and interdependent poses a threat to the late capitalist, neoliberal fantasy of the independent individual. Rejecting the myth of the individual threatens the status quo because it reveals the ways in which, to borrow Johanna Hedva's words in their essay "Sick Woman Theory," it's the world that needs fixing. Hedva describes the impact of the neoliberal, white-supremacist, imperial-capitalist, cisheteropatriarchy when they write: "Sick Woman Theory maintains that the body and mind are sensitive and reactive to regimes of oppression. . . . It is that all of our bodies and minds carry the historical trauma of this, that it is *the world itself* that is making and keeping us sick." Hysterical intimacies reveal the ways in which the oppressions we experience do not come from our individual shortcomings, but rather are the direct result of the structures of oppression that produce great trauma. Hysterical intimacies recognize that interdependence enables us to resist and heal from the systemic and individual traumas that have made us sick. Within the landscape of hysterical intimacies, the sick person receives the care and intimacy they have been denied.

This longing for intimacy, and more specifically touch, is something that Audre Lorde reflects on in *The Cancer Journals*. After having a mastectomy, Lorde writes: "The status of untouchable is a very unreal and lonely one." For Lorde, the status of untouchable protects her as she heals: "It does keep everyone at arm's length, and protects as it insulates." And yet, her desire for touch renders its lack harmful: "You can die of that specialness, of the cold, the isolation. It does not serve living." Lorde thus "began quickly to yearn for the warmth of the fray." While Lorde may have been rendered untouchable for practical reasons here, under the surface of her reflection, of her yearning, is the recognition that sick bodies are always positioned as bodies to be kept "at arm's length." Intimacy, figured here as "the warmth of the fray," withdraws from the sick woman, and she is left cold and isolated.

I read Lorde's writing and I think of the hysterical women at the Salpêtrière Hospital at the turn of the twentieth century. The only intimacy they experienced was with the doctors who studied them and the audiences they were performing in front of during Jean-Martin Charcot's weekly lectures. I'm also reminded of today's chronically ill woman, trapped in a hospital bed or at home, who experiences contact largely through a phone screen and social media. In these isolated landscapes, what does intimacy look like? What if the intimacy that you so desire cannot be spoken without risking pathologization? How might we reimagine intimacy in a world that seeks to isolate the sick, traumatized, and hysterical from the "warmth of the fray"? In asking these questions, I want to create roadmaps for healing that refuse to pathologize the forms of intimacy and care that do not read as normative. It is my belief that those of us who're sick and traumatized are creating those roadmaps. We are the ones calling out, again and again, *Touch me, I'm sick.*

☾

Sexual trauma wasn't the only root of my sickness. The trauma of being a caregiver also made me sick. And so I have ambivalent feelings about care. When I read Leah Lakshmi Piepzna-Samarasinha's book *Care Work: Dreaming Disability Justice*, I found myself getting angry when she proclaims that it is our duty to care for one another. Resistance, I have learned, is a lantern that can illuminate our trauma.

I'm lying on a thin mat on the floor, naked except for my underwear, a thin white sheet spread across my body. I've been receiving free sessions with a Zen shiatsu massage therapist, who happens to be the mother of my ex-partner, in exchange for acting as her test body. This offer came after I told her about the ongoing and seemingly disconnected health problems I'd been dealing with for many months—colds, flus, infections, chronic fatigue, anxiety—and my inability to pay for alternative forms of care. She thinks that my physical symptoms are the result of emotional stress caused by the twenty years that I've acted as a caregiver to my disabled father. I am not ready to entertain her hypothesis, and so I shrug it off.

Over a year later, a week after my father's death, I'm sitting across from my therapist. I've just finished expressing how angry I am at my father for his sudden departure. The day of his death, I received a call from the hospital where he'd been living for the last three years:

"As you know, your father had a routine bronchoscopy today. He hasn't recovered and we think you should get here soon."

My father had been dying for more than twenty years. I want to say that it wasn't a surprise when he died. I'd long been doing the work of anticipatory grief. But when I received this phone call I was caught off guard. What do you mean *as you know*? What do you mean *hasn't recovered*? My father failed to mention this procedure during our weekly phone call.

I'm trying to process the shock, anger, and grief that have all hit me at once in the wake of his death. And then comes the guilt:

"What if there is a heaven, which I'm not sure there is anyways," I say to my therapist, "but what if there is and he's listening to me talk about how angry I am at him? Won't he feel hurt?"

With all the gentleness she can muster, my therapist tells me, "It's okay for you to stop caring for him now. It's time for you to start caring for yourself."

While I'm grateful for this permission, I can't begin to imagine how such a thing might be possible. After my mother's death when I was eleven, I became a surrogate mother. My brother was only nine and not yet to be trusted in the kitchen. So I cooked all the meals, did the laundry, made sure he got to school each morning. And then a year later, I began my role as my father's caregiver too. When I moved out at the age of twenty-one, I was wracked with guilt. How could I leave my brother? How selfish of me. And, what a relief. My days no longer punctuated by acts of care that I had no say in, no way to refuse. Eight years later, after pneumonia almost killed him, my father moved to a long-term care facility in Toronto, and my caregiver duties resumed. Now being close in proximity once again, I was expected to visit him weekly.

These visits filled me with dread. Ever since moving out, my conversations with my father followed a formula:

HIM: "How are you?"
ME: "I'm good. How are you?"
HIM: *Spends the next hour talking about all of the things that he's doing before we inevitably start to discuss hockey (a game that I have never watched or enjoyed), and then he*

*asks me to do a few things for him before I go ("Can you
clip my nails?" "Can you fill out this form?" "Can you
take my laundry?").*

He rarely asked me questions about my work or about my personal
life. When he did ask, or when I chose to volunteer some information,
his response usually didn't go much further than "Oh, good for you"
or "Oh, that's interesting." (From what I was told by his nurses after
his death, my father never stopped talking about how proud he was
of me. *If only he could have shared those sentiments with me*, I think,
wishing that they'd kept this information to themselves. For it just
adds to my grief, all of the "could've beens" that accumulate when
someone dies and you realize that you're not just grieving the person,
but all of the possibilities that existed alongside them.)

My visits became harder after I started to get sick. I felt that my
pain had to be kept hidden. Perhaps because I was afraid that it
would upset my dad. But also, perhaps because I was afraid that it
wouldn't. I'd spent years in therapy trying to decide whether it was
possible to shift our dynamic or if I should just accept that this was
the best I'd get from him. Time and time again I went with the latter.
And yet, I couldn't accept our dynamic. I visited my father but never
felt seen. Instead, I felt like another nurse—except, of course, that I
also happened to be his daughter.

The reason that I was unable to address my dissatisfaction with
our relationship? Trauma. As a teenager, I would often come to
my dad after my brother and I fought. A typical scene: My brother
comes home at 3:00 a.m. and decides to microwave some food. This
wouldn't be a problem except that the microwave is in the living
room. This wouldn't be a problem except that my bed is also in the
living room. This wouldn't be a problem except that at some point
after we were evicted from the home I grew up in, a decision was
made that my brother and father would each get a bedroom and
my bedroom would be the living room. Who made that decision?
And why was I so quick to acquiescence? After coming home from
a fifteen-hour day of school and my full-time job, I would try to tell
my brother that microwaving food at 3:00 a.m. woke me up. Made
it difficult for me to concentrate. He would yell, call me names, slam

doors (his grief came much later than mine and took the form of rage and entitlement). My father would sit there, face clenched, and tell me, "You know how your brother is. You shouldn't have said anything," and I would cry.

I was met with rejection any time I attempted to address how my brother's actions and my dad's inaction made me feel. And so in order to protect myself, I began to say nothing. I no longer believed that my needs should be heard, let alone respected. Despite all of the years I've spent in therapy, some part of me still believed that my needs didn't matter. As soon as I thought about trying to broach this subject with my dad, to tell him what it is that I need, panic set in. My body says no.

In his national bestseller *When the Body Says No*, trauma specialist Dr. Gabor Maté argues that those with chronic illnesses share similar character traits: namely, the repression of emotions and the inability to say "no." Among the illnesses cited by Maté are multiple sclerosis, Crohn's disease, autoimmune disorders, fibromyalgia, endometriosis, and ALS. In these descriptions I see my father, and I see myself.

> The life histories of people with ALS invariably tell of emotional deprivation or loss in childhood. Characterizing the personalities of ALS patients is relentless self-drive, reluctance to acknowledge the need for help and the denial of pain whether physical or emotional. All these behaviors and psychological coping mechanisms far predate the onset of illness.

In the margins I've made a note: *What if my mom's death triggered the trauma of being abandoned as a child?*

Growing up, I always rejected the idea that I was anything like my father. I was my mother's daughter: rebellious, flying in the face of convention; she would have approved of my decision to dye my hair pink when I was fifteen. In my favorite story of my mother and father, they are fighting over a coffee table. On their drives to Florida in the winter, they would stop in antiques shops along the way, always finding some strange old relic to bring home with them. This time there's contention. My mother has fallen in love with a coffee table, and my father tells me how this is one of the only times he ever said no to her. But why? The coffee table used to be an old chicken coop. And inside of this refurbished coop is a taxidermy bird. I'll never understand how my father could have said no to such an incredible piece of furniture.

After his death, almost twenty-one years to the day that my mom died, I sat down to write his eulogy. It was then that I realized that we have a lot more in common than I thought: a desire to build community, a type-A personality that loves lists and spreadsheets, and an inability to say "no." I always thought of my dad as a man all too comfortable saying no, but as his illness progressed I watched as he said yes when he should have said, "No, I'm sorry, it's not possible for me to do that." And so when a friend made a request, my father would sign my brother or me up to complete the task. We became his surrogate bodies.

His death came as a relief, for it released me from being his caregiver. And, at the same time, I was left adrift, not knowing who I was if I wasn't caring for him. This identity crisis is all too common among those of us who became enmeshed with our parents early on through parentification. A term coined by family therapist Ivan Boszormenyi-Nagy, *parentification* occurs when a child is forced to take on tasks that are not age appropriate, such as grocery shopping (check), taking care of siblings and other family members (check), cooking meals for the family (check), paying bills (check), and figuring out the emotional needs of a parent (check). My sense of self and self-worth became inextricably linked to providing care to anyone but myself.

After reading Freud's case study of Dora, I turned to the other most famous case study of hysteria in psychoanalysis: Joseph Breuer's patient Bertha Pappenheim, later named Anna O. In the 1880s, Breuer began to see Anna, who had fallen ill during the course of caring for her father who had tuberculosis. Breuer describes a whole host of symptoms impacting Anna's health. Like Dora, Anna has a cough. But while at her father's bedside, Anna also experiences hallucinations and heightened anxiety. In one such hallucination, or what Breuer called an "absence," Anna is sitting beside her father's bed when a black snake appears out of nowhere. Anna wishes to protect her father, and goes to move her right arm, but it has fallen asleep.

To make matters worse, the fingers on her right hand transform into snakes. Not only is she unable to save her father from this attack, but the very hand that would save him has transformed into the danger that she wished to fend off.

Can there be a better analogy for the guilt a caregiver feels than this? Not only is there nothing you can do to save your loved one. But you can actually do them harm with your hand of snakes. If sickness is the snake, and Anna herself is falling ill, then perhaps there's another reading of this hallucination I can offer. It takes tremendous effort to care for your self, especially when your life has been defined by caring for others. As I continued to put my father's needs before my own, I had little energy left to take care of my own needs. I became sicker. Let's imagine that when Anna looks at her hand, she sees just one snake finger at first. As she tries to move her arm to save her father, another finger transforms into a snake. And then another and another, until all five fingers are metamorphosed. What can be done, then, with this reptilian hand?

To consciously acknowledge the possibility that my own illness has been caused or amplified by the twenty years that I cared for my father is too much. It's as though my brain has said, "Well, you haven't listened to me yet, and so maybe you'll listen to your body." For if I'm too exhausted to make myself dinner, how will I go to the store to procure the items on my father's grocery list? If it takes great effort to lift my arms up, the pain like little shocks in my wrists, how will I be able to put the food up to his mouth to eat?

And so I understand why Anna is unable to drink water for days and weeks at a time. It is not, as Freud proposes, because she witnessed the nanny's dog drink from a glass of water (although I love that this is Freud's best guess). Perhaps Anna wished to deprive herself of this life-sustaining force because it would not, in the end, be able to save her father. Because, perhaps, she wouldn't be able to save him either. I wonder if Anna wanted to suffer alongside him, to be in sympathy with him, even if it harmed her. Had I been doing the same thing?

As I look for the many sick mothers of my heart, I'm forced to confront the fact that not only did Anna O. care for her sick father, but Dora did too. By the time Dora was six, her father had fallen ill with tuberculosis. He remained sick for another decade. Freud also refers to an aunt who exhibits clear markers of psychoneurosis, and who will die of marasmus—a form of severe malnutrition that usually occurs in children. I pause as I read the following sentence: "The sympathies of the girl herself, who, as I have said, became my patient at the age of eighteen, had always been with the father's side of the family, and ever since she had fallen ill she had taken as her model the aunt who has just been mentioned." Freud makes this assessment of Dora's sympathies without having ever met Dora's mother, for she was always absent. Missing mothers and sick fathers. Then sick daughters.

I was never able to tell my father how much I resented his inability to accept his new limitations, which I now understand were the workings of internalized ableism, of the belief that one holds no value outside of what one can offer to others. Many therapists through the years suggested that maybe I could talk to him about how years of being his surrogate body had impacted me, but the trauma of so many rejections from my father made this feel like an impossibility. There was no way he would understand. My needs didn't matter when I was twelve, fourteen, seventeen. So how could they possibly matter now?

Part of me will always wish that I could have said, "It was enough that I had to bathe you and feed you and dress you before I was even an adult. But now that I'm sick, I can no longer do the things you ask of me. And I'm angry that you've never understood that you were asking me for too much. That you collapsed me into you." Instead, I blamed my body for my new limitations. "I'm sorry. I can't. My fingers have become snakes." *I cannot touch you. I have become sick.*

☾

My sun sign, Cancer, is in my eighth house of grief and trauma. Astrologer Chani Nicholas writes that people with this astrological placement are destined to be therapists and caregivers. They may also suffer from trauma caused by care: a lack thereof in the wake of grief and trauma, an overburdening of care, or, as in my case, both. And so, while I carry this caregiver trauma with me, it is despite and because of this trauma that I am deeply invested in dreaming up forms of care that are not shaped by a lack of consent and the absence of reciprocity. What I needed was a redefinition. "Care," writes kamra sadia hakim in *care manual: dreaming care into being*, is "intentional and informed giving and receiving of abundance." Caring, it follows, is "the act of consensually delivering care."

For the Care Collective, originally formed in 2017 as a London-based reading group, and later authors of *The Care Manifesto*, care is

> also a social capacity and activity involving the nurturing of all that is necessary for the welfare and flourishing of life. . . . Care is our individual and common ability to provide the political, social, material, and emotional conditions that allow the vast majority of people and living creatures on this planet to thrive—along with the planet itself.

I am relieved to learn that one cannot speak about care without acknowledging that care evokes great ambivalence. As the Care Collective notes, "The word care in English comes from the Old English *caru,* meaning care, concern, anxiety, sorrow, grief, trouble—its double meanings clearly on display. This reflects a reality where attending fully to the needs and vulnerabilities of any living thing, and thus confronting frailty, can be both challenging and exhausting."

María Puig de la Bellacasa's *Matters of Care: Speculative Ethics in More Than Human Worlds* illuminates how care is a vexed topic with competing definitions when she asks: "But what is care? Is it an affection? A moral obligation? Work? A burden? A joy?" We've been taught that care should produce a "warm pleasant affection or a moralistic feel-good attitude." But, as Bellacasa notes, feminists have worked hard to complicate such a definition of care, as it supports the ongoing exploitation of the emotional labor and care work performed by women and femmes. When care is thus framed as an obligation, it will certainly leave us with some bad feelings.

The reality is that not everyone is obligated to care. In her book *The Care Crisis*, sociologist and political scientist Emma Dowling shares the results of a study conducted by the Overseas Development Institute in 2014, reporting that "on average across 66 countries representing two-thirds of the world's population, women spent 3.3 times as much time as men on unpaid care." Dowling goes on to note how "the ratio varies by region, but everywhere in the world without exception, women do significantly more unpaid care work than men" and when it comes to paid work, care work makes up 19.3 percent of global female employment and 6.6 percent of global male employment." Despite just how necessary care work is for our survival, "caring activities are some of the most undervalued and invisibilized activities of all, while those who perform them are some of the most neglected and unsupported people in our societies." It is no wonder, then, that we feel ambivalent about care. I want us to hold space for that ambivalence, rather than strive to eliminate it. And, when it comes to the global care crisis, which has been made all the more evident in the wake of the COVID-19 pandemic—which, as of this writing, is still very much ongoing—we must figure out how to make care work more pleasurable and more sustainable.

Those in the disability justice movement have been at the forefront of reimagining care work. *Disability justice* is a term coined by the Disability Justice Collective in 2005. Made up of mostly QTBIPOC, the founding members of the Disability Justice Collective are Patty Berne, Mia Mingus, Stacey Milbern, Leroy Moore, Eli Clare, and Sebastian Margaret. The disability justice movement emerged out of a shared recognition that disability rights alone are not going to produce the change necessary for building an anti-ableist world.

Mia Mingus summarizes the difference between disability rights and disability justice as follows: "Disability rights works to bring disabled people to the table, whereas disability justice seeks to question the ways that "the entire 'table' or 'system' might need to change." Leah Lakshmi Piepzna-Samarasinha explains how disability rights places a white, male, cisgender, straight subject at the center, whereas disability justice centralizes sick and disabled QTBIPOC.

While those in the disability justice movement require the very things that disability rights is fighting for, such as the Affordable Care Act and the Americans with Disabilities Act, Piepzna-Samarasinha wants us to recognize that "our focus is less on civil rights legislation as the only solution to ableism and more on a vision of liberation that understands that the state was built on racist, colonialist ableism and will not save us, because it was created to kill us."

Philosopher and academic Jasbir K. Puar makes a similar argument in *The Right to Maim.* For Puar, the problem with rights discourses is that they "produce human beings in order to give them rights; they discriminate which bodies are vested with futurity, or more accurately, they cultivate (some/certain) bodies that can be vested with futurity." Puar puts forth the concept of debility to help us understand how marginalized communities are slowly worn down through debilitation, which is a "practice of rendering populations available for statistically likely injury." Disablement has a before and an after, whereas debility "comprehends those bodies that are sustained in a perpetual state of debilitation precisely through foreclosing the social, cultural, and political translation to disability." Debilitation is thus the terrain of the endemic, systemic, and chronic.

The Centers for Disease Control and Prevention defines endemic as "the constant presence and/or usual prevalence of a disease or infectious agent in a population within a geographic area." In contrast, an epidemic is "an increase, often sudden, in the number of cases of a disease above what is normally expected in that population in that area." The epidemic marks that which is exceptional, while the endemic is banal and quotidian. What escapes these definitions is the reality that the endemic, while seemingly banal, is no less threatening than the epidemic. In fact, for so many oppressed groups, the endemic is inherently more violent and traumatizing because it is woven into the very fabric of everyday life.

In our cultural moment, anti-Black violence is endemic, poverty is endemic, and violence against women, and trans women of color in particular, is endemic. Remembering that endemic refers to "the constant presence and/or usual prevalence of a disease or infectious agent in a population within a geographic area," we can see how, within Black communities, anti-Black racism is a "constant presence," an "infectious agent," embodied by police brutality and the state-sanctioned murders of so many young Black people. These events are not exceptional within the Black community but are framed as such by the state in order to excuse the behavior of those responsible for these killings. The endemic nature of anti-Black racism is traumatic and highlights the ways in which trauma is caused not only by shocking events but also by events that are now so banal that they fail to shock.

The concept of the endemic is connected to the chronic. Coming from the Greek word *khronos* (of time), chronic marks that which is continual, ongoing, forever present. Chronic illnesses have no cure. There may be periods when the symptoms disappear, or the disease goes into remission, but there is always the possibility that they'll return. The sicknesses I discuss in this book, which include complex trauma and chronic pain, become endemic in the lives of girls, women, and femmes—and this is especially true for women of color, and for Black people in general. It thus makes sense that Puar begins her discussion of debility by referencing the rise of the Black Lives Matter (BLM) movement. BLM is a direct response to the shootings of Michael Brown, Trayvon Martin, Philando Castile, Alton Sterling, and so many other Black people in the United States. These shootings have placed Black subjects in a state of debility, in which one is afraid to leave the house from fear that anything they do might result in their death.

Thus, writes Puar, "We will not all be disabled. Some of us will simply not live long enough, embedded in a distribution of risk already factored into the calculus of debilitation. Death's position." Debility draws attention to how "while some bodies may not be recognized as or identified as disabled, they may well be debilitated, in part by being foreclosed access to legibility and resources as disabled." Here we must confront the problems rendered by visibility and invisibility, of who gets read as disabled and who doesn't. For the state, this lack of recognition enables the slow deaths, to borrow Lauren Berlant's term, of those who're already marginalized. The systems of care that we have in place—charity, social services, aid—will not save us. In fact, these systems support the creation and sustainment of the endemic.

Care, as understood through disability rights, emphasizes charity, whereas disability justice focuses on mutual aid. In his book *Mutual Aid: Building Solidarity During This Crisis (and the Next)*, Dean Spade explains how mutual aid (unlike charity, aid, relief, and social services, in which "rich people of the government mak[e] decisions about the provision of some kind of support to poor people") does not seek to determine "who gets the help, what the limits are to that help, and what strings are attached." For Spade, "mutual aid projects mobilize lots of people rather than a few experts; resist the use of eligibility criteria that cut out more stigmatized people; are an integrated part of our lives rather than a pet cause; and cultivate a shared analysis of the root causes of the problem and connect people to social movements that can address these causes." Some examples of mutual aid include crowdfunding to help someone pay their rent or other living expenses, fundraising for top surgery or other kinds of gender-affirming care, and dropping off food to encampments protesting for a free Palestine.

I see mutual aid as a form of *promiscuous care*, a term used by the Care Collective to describe how "all forms of care between all categories of human and non-human should be valued, recognised and resourced equally, according to their needs or ongoing sustainability." They are quick to clarify, "In advocating for promiscuous care, we do not mean caring casually or indifferently. . . . For us, promiscuous care is an ethos that proliferates outwards to redefine caring relations from the most intimate to the most distant. It means caring *more* and in ways that remain experimental and extensive." In other words, we need to get slutty with our care. And who better at promiscuous care than the hysterics?

What promiscuous care recognizes is our fundamental interdependence. In *Emergent Strategy*, adrienne maree brown defines interdependence as "mutual reliance" that requires a shared commitment to vulnerability, and to the decentralization of power. This commitment takes shape in "a series of small repetitive motions" that we do again and again, when we have the capacity to do so. Working from a disability justice framework, brown is careful to acknowledge how "interdependence is not about the equality of offers in real time." We may have to ask someone to support us, knowing that it might take a really long time before we can offer anything in return.

Piepzna-Samarasinha argues for a similar definition of interdependence when she proposes "the radical notion that providing care is work" that "is essential to building movements that are accessible and sustainable." In her essay "A Modest Proposal for a Fair Trade Labour Economy (Centered by Disabled, Femme of Color, Working-Class/Poor Genius)," she'll go on to outline seven tenets of a fair-trade emotional labor economy, including a shared belief that care is reciprocal. But reciprocity isn't necessarily a fifty-fifty trade: "In disabled communities, we talk about the idea that we can still offer reciprocity to each other, even if we can't offer the exact same type of care back. . . . If my disabled body can't lift yours onto the toilet, it doesn't mean I can't be reciprocal—it means I contribute equally from what my particular body can do."

We're not here to tally up the number of hours spent on an act of care so that we can compare it to how many hours we've put in. In practicing interdependence, we must accept that we live in a responsive ecosystem of flux and change. While I may have been able to lift you onto the toilet last week, when my body was relatively pain-free, you cannot expect that I should always be able to do so.

In an essay entitled "what happens when we can't live interdependently all the time?" the anonymous author grapples with what it means for interdependency to ebb and flow:

> If interdependency is in our DNA, what does it mean when we fall out of whack with it? How do we handle the realities of our bodies and minds that need what they need when they need it? What does it mean when I can't support you in the ways you're supporting me? Does interdependency mean we do the same for one another at all times, as though there's even such a thing as 'the same' when it comes to this stuff? Is it a gentle ebb and flow? What if my ebb will never match your flow? What if it's sometimes a torrential downpour and one of us is drowning? What do we do then?

One possible response to the final question is that we must build our capacity for what brown calls "intentional adaptation." To allow others to meet you where they're at, and to be grateful for what they can offer you, is integral to living interdependently. And what's so incredible about committing ourselves to interdependence in this way is that we become less afraid of change and more able to embrace the messiness of failure. Because inevitably things will change and we will fail. What matters is that we can work together, that we can adapt and create new strategies for surviving and thriving through acts of care.

☾

What might my life have been like if my mother hadn't gotten sick? Would she have talked to me about consent? Would she have reminded me, day in and day out, that I was beautiful, lovable, and much too magical for the boys who just wanted to use me? Would I have been raped and slut-shamed? And, if I was, how might I have healed from those traumas with her care?

What might my life have been like if my mother's death hadn't made my father sick? Would he have been able to give me the love I needed? Would he have been able to hold me when I cried about breakups and fights with friends? Would he have not just accepted but celebrated me for wanting to be my own person?

What might my life have been like if my family had access to the forms of care we needed in the wake of my mother's death and my father's illness? Would I have processed the trauma of losing my mother? Would I have learned that my self-worth didn't depend on being a caregiver? Would I have needed to turn to drugs to help me escape traumas that couldn't be named, let alone processed? Would my father have had the capacity to love my brother and me? Would I have gotten sick?

All of these what-ifs. They haunt me. And at the same time, these questions become portals to possibility. This isn't the same thing as silver-lining my trauma. Each time I ask myself what life could have been like, I am acknowledging that I deserved more—that we all deserve so much more than the paltry offerings of care and intimacy that we've been given. I'm no longer willing to pathologize myself and the forms of intimacy and care that I have sought out and that have enabled me to survive.

And so, as a final question, I ask: What might happen if we moved toward the call of *touch me, I'm sick*?

AMBIVALENT DESIRES, UGLY SEX

I feel called to start with a confession: I have had ugly sex. No, I do not mean bad sex (although I've had plenty of that too). I'm talking about the sex that you desire but also feel a bit repulsed by. Sex that gets you off but leaves you feeling unsettled afterward. Sex that is messy and ambivalent, and thus different from the so-called fully empowered, unequivocally "yes!" sex that feminists are supposed to have. I used to suffer so much shame every time I recalled how these ugly sexual encounters were all I really knew for my first decade of having sex. From ages fourteen to twenty-four, I'd sleep with boys whose sloppy kisses disgusted me and turned me on at the same time. Their hands always moving too fast as we went from kissing to fucking on bathroom floors or in dark bedrooms illuminated by strings of white Christmas lights. They'd always get up and walk out first. I'd leave feeling used and abandoned. And yet, there was something that compelled me to return again and again to these boys. I was a repeat offender.

I've made this confession before, and so it wasn't surprising that so many of my friends messaged me when Kristen Roupenian's short story "Cat Person" went viral. Published in *The New Yorker* in December 2017, "Cat Person" follows a twenty-year-old woman named Margot (the similarity of our names was not lost on me) who goes on a few dates with the thirty-four-year-old Robert, a man who frequents the cinema where she works. After weeks of exchanging text messages, Margot meets Robert for one of the most awkward dates in history, in which he takes her to "a very depressing drama about the Holocaust, so inappropriate for a first date."

After the movie, Robert asks her if she'd like to have a drink and Margot agrees, only to be turned away at the door because she's one year shy of legal drinking age. They find a different bar and after three drinks Margot starts to think about what it would be like to have sex with Robert: "Probably it would be like that bad kiss, clumsy and excessive, but imagining how excited he would be, how hungry and eager to impress her, she felt a twinge of desire pluck at her belly, as distinct and painful as the snap of an elastic band against her skin." That Margot imagines this encounter as both "clumsy and excessive . . . distinct and painful" and also capable of causing a "twinge of desire" reveals a lot about the ambivalence at the heart of the things we want and don't want. But this ambivalence does not deter her from having sex with Robert. In fact, it's just the opposite.

The two go to Robert's place, where Margot is forced to confront the sexual encounter awaiting her:

> When Robert was naked, rolling a condom onto a dick that was only half visible beneath the hairy shelf of his belly, she felt a wave of revulsion that she thought might actually break through her sense of pinned stasis, but then he shoved his finger in her again, not at all gently this time, and she imagined herself from above, naked and spread-eagled with this fat old man's finger inside her, and her revulsion turned to self-disgust and a humiliation that was a kind of perverse cousin to arousal.

The only way for Margot to get through her "pinned stasis" beneath the man who throws her around, "as if they were in a porno" and growls, "'I always wanted to fuck a girl with nice tits' in her ear" is to dissociate. Imagining herself "from above" allows her to transform her revulsion—which comes less from Robert's body and more from how he treats hers—into feelings that are more bearable. By shifting the focus away from Robert and onto herself, Margot transforms revulsion into self-disgust and humiliation, and these feelings enable her to get a bit closer to feeling aroused.

After the act is over, and Robert drops her off at home, Margot stops responding to his texts. She wants to figure out how to break things off without hurting his feelings, and after a few days of torturing herself, her roommate steals her phone and texts Robert "Hi im not interested in you stop textng me." Robert responds back with more kindness than you'd expect from a man who got a girl, fifteen years his junior, drunk at a bar and then took her home and proceeded to not think at all about her desire as he had sex with her. The story ends with Margot spotting Robert in a bar a month later. Not wishing to be seen by him, she leaves with her friends. Later that night she receives a series of text messages from Robert, which start out benignly ("I just wanted to say you looked really pretty" and "I really miss you") before getting increasingly aggressive, ending with "Whore."

I immediately fell in love with the story for all of the ways in which it dares to represent sex that is ugly and ambivalent. But the responses to "Cat Person" were wide-ranging. Women quickly flocked to Twitter to proclaim #metoo. @alanalevinson tweeted: "So much of hetero dating is based on a very sick, sad contract: you (woman) better like the holocaust documentary & when he sucks at fingering you that's somehow your fault." The response from male readers was decidedly different and vacillated between judgment and confusion: "Some guys are bad at kissing, and bad at relationships. Having sex very soon after meeting someone is usually not a good life decision imo," tweeted @RossGellar482 while @logankugler asked, "What are all of you relating to in this? I'm confused. Can a sister enlighten a brother?"

One man was so confused by Margot's actions that he penned an open letter to the character entitled "Dear Cat Person Girl." In his open letter to Margot, Kyle Smith tells the fictional character, "I don't think you have thought through how you got into a terrible situation." Then the slut-shaming begins with Smith questioning Margot's previous sexual history (she's had sex with seven men and seven is too many for her age) and explaining that her choice to sleep with Robert after "1.5 dates is a bad idea." Had they spent more time developing an emotional connection, Margot "could have made it clear that [she] didn't like being treated like a porn star." The claim that emotional connection is necessary for good bedside manner is problematic. This logic works to blame the girl for not fostering an emotional connection before choosing to have sex and removes any onus from the man (wasn't he at all interested in creating that connection?). This claim also promotes the false belief that emotional connection is the key to good sex while simultaneously ignoring the fact that bad and nonconsensual sex occurs both with and without emotional ties.

Unsurprisingly, then, the responsibility for good sex is placed on Margot. And the same holds true for her choice to have three drinks, which, as Smith notes, "is another bad idea." What Smith fails to acknowledge, alongside so many others wishing to defend Robert's actions, is that Margot is confronted with a lose-lose situation: Does she say no to having sex with Robert and risk being viewed as a tease, or does she choose the ugly sex to come?

> But the thought of what it would take to stop what she had set in motion was overwhelming; it would require an amount of tact and gentleness that she felt was impossible to summon. It wasn't that she was scared he would try to force her to do something against her will but that insisting that they stop now, after everything she'd done to push this forward, would make her seem spoiled and capricious, as if she'd ordered something at a restaurant and then, once the food arrived, had changed her mind and sent it back.

Prioritizing his pleasure over her own, Margot chooses to go through with the act.

Her decision marks the ways in which, as Juana María Rodríguez poignantly puts it, "coercion is rarely absolute." Rodríguez goes on to point out that

> most of the sexual contracts we enter have everything to do with various forms of coercion mandated by the social bonds we inhabit. Whether with a partner, date, trick, or wife, sex can become a social obligation that is offered in exchange for dinner, domestic harmony, rent, safety or our own sexual pleasure. . . . Whether in overt commercial exchanges, casual anonymous encounters, or intimate relations structured around love and care, sex functions as a kind of trade.

Margot finds herself faced with a social obligation: In choosing to go through with sex with Robert, she avoids the discomfort that comes with rejecting his advances and the possibility that he'll decide that she's "spoiled and capricious." More importantly, Rodríguez's insight points to the ways in which this trade can and does take place in casual encounters and long-term intimate relationships.

Melissa Febos shares a similar reflection in her book *Girlhood* when she writes about "empty consent": scenarios in which we consent, but we don't necessarily want to. "During fleeting casual sexual encounters, women and girls are expected to place a man's physical and emotional interests above their own, to assume responsibility for ensuring that they are met. But in committed relationships, they are often expected to do this every minute of their lives." One of the ways that women prioritize the needs of men over their own is through empty consent. There are other reasons we engage in empty consent: "the need to protect our bodies from the violent retaliation of men and the need to protect the same men from the consequences of their own behavior, usually be assuming personal responsibility"; we may offer a blowjob in order to avoid being forced to have sex; we may feel exhausted at the end of a long day, a long week, a long month, but also desire connection with our partner.

"Cat Person" is a story about empty consent and ugly sex—and how easily the two can overlap in the same sexual experience. What I love about this story is how it depicts consent as a messy space that cannot always be defined by a yes or a no. Why we say yes matters, and empty consent does not negate the pleasure we may have experienced by engaging in an act that we didn't necessarily feel 100 percent enthusiastic about. There is a way in which we pathologize experiences that fall short of an uncomplicated, unequivocal yes. I spent years and years of my life feeling ashamed of my early sexual experiences once I recognized that consent couldn't really exist if I wasn't sober. Was I harmed by these experiences? Yes. And, at the same time, ugly sex and empty consent enabled me to access the intimacy and connection that I desperately needed to survive.

Ugly sex is a term I am using to refer to sexual encounters that might be degrading or humiliating, that might leave you feeling not so great afterward, but that are still pleasurable in the moment and might cause you to want more. Part of the reason I have chosen the word *ugly* to describe these sexual encounters is because ugliness is an aesthetic category, defined by its opposition to the beautiful. What constitutes beauty and ugliness has a long history of debate, one that I won't rehash here because I'm not interested in subjective definitions (though many philosophers will try to tell you that beauty is objective). Rather, I'm drawn to ugliness for the ways in which it marks certain bodies as unworthy of desire and certain acts as abhorrently undesirable.

In *On the Politics of Ugliness*, Sara Rodrigues and Ela Przybylo point out,

> Ugliness or unsightliness is much more than a quality or property of one's appearance. In Western contexts and histories especially, ugliness has long functioned as a social category that demarcates one's rights and access to social, cultural, and political spaces. People who are unsightly are framed as not only unworthy of being seen or of having eyes set upon them, but they then become the target of interventions to curb the possibility of their causing aversion and discomfort in others.

Included in the list of those marked as ugly are the disabled, queer, trans, gender nonconforming, fat, aging, and racialized. Marking those whose ugliness is visible by way of physical appearance (disabled, fat, aging, racialized, trans) and those whose ugliness is invisible but marked by their desires (queer, trans, gender nonconforming), ugliness is as much about what a body chooses to do as it is about that body's appearance.

Marie Calloway, whose writing I'll turn to shortly, is a conventionally beautiful person writing about conventionally attractive humans. And yet, critics of her writing proclaim that "her female characters are so fucking ugly" due to their lack of morality and the sexual practices they engage in. Ugliness, then, is "attributed to those bodies that deviate from a given society's norms" and is just as much about "behaviors that depart from the social norms acceptable in and to capitalist patriarchy" as it is about appearance. In other words, that which is ugly is viewed as being morally offensive or repulsive; the ugly is base, degraded, and highly objectionable.

The ugly is thus not only an aesthetic category but an affective one as well. Ugliness evokes feelings of fear or dread, and these reactions, Tobin Siebers writes, "reveal the ease or disease with which one body might incorporate another." Rodrigues and Przybylo expand upon Siebers's evocation of ease and disease, writing: "Our visceral responses to dirt, the grotesque, plainness, and/ or monstrosity, are about maintaining social relations and social margins. These and other 'ugly feelings' are indicative of culturally and materially shaped inclinations to the world around us that are grounded in the 'ease or disease' with which we relate to one another."

I can't help but pause at the double meaning of disease being employed here: a body that is diseased, and the lack of ease. It's not just that ugliness makes us feel things; but there are feelings that we have decided are ugly: shame, grief, anger, pride, self-love (depending on who is feeling and/or expressing them). Sianne Ngai's book *Ugly Feelings* adds other ambivalent and other "minor feelings" to this list, such as envy, irritation, anxiety, and paranoia. Placing us all in a bind, it is also ugly to not feel certain things: If you aren't sad enough in the face of grief, or you aren't disturbed by something that is meant to shock, or you don't smile when something good happens, you are marked as pathological. Which is just another way of saying ugly.

Ugly sex might be offensive to "good feelings," but it does not have to occupy an exclusively "bad" position. Ugly sex can bring us joy even as it makes us feel a whole host of "bad" feelings. And so when I talk about ugly sex, I am referring to an experience that can feel pleasurable and devastating all at once. Ugly sex captures the oscillation between empowerment and devastation, attraction and repulsion, agency and subordination. Ugly sex is the sex that we are not supposed to talk about, especially as feminists, because the only kind of feminist sex is the sex that empowers you.

Despite my invocation of Febos's "empty consent" earlier, it feels important to name that ugly sex is not the same as nonconsensual sex, nor is it the same as bad sex. Katie Roiphe uses the term *bad sex* to refer to the blurry line between consensual and nonconsensual sex—like the sex that one has while intoxicated. But bad sex might also refer to sex that is not fulfilling. When we say "bad sex," as Rebecca Traister does, we might be characterizing the "joyless, exploitative encounters that reflect a persistently sexist culture and can be hard to acknowledge without sounding prudish." I agree with Traister that we exist in a "halved sexual universe, in which there is either assault or there is sex positivity," and thus we need to explore the space in between. But where Traister and I differ is that there is little to no pleasure in the gray-area sexual encounters that she discusses. In my experience, ugly sex can be and often is pleasurable, if not fulfilling, and also difficult (which is to say: ambivalent).

Sloppy kisses and smelly boys. Hands that move too fast or too rough. Pants down around ankles on bathroom floors, and just a few thrusts in, he's done. Hand over your mouth in his bedroom, stifling your moans so his parents won't hear. Always you going down on him and barely, if ever, him going down on you. The location of the clitoris lost on him. Sometimes, you can get on top of the boy and ride him until you come. Wash, rinse, repeat. The pleasure doesn't always come from the quality of the sex but arises from the very fact of being touched by another. A touch that is all you've desired, and that is utterly terrifying.

Ugly sex reminds me of the unbearable sex that Lauren Berlant and Lee Edelman theorize in *Sex, or the Unbearable*. For Berlant and Edelman, sex (and, I would argue, any form of intimate encounter) is unbearable because it threatens our sovereignty; sex is always an encounter "with what exceeds and undoes the subject's fantasmatic sovereignty." In other words, sex reminds us that, for better or worse, we are impacted by our encounters with others. Berlant and Edelman claim that sex is a site where "relationality is invested with hopes, expectations, and anxieties" that the subject may experience as unbearable.

It is for this reason that sex—any sex—cannot be divorced from negativity, which Berlant and Edelman define as the "psychic and social incoherences and divisions, conscious and unconscious alike, that trouble any totality or fixity of identity." Negativity thus works to produce the feeling of non-sovereignty that we experience in the moment of sex. Berlant and Edelman's investment in negativity is compelling: intimacy can leave us feeling undone.

Berlant is deeply interested in sexual encounters that are puzzling and ambivalent. Differentiating themselves from Edelman, they write, "Excitement is disturbing, not devastating; ambivalent, not shattering." I am less interested in how one is shattered by sex, and more interested in how we might shatter normative narratives of what sex should look like, how sex should feel, and how those feelings should be described. What does it mean to tell a story about sex that does not pathologize desire? Can we address the ways in which sexual experiences can be pleasurable and filled with shame, disgust, and other supposedly negative affects?

If there's anything we can rescue from Freud's analysis of the hysterical Dora, it's his assertion that our desires are always deeply ambivalent: "Thoughts in the unconscious live very comfortably side by side, and even contraries get on together without disputes." And yet we all feel the injunction that, when it comes to desire, we should only experience positive feelings. But what would happen if our ambivalent desires could exist at the same time without leading to pathology? Ugly sex is one space in which ambivalence pivots from negativity to possibility.

What do we miss when we choose to pathologize these ugly sexual encounters? The focus on why we have ugly sex is a critical distraction, yielding only two possible outcomes—either, from the popular viewpoint, we are individually at fault for our bad choices or, from a more feminist perspective, patriarchal structures of inequality make it incredibly difficult, if not impossible, for us to choose otherwise. Instead, we need to shift our focus to a different set of questions: Why are we so quick to pathologize those who have ugly sex and what does such a reading foreclose?

I have spent so much of my life ashamed of the ugly sex I've had. At the root of this shame is the reality that ugly sex presents a problem for feminist articulations of power and self-determination. In the world of feminist criticism and the sex-positivity movement, sex is framed in binary terms: sex either makes you feel pleasure (at worst) or empowered (at best); or sex makes you feel violated, devastated, and traumatized. This polarizing view of feminist sex emerged during the second wave of feminism with the now infamous pornography wars of the 1970s and '80s. Andrea Dworkin and Catharine MacKinnon were at the center of this debate.

For Dworkin, who penned *Pornography: Men Possessing Women*, pornography was inextricably tied to the domination of women and therefore was anti-feminist. Susan Brownmiller made similar claims, arguing that "there can be no 'equality' in porn, no female equivalent. . . . Pornography, like rape, is a male invention, designed to dehumanize women, to reduce the female to an object of sexual access, not to free sensuality from moralistic or parental inhibition." Laura Kipnis summarizes the sentiments of anti-pornography feminists as follows: "What pornography both portrays and endeavors to perpetuate is the deployment of male power over female bodies; while violating women through representation is just one instance of the male desire to violate women generally, it is the sole purpose of porn." And yet, as Kipnis points out, the anti-porn feminists were just as guilty of deploying power over female bodies: "Anti-pornography feminism," she writes, "shares a highly questionable alliance with the Right and the state to the extent that both see sexual representation as a potential site of regulation and law."

In her canonical 1981 essay "Lust Horizons: Is the Women's Movement Pro-Sex?" Ellen Willis expands upon Kipnis's claim, writing: "The movement's attacks on sexual exploitation and violence, male irresponsibility, pornography, and so on have often reinforced right-wing propaganda by giving the impression that feminists consider the loosening of controls over sexual behavior a worse threat to women than repression." The cost of these arguments from anti-sex feminists is the moralizing of what constitutes good and bad sex, and the further restriction of desires for those of marginalized genders.

On the other side of the pornography debate were sex-positive feminists, including Gayle Rubin, whose formative essay "Thinking Sex: Notes for a Radical Theory of the Politics of Sexuality" has become a touchstone for those offering more reparative readings not just of pornography but of a fuller spectrum of consensual sexual practice more generally. For Rubin, "a radical theory of sex must identify, describe, explain, and denounce erotic injustice and sexual oppression." In order to do so, we must challenge the pervasive assumptions that structure how sex is understood. The first assumption she discusses is sexual essentialism, which claims that sexuality is a "biological phenomenon or as an aspect of individual psychology" and is thus not shaped by our social worlds. Rubin goes on to name five other ideological formations that must be addressed: "sex negativity, the fallacy of misplaced scale, the hierarchical valuation of sex acts, the domino theory of sexual peril, and the lack of a concept of benign sexual variation." Of these, Rubin names sex negativity as the most important site for interrogation. Under the logic of sex negativity, any sex that isn't purely procreative is deemed suspicious if not dangerous, "presumed guilty until proven innocent."

This belief creates a socio-sexual hierarchy, in which heterosexual reproductive sex holds the highest value, with the lowest value attributed to "transsexuals, transvestites, fetishists, sadomasochists, sex workers such as prostitutes and porn models, and the lowliest of all, those whose eroticism transgresses generational boundaries." Desires outside of the "charmed circle" of reproductive heterosexuality are read as increasingly pathological and in need of state control—either in the hands of medical professionals or the courts, and sometimes both. And yet, Rubin will go on to note how, despite the fact that "the legal apparatus of sex is staggering most everyday social control is extralegal." By this she means that every day, informal practices of social policing are consistently deployed against minoritized sexual populations. And it is here that we find ourselves confronting the injunctions on pornography from the anti-porn feminists of the second wave.

That anti-pornography feminists were particularly concerned with representations of sadomasochism should not be surprising. Rubin summarizes this attack on S/M pornography as follows: "A great deal of antiporn propaganda implies that sadomasochism is the underlying and essential 'truth' toward which all pornography tends. Porn is thought to lead to S/M porn which in turn is alleged to lead to rape." For Rubin, "this discourse on sexuality is less a sexology than a demonology." Rubin highlights how the logic at play in the vehement opposition to S/M pornography implies that the pornography will cause sexist relations, when in fact it's the other way around: the sexist world we live in creates forms of pornography that reflect it. Unfortunately, the moral panic surrounding pornography—and S/M porn in particular—hasn't changed all that much since Rubin's essay was published in 1984.

I am grateful for the reparative scholarship on BDSM pornography by queer women of color, which has challenged this panic in ways that expand on Rubin's initial arguments about sexual negativity and its pleasures. Ariane Cruz notes that in the history of Black feminists' discussions of BSDM, there is a tendency to privilege a reading of BDSM and BDSM pornography as injurious, thus eradicating the life of pleasure present in these practices. This attention to injury and harm is tied to the history of sexual trauma experienced by Black women and other women of color. In *The Color of Kink: Black Women, BDSM, and Pornography*, Cruz intervenes in these discussions by offering a nuanced reading of the dynamics of pleasure and power imbued with the memory of chattel slavery: "Performances of black female sexual aggression, domination, humiliation, and submission in pornography and BDSM [are] crucial modes of black women's pleasure, power, and agency."

Cruz describes race play as "a practice that explicitly uses race to script power exchange and the dynamics of domination and submission." She emphasizes that we must recognize that the pain of chattel slavery need not negate the pleasure that can come with this BDSM reimagining. Engaging with the work of Mireille Miller-Young, Cruz continues:

> Black women's history of racial-sexual violence and 'exploitation' nuances their labor in pornography, a visual domain in which they are "ambivalently mythologized as sources of both fascination and disgust in a system organized around the marking and marketing of their absolute difference." Conveying this ambivalence "illicit eroticism" encompasses how black women capitalize on their "mythic racialized hypersexuality in the sexual economy."

What Cruz illuminates here is the ways that Black women are produced by white culture as ambivalent objects marked by both "fascination and disgust." The practices of race play and rape play in BDSM can function as examples of "BDSM's therapeutic possibility," for it is through reenacting past sexual traumas "on their own terms," that the Black women engaging in these practices "become agents of their own sexual pleasure and pain." Note here that pain is not transformed into pleasure; rather, in Cruz's theorization pleasure and pain exist side by side. Pushing back against the politics of respectability that forecloses the potentiality of pleasure in these sexual acts, Cruz thus reveals how race play opens up "innovative new modes of accessing pleasure."

Juana María Rodríguez offers another reparative reading of the fantasies of sexual objectification. In *Sexual Futures, Queer Gestures, and Other Latina Longings*, Rodríguez asks: "How do we begin to make sense of willful sexual fantasies of violence and abjection that sometimes creep into our psychic and erotic imaginations, and the shame, delight, or confusion that these thoughts generate?" Rodríguez believes that it is possible to "activate abjection as a resource for a reclamation of erotic-self-determination and world-making." "To deny our fantasies because they are too twisted, too painful, or too perverse, to erase their presence or censor their articulation in public life," she argues, "constitutes a particular kind of insidious violence that threatens to undermine our ability to explore the contours of our psychic lives and imaginary possibilities of the social worlds in which we exist." Within the world of fantasy, "we can rewrite scripts of sexualized objectification, subjection, and racialized violence" and "we can make familial shame sexy and state discipline erotic."

What I appreciate about Rodríguez's work is her attention to the ways in which BDSM fantasies—and their enactments—are not the only sites where "the coercive deployment of power" might play out. Rodríguez urges us to recognize "how fantasies of domestic bliss are likewise predicated on multiple forms of corrosive power." For Rodríguez, power's operations are insidious and can be found not just in the exceptional scenes of race play or daddy play in BDSM pornography, but also in quotidian social exchanges as well. Rodríguez's words point us away from the hyperfixation on the individual and their desires—which we see in the anti-sex feminists—and toward an understanding of the ways in which our desires are shaped, for better and for worse, by the world we live in.

I am curious about the ways in which many feminists are fixated on the sex that other people are having and see it as their job to determine whether or not that sex is okay—an imperative that continued through third-wave feminism and is alive and well today. In "Lust

Horizons," Ellen Willis responds to Pat Califia's essay "Feminism and Sadomasochism" in which Califia argues that he doesn't need to interrogate his desire for S/M—all that matters is that it turns him on. Willis asks the following questions:

> Does the need to act out fantasies of debasing oneself or someone else really require no further explanation? Does it have nothing to do with buried emotions of rage or self-hatred? Nothing to do with living in a hierarchical society where one is "superior" to some people and "inferior" to others, where men rule and women serve? Can the need to connect sexual pleasure with pain and humiliation be unrelated to the fact that our sexual organs and their function are still widely regarded as bad, contemptible, and embarrassing, a reproach to our higher spiritual natures? Is it irrelevant that our first erotic objects were our all-powerful parents, who too often hurt and humiliated us by condemning our childish sexuality?

These questions are important, for sex is political and our desires are shaped by the world. Yet, I am concerned by how easily Willis's questions pathologize sex as merely representing our "buried emotions" or our relationships with our parents (though, of course, these may have their own roles to play). At the same time, I too "don't believe our sexual desires are ever just arbitrary tastes." How can they be, when we are humans living in a world that tells us who and what to desire?

While I believe that it is important to look at how our desires are shaped by a world of systemic oppression and violence, I am wary of moralizing what sex is good and what sex is bad, for when we do that we fall back into a patriarchal, colonial logic of control. It also is imperative that our discussions of sexual desire take into account the ways in which those with more privilege—for example, white feminists—make grand, sweeping declarations that do not serve, and often harm, those with less privilege, in this case Black women and femmes. I want us to turn the focus inward. To borrow the words of those in the BDSM world, I don't need to yuck your yum.

Willis comes to a similar conclusion at the end of "Lust Horizons," arguing that "consenting partners have a right to their sexual proclivities, and that authoritarian moralism has no place in a movement for social change" before she goes on to argue that "a truly radical movement must look (to borrow a phrase from Rosalind Petchesky) beyond the right to choose, and keep focusing on the fundamental questions. Why do we choose what we choose? What would we choose if we had a real choice?" I can't help but feel as though we're caught in a game of what came first: the chicken or the egg? Do I desire objectification because it's what I have learned to desire as someone who was socialized as a woman? As a feminist who has spent countless hours exploring, critiquing, and unpacking my desires, I am not sure if we can ever fully disentangle our desires from our social and political realities.

I find myself wanting a both/and: we can and should see our desires as political and thereby question why it is that we desire what we desire. And, at the same time, there must still be space for play, pleasure, sex, and desire to exist outside of constant interrogation, so long as all parties are consenting. I too am curious about the answer to Willis's question: "What would we choose if we had a real choice?" The reality is, I don't know. The best I can do, while still living under the patriarchy, is root into my agency, choicefulness, and values as much as is possible (remembering that our values are often in conflict with what we desire), ensure that everyone is consenting, and continue to dream up pleasures that aren't shaped by systems of oppression—the intimacies to come.

☾

During my PhD, I took a course called Girls and Sex in the 21st Century. I thought I would feel at home in a class dedicated to exploring representations of sex and girlhood. Instead, I felt like an alien. Each time we read a book with a girl who didn't neatly fit into the box of the exemplary feminist, I felt seen. My colleagues, on the other hand, were enraged, frustrated, and dismissive. For them, these girls and women were unredeemable. My classmates desired perfection and felt repulsed by anyone that was messy or problematic. The person that most displeased them was Marie Calloway.

In 2011, an unknown writer pseudonymously named Marie Calloway published an essay entitled "adrien brody" and became an internet sensation overnight. The story was originally published as nonfiction on Calloway's blog and included the real name of the man she slept with and a photo of his cum on her face. Calloway (age twenty-one at the time) sent the piece to alt-lit writer Tao Lin and he published it on his website, Muumuu House, under the name "adrien brody," which is the pseudonym for the forty-something-year-old writer whom Calloway meets online and sleeps with in New York City. In this fictionalized account of a real story, Calloway arranges to meet up with a semi-famous literary critic in order to have sex; he comes on her face, she asks him to take a photo, and the story is born.

In 2013, Calloway published a collection of first-person sexual odysseys entitled *what purpose did i serve in your life*. While Calloway has classified the collection as a novel, the text invites us to read it as memoir: It is Calloway's face that stares at us on the front and back covers. In between these black-and-white images of Calloway's defiant face are thirteen stories in which the narrator, also named Marie Calloway, loses her virginity to a stranger, engages in sex work, and has a threesome with two male fans who she met on the internet. Each story is punctuated with Marie's age (eighteen in the first story and twenty-two in the last), and many of the stories include screenshots of Marie in various stages of undress as well as images of iPhone and Facebook cybersex messages. In each of the stories, Marie recounts feeling humiliated, objectified, and degraded during these sexual encounters—and also excited.

One cannot talk about Marie Calloway without discussing the polarized response to her work. In one camp there are critics and writers who proclaim that her writing is an attempt to get attention and describe it as boring, flat, and showing no talent. As Lisa Carver of *Vice* magazine notes, Calloway has been labeled "'a fame whore, with the accent on the whore.' Her 'lazy, Penthouse Letters style' is 'offending to real writers.'" In *what purpose did i serve in your life*, Calloway responds to these bad reviews and nasty online criticisms by appending these comments onto images of her own face in her essay "criticism." The comments range from "slut"—which is superimposed over a photo of Calloway drinking coffee—to longer diatribes, in which the anonymous author writes: "As a female myself I find her annoying not because she's writing about sex or insecurities or popularity (yawn yawn yawn, that is what shitty-ass TV is for) but because she's kind of a moron. . . ." and it goes on. Calloway's gesture of overlaying these comments on her affectless face resonates with her flat descriptions of sex. She continues to deny her readers and critics the affective responses they so desperately seek.

Others have been quick to claim that what Calloway is doing is not anything new, thus denying her any claim to creative originality. Hamilton Nolan dismissively writes: "Blah blah blah. It's a case of internet oversharing-turned-emotionally-hurtful not seen since . . . I dunno, yesterday probably, when some overeager teenager somewhere sent sexy photos to some more famous man upon whom she had developed a crush. It will happen again, somewhere else, tomorrow." In his dismissal of Calloway, Nolan fails to acknowledge that literature is rarely, if ever, new. In response to Nolan's article, and the claim that there is nothing new about Calloway's project, Melissa Petro notes,

> Seeing that women have been historically and contemporarily excluded from conversations about our bodies—and that such bodies are the epicenter of all existence, our sex being the conduit to life—I'd argue that what happens to a woman's body—what is done to them or what we choose to do with them—holds a special significance. Our bodies are politically contested territory, and so when a woman chooses to step forward and tell her stories in the first-person, I'd say that's pretty fucking significant.

Petro goes on to wonder: If there is nothing new or significant about Calloway's writing, then why is everyone talking about it so much?

An anonymous contributor to the now defunct literature blog *HTMLGIANT* sums up what they call "The Marie Calloway Problem" as follows: "We live in a society in which the mechanisms of commerce are designed to encourage us to believe that young women are randy hot sex machines, but we have a collective meltdown when one of them actually writes about sex that is anything other than vanilla. It breaks discourse. We're that unevolved." And the sex that Calloway has is anything but vanilla. In "bdsm" we see multiple screen shots of Marie's iMessage exchanges. In the image on the title page for the story, Marie writes, "Mew are you going to make me cry" to which her interlocutor responds "Yes. It will be glorious." Inside the pages of this story, there is a photo of Marie's bruised breast and descriptions of her vomiting during the BDSM sex she has.

Marie does not just have sex: She has ugly sex, and she does not appear to be too worried about the impact these encounters have on her emotional, physical, and psychic well-being. It's not so much the content—Marie's depictions of ugly sex—that has shocked and appalled readers and critics (although it certainly has); rather, it is the way that Calloway describes these experiences with a flat affect that makes critics feel so unsettled. Critics have tried to place Calloway's writing style within a particular genre. Hazel Cills refers to "adrien brody" as a "dispassionate account" of physical intimacy, while Stephen Marche describes Calloway's style as "calm, clinical . . . utterly pared down and horrifyingly bald." Michelle Orange at *Slate* proclaims that Calloway "joins a new chapter in the literature of disaffection. Here self-consciousness, far from a new literary toy, has flattened into landscape, an airless plane where stunted characters pass the occasional pebble back and forth like a cold potato."

In her essay "But Is It Good? The Problem With Marie Calloway's Affectless Realism," Elizabeth Spiers places Calloway's writing in a new—and problematically titled—genre called "Asperger's realism," a term coined by critic Christian Lorentzen to describe the work of Tao Lin. Spiers locates "Asperger's realism" within Calloway's writing as the "suggestion of mournful detachment [which is] characterized by affectlessness and a stilted literalism that gives the impression of a semi-robotic narrator that can only convey emotion by prefacing descriptions with 'I feel.' *This happened, then this, then this. I felt . . .*" Pushing back against these criticisms, Alexandra Molotkow offers a more capacious reading of Calloway's style, arguing that it is "flat, declarative, and personal. It's the language of *Livejournal* updates, which is as legitimate, as far as I'm concerned, as the language of leather-bound diarists etching in quill pen by candlelight."

Instead of reading Calloway's flat affect through the category of "Asperger's realism"—a term that I find quite ableist—I see Calloway's "dispassionate" accounts of sex more generatively, as a reminder that excessive emotions and flatness, so often caused by dissociation, are both signs of hysteria. Our feelings are either deemed "too much" or "not enough." In this case, what readers want from Calloway is over-the-top emotions. She should be feeling so much more than what she conveys via her flatness.

In this way, Calloway challenges the commonplace interpretation of symptoms (such as ambivalence, flatness, and excess) as leading to or being caused by pathology. Such interpretation lends itself all too easily to the logic of the cure. Through Marie's flat affect, Calloway pushes back against the history of pathology attached to hysterics. She exposes the subject's desire without feeling the need to get rid of the so-called symptoms.

Calloway's story "adrien brody" embodies her call toward flatness. This story is much tamer than many of the others in the collection, and that tameness is part of the reason why I feel that it is a more surprisingly generative site for thinking about ugly sex. On the surface, what makes "adrien brody" a story of ugly sex is that Marie messages a writer she admires but has never met before and tells him that she wants to have sex with him when she is visiting New York City. The man is twice her age and is not very attractive. He also happens to have a girlfriend, but he does not tell her until they are en route to his apartment. This confession causes Marie to question the image of this man that she had created, in which he "seemed to uphold human dignity and the sacredness of human feeling and connection. And so it seemed unbelievable that he would cheat." But the disillusionment that Marie feels causes her to feel "sexually excited, because he was betraying those values." Adrien Brody's admission and his justification for not telling her (he was afraid Marie would not meet him if he told her in advance) results in a host of ambivalent feelings: disillusionment and excitement, "the feeling of being flattered" and an "abstract feeling of disgust." And yet Marie tells the reader that she "couldn't pass up the chance to sleep with [her] intellectual idol" and so she leans her head against his chest as the cab drives up to his apartment building.

After arriving at Adrien Brody's place, Marie inspects his apartment while they discuss pornography. Marie asks him to show her the porn that he looks at and is delighted when he proclaims, "I think that you can tell a lot about a person depending on what kind of porn they watch.' 'I always thought that too!' I was excited someone shared my strong held belief about personality and porn habits." But she's disappointed when Adrien Brody shows her the porn he enjoys looking at: "It was all pictures of modelesque brunette women posing. They didn't look like typical pornstars, but they were all very thin and kind of generic looking. And there was the usual feeling of objectification in the photos. So I judged him."

Marie is acutely aware of the ways that men objectify women, and at every moment during their sexual encounter she is aware of her position in their exchange, at one point remarking, as she gives him a blow job, "I've never been able to figure out why I get off on being used as an object." A page later she explains how she feels frustrated by how "strange and unfair" it is that "the possibility of sex relies on just one thing, the man's ability to get an erection." She goes on to tell the reader: "I thought then how it's really unfair how men want and expect you to be really slutty and wild in bed, but they then laugh at you for it. You're either frigid and boring or you're unintentionally funny and crazy." Marie has a hard time figuring out how to occupy a space in between these poles, which leads her to admit: *"I'm totally powerless in the face of men."* It is worth noting that she makes this statement right after slapping Adrien Brody's face.

While Marie has moments of feeling powerless or threatened in front of men, she is also an active player in her sexual exchanges, making requests that are all too easy to judge as a reflection of her own disempowerment. The perfect example of this is the infamous scene in which Adrien Brody comes on Marie's face. It is unclear who brought up the idea, but it is Marie who feels "vaguely annoyed" at her partner's ambivalence. Her feelings of annoyance continue after the act has taken place, when Adrien Brody tells her, with his voice shaking, "I feel so vulnerable." Marie, with great poignancy and flat affect, states, "I felt annoyed that he was only focused on his own feelings, after he had just shot a load in my face." In an attempt to shift the focus back onto herself, she asks him to take a photo of her with his cum still on her face, and he acquiesces.

Marie might feel powerless in the face of men, but here we see her adjusting her relation to her face, turning it into a site where she can encounter her desire. And her desire for ugly sex is nowhere better embodied than in the cum drying on Marie's face and her refusal to make much, if anything, of the fact that Adrien Brody just came on her face. Instead of getting up to wash her face, and thus washing away her desire, Marie lets the cum dry, as she and Adrien Brody "talked more about Gramsci, and then our feelings." Marie wonders how Adrien Brody could respect her and "have this intelligent conversation with me, when I was laying there with his cum all over my face." Marie's flat affect turns this scene of ugly sex into a moment of dark comedy, where the act of sex is almost instantly forgotten, but still lingers on Marie's face.

When she does get up to wash it off, she grabs Adrien Brody's hand and brings him with her to the bathroom: "Come with me," she commands him. Marie transforms the act of coming on her into an act of coming with her. She wants him to witness this act. By bringing Adrien Brody into the bathroom with her, Marie turns the act of washing into an intimate encounter with both Adrien Brody and her desire. In Calloway's words, this act can be read as "an elaborate strategy of purification, to blend honesty and revulsion until they are no longer separable." What makes this strategy—this ritual of purification—elaborate is that Marie refuses to rid it of revulsion. While she literally washes the cum off her face, her act of washing beside Adrien Brody can also be seen as an attempt to blend the honesty of her desire with revulsion or a sense of self-loathing.

In a disarming moment of metafictional self-reflection and narrative dissociation, Marie shifts into third person to describe and perhaps even attempt to explain her desire to the reader:

> She works under an assumed name. She once wished she were in Japan, but now she subjects her fascination with Japanese culture—its preoccupation with reified cuteness, with fastidiousness, with compliant femininity—to elaborate scrutiny, with a variety of unconventional tools: submersion, revulsion, role-playing, obsession, ridicule, mimicry. She writes with stark and troubling ambivalence. It can be easily misread as apathy, numbness; this is part of what she risks. An elaborate strategy of purification, to blend honesty and revulsion until they are no longer separable, until readers must begin to shut down themselves. She is sure enough of herself to confront and even

invite misunderstanding, as though misunderstanding might offer a way forward toward an authenticity beyond the deceptive surfaces of exhibitionism.

Marie does not judge her fascination with Japanese culture—it is worth noting here that Calloway is part Japanese—or its preoccupations. When she uses the term *scrutinize* she is not referring to an act of critical judgment. Rather, she uses the term to denote the act of "looking searchingly at something; a searching gaze." The tools she uses—submersion, revulsion, role-playing, obsession, ridicule, mimicry—are, we are told, "unconventional." Instead of distancing herself from the cultural fascination with reified cuteness, with fastidiousness, with compliant femininity, Marie opts instead to immerse herself in these forms of idealized femininity through submersion, role-playing, obsession, and mimicry. In fact, when Marie recognizes that Adrien Brody is nervous, in order to help make him come she reenacts a Japanese pornography scene she had once watched: "I opened my eyes and looked into his and smiled."

When she comes face to face with her desire, which for Marie is located in the ambivalence of ugly sex, she becomes aware of how desire and repulsion are intimately linked—not just for her, but for all subjects. For Calloway, when it comes to ugly sex, the repulsion you feel in the moment might be an integral element of your desire and thus increase your feelings of attraction. In fact, one might even desire the same thing she finds repulsive. In approaching her desire—embodied in the ugly sex she has—through a flat affect, Calloway refuses to pathologize herself. Her flatness just lets her desires be.

Marie is aware of the ambivalence running through all her sexual encounters, and she understands how that ambivalence might trouble the reader, might cause them to read her as numb or apathetic. While Marie describes ugly sex via flat affect, she recognizes the potential that such a project holds: "Misunderstanding," she writes, "might offer a way forward toward an authenticity beyond the deceptive surfaces of exhibitionism." Marie's statement is reminiscent of the psychoanalytic axiom that truth emerges from the mistake. Marie is asking us to read below the deceptive surfaces, to get underneath the symptom, to get beneath our desire to cure hysteria, and to come face to face with the authenticity that lies below. Confronting the ambivalence of Marie's desires, then, can lead to an encounter with the truth of one's own desires—which might be just as ambivalent as Marie's.

☾

Ugly sex is not a strictly a cisheteronormative experience. While much of the sex I had throughout my adolescence was with cis men, I have always known that I was queer. When I discovered the porn channels on our family's satellite TV, I was only interested in watching people with vulvas have sex. My first sexual encounters were with my elementary school friend Jessica. One day we were in her bedroom reenacting a scene from a movie (I can't remember which) where a man and a woman tossed each other around in bed. As I pinned Jessica to the bed, our bodies started to move against one another, and eventually we kissed. For months, we'd make out and explore each other's bodies. Unfortunately, growing up in the suburbs in the late '90s and early 2000s meant that no one was out as queer. And so when high school started, Jessica stopped talking to me. It wasn't until I started university that I was with another human with a vulva.

It is true that I have found far more representations of ugly sex among presumably cis straight folks than I have in queer literature. This does not mean that queers do not have ugly sex—it's just that they're reticent to talk about it. In her book *Body Work*, Melissa Febos writes: "While it's well-known that straight sex is full of fake female orgasms and that homophobic bigots think that all queer sex is depraved, there are few depictions of realistically bad queer sex. This is in part because there are so many fewer descriptions of queer sex overall, but it is also due to the phenomenon of image management that often occurs in representation of marginalized communities." Despite the fact that "all of us queers know that not all of our sex is healthy and satisfying," we are beholden to policing by "our own communities to represent our sex in an idealized way."

Torrey Peters's novel *Detransition, Baby* is one of the few places where I have found representations of ugly queer sex. Peters's novel follows Reese, a trans woman; her ex-partner Ames/Amy, a trans woman who has detransitioned; and Ames's new partner Katrina, who is pregnant with his child. The central plot line is that Ames doesn't feel like he can be a father to this child without erasing his transness and so he asks Reese, whom he hasn't spoken to since they broke up three years prior when he began to detransition, if she would consider joining him and Katrina in raising this child together. While this is the drama that propels the book forward, the novel begins by introducing us to Reese and her desire for ugly sex.

"The question, for Reese," the novel begins, is "Were married men just desperately attractive to her? Or was the pool of men who were available to her as a trans woman only those who had already locked down a cis wife and could now 'explore' with her?" Reese asks herself these questions as she waits in a Beamer while the married man she is with goes to buy condoms. This man, "was similar to her others. A handsome, married alpha-type who put her on a leash in the bedroom. Only this one was better, because he was an HIV-positive cowboy-turned-lawyer." When her "cowboy" returns to the car, condoms and lube in tow, he asks Reese "'Do we really need these tonight? You know I'm gonna want to knock you up.'"

This question, and his desire to bareback with Reese, is

> why she put up with him: He got it. With him, she'd discovered sex that was really and truly dangerous. Cis women, she supposed, rubbed against a frisson of danger every time they had sex. The risk, the thrill, that they might get pregnant—a single fuck to fuck up (or bless?) their lives. For cis women, Reese imagined, sex was a game played on the precipice of a cliff. But until her cowboy, she hadn't ever had the pleasure of that particular danger. Only now, with his HIV, had she found an analogue to a cis woman's life changer. Her cowboy could fuck her and mark her forever. He could fuck her and end her. His cock could obliterate her.

The possibility of exposing herself to the danger of contracting HIV turns Reese on, as it allows her to feel some proximity to the fear that cis women experience when it comes to the risk of pregnancy— in addition, of course, to the risks of getting STIs and getting hurt or even killed.

Reese experiences a similar draw to ugly sex in her relationship with Stanley, another married cis man whom she dates before Amy.

After Stanley hits Reese for the first time, she reflects on how she desires him "but she wouldn't say that she liked him. She liked his jealousy, his controlling behavior, the way he told her how to dress. She liked seeing herself through his eyes: vulnerable, fragile, prone to the exasperatingly feminine qualities. . . . She liked how he called her a whore, and then bought her expensive gifts. . . . The more he demeaned her, she knew, the more she'd hooked him." We're told how Reese "had long since discovered that most talk about owning her turned her stomach liquid with desire."

She doesn't care that she met Stanley "on a fetish site with the word 'tranny' in the name." According to Reese, "It's a mark of prudish inexperience to think that being fetishized and objectified isn't the hottest thing going in the bedroom." She doesn't care that Stanley refers to her genitals as "purely decorative"; in fact, "instead of being offended, she was turned on." While Reese knows that she should be disgusted and appalled by Stanley, and her desire for him, she also believes that, as a trans woman, "You don't get to choose who you fuck, you get to choose from among those who want to fuck you." What Reese's proclamation highlights is the truth of desirability politics: some bodies get to choose who they fuck, and others—fat, disabled, poor, non-white, ugly, older, or trans—are left to pick from what's on offer. Put another way, as Amia Srinivasan poignantly notes in her essay "The Right to Sex": "Sexual self-objectification may mean one thing for a woman who, by virtue of her whiteness, is already taken to be a paradigm of female beauty, but quite another thing for a black or brown woman, or a trans woman."

Srinivasan's essay led me to another: Andrea Long Chu's "On Liking Women." In a passage strikingly similar to Reese's proclamations about what's at the root of her desire to be treated, as the phrase goes, "like a woman," Chu explains her desire to transition:

> I transitioned for gossip and compliments, lipstick and mascara, for crying at the movies, for being someone's girlfriend, for letting her pay the check or carry my bags, for the benevolent chauvinism of bank tellers and cable guys, for the telephonic intimacy of long-distance female friendship, for fixing my make-up in the bathroom flanked like Christ by a sinner on each side, for sex toys, for feeling hot, for

getting hit on by butches, for that secret knowledge of which dykes to watch out for, for Daisy Dukes, bikini tops, and all the dresses, and, my god, for the breasts.

In a statement reminiscent of Ellen Willis's observation that "our most passionate convictions about sex do not necessarily reflect our real desires," Chu quips: "But now you begin to see the problem with desire: we rarely want the things we should." At the same time, "Nothing good comes of forcing desire to conform to political principle," Chu writes. As Amia Srinivasan points out, in her discussion of Chu's essay, "This declaration, as Chu is well aware, threatens to bolster the argument made by anti-trans feminists: that trans women equate, and conflate, womanhood with the trappings of traditional femininity, thereby strengthening the hand of patriarchy."

Reese's desires are only a few steps away from Chu's. What Reese wants, and what she experiences via ugly sex, is the banality of violence against cis women. Statistically, we know that trans women experience violence at disproportionately higher rates than cis women—especially Black trans women and women of color. And yet it would be a mistake to claim that the root cause of that violence is the same. Transmisogyny is not the same thing as misogyny, and it is the latter that Reese wants access to: "Reese spent a lifetime observing cis women confirm their gender through male violence. . . . Hear women define themselves through pain, or rage against the assumption that they do, which still places pain front and center. Hear the strange satisfaction when they talk about the men who have hurt them—the unspoken subtext of it being *because I am a woman.*"

She is quick to acknowledge how admitting these desires will lead the "liberal feminists—especially the trans-hating variety" to "accuse her of misogyny, of being a secret man, a Trojan horse in slutty lingerie who sought to recapitulate under the guise of womanhood all the abusive tropes that they, in the second wave, had sought to put in the past." For Reese, it is unfair that she, a trans woman, be expected to uphold "impeccable feminist politics that barely served her." Instead, "she'd be over here, getting knocked around." What Reese recognizes is that feminists put one another in a bind when they proclaim that feminist sex must be empowering. We live in a world where our bodies are objectified against our will no matter what. And so we might as well find a way to get off.

Reese's desire for ugly sex makes all the more sense when you look at the history of trans exclusionary radical feminists (TERFs). In "Liking Women," Chu offers an example from the West Coast Lesbian Conference of 1973, in which trans singer Beth Elliott's performance was interrupted by protestors who wanted her to leave the stage. Chu explains how "the following day, the radical feminist Robin Morgan, editor of the widely influential 1970 anthology *Sisterhood Is Powerful*, delivered a hastily rewritten keynote [that was] soon printed in the short-lived underground newspaper Lesbian Tide." Morgan proclaims:

> I will not call a male "she"; thirty-two years of suffering in this androcentric society, and of surviving, have earned me the title "woman"; one walk down the street by a male transvestite, five minutes of his being hassled (which he may enjoy), and then he dares, he dares to think he understands our pain? No, in our mothers' names and in our own, we must not call him sister. We know what's at work when whites wear blackface; the same thing is at work when men wear drag.

In Morgan's words, trans women can never be women unless they experience the objectification that cis women have experienced their whole lives. And so the best way to do that is to put on "the Daisy Dukes, bikini tops, and all the dresses" and have ugly sex.

In Peters's novel, Amy's sexual desires are similarly shaped by her desires for the quotidian and the feminine. When she is nineteen, Amy meets the thirty-six-year-old Patrick after the two connect on a Yahoo group for cross-dressers. In the car ride over to Glamour Boutique, Patrick asks Amy if she "likes the same kind of *stories*" that he does: erotica from Fictionmania, an online archive filled with over twenty-thousand stories "of women forcing boys into girlhood." We're told that "The stories were dangerous. But she knew, from the self-evident existence of the site, that all over the world eyes were eating up the text and penises were spurting at the climaxes of the stories of when the cross-dressers themselves first took dick, or when a former-boy-now-buxom-shemale was humiliated and raped, or when a strong man was feminized against his will." On Fictionmania, the stories replicate the subordination and humiliation that Reese gets off on. Amy understands that "the femininity forced upon the males was the ultimate in degradation and humiliation" and wonders "what did that say about her opinion of femininity?" She recognizes that she would be judged by others who'd "just think she hated femininity and equated it with humiliation" and it is not until she transitions, "until she met women into rape-play, into servitude and infantilization, women who had eroticized and sexually defanged every unspeakable shame and violation life had thrown at their womanhood," that she understands her desires.

But what Amy loves the most is perhaps the softest and tamest of them all: "the *Wedding Dress or Married* category." She explains to Patrick:

> Weddings are so kinky. I think most non-kinky people just never realize it. Think about it! You put a woman in a special elaborate outfit, and then one man gives her to another man like some kind of BDSM scene, and then they put like a symbolic collar on the woman's finger. . . . Then he picks her up and takes her away to fuck her while everyone else knows it's happening! It's so dirty. It's like the kinkiest thing I could ever imagine and it actually happens all the time. So I like to think about it happening to me.

Recalling Rodríguez's claim that "fantasies of domestic bliss are likewise predicated on multiple forms of corrosive power," it is not surprising that what gets Amy off is the most mundane and cishetero scene of all.

After Patrick and Amy acquire new dresses and bust forms, they go back to Patrick's place to have sex. Amy remembers "the day at the Glamour Boutique as erotically charged. But she would remember very little about the sex that she and Patrick had, only that it was not erotic. . . . The erotic part lay in the dressing up, the foreplay, the mental switch into the female role." The sex that she has with Patrick is "a distant faraway sex—one that Amy felt like she hadn't participated in" as Patrick "vacantly" fucks Amy while watching "the shemale porn DVD playing on the TV." While Amy is repulsed by Patrick, she imagines Jen, the transgender clerk from Glamour Boutique, fucking her. And it is in this "faraway place" that "she could enjoy herself for once, she could feel everything as it should be." In order to engage in ugly sex, the sex that is the closest she can get to what she truly desires, Amy dissociates.

Aware of her tendency to dissociate during sex, Amy remarks that "the word 'dissociate' sounded pathologizing to her at first—why should she be accused of dissociating when normal people get to call it fantasizing, and talk about how fantasy must make their sex better and better?" Amy's question points to the ways in which the strategies we use to engage in intimacy can be read differently based on someone's subject position and desires. At the same time, "pathology felt more and more apt the more sex that she had" for Amy recognizes how connecting with another requires an act of disappearing, and that this disappearing act hurts those that she cares about. And so she "grew to dread and avoid sex with specifically those most-liked people," eventually resulting in the end of those relationships, "concluding in a final angst in which the loneliness that had made her want to connect with someone in the first place returned upon her tenfold with every attempt to have sex." Thus, it makes sense that when she first has sex with Reese, Amy cannot stop crying. The poppers that she and Reese took enable her to let down her guard, to be present with Reese, which "felt like some kind of healing, some kind of redemption." Eventually, however, Amy's wall will come back up and she will stop having sex with Reese.

Like Amy's, my earlier sexual experiences were shaped by conflicting desires to connect and to flee. A part of me wants to turn, desperately, toward another, while another part of me wants, so urgently, to run away. While talking about these conflicting desires, a friend refers to these moments as "the emotional hunger games." Confusion, ambiguity, and ambivalence, I have learned from Janina Fisher, are "manifestations of struggles between parts triggered by each other as well as by trauma-related stimuli." The desire for connection, activated by the trauma of my mom's death and my father's emotional abandonment; the need to flee, activated by the trauma-related stimuli of rape: This is the terrain of my ugly sexual experiences.

In using the language of parts, I am invoking the work of therapist Richard C. Schwartz. In his book *No Bad Parts*, Schwartz, the developer of Internal Family Systems, explains that the mono-mind belief system has us thinking that "you have one mind, out of which different thoughts and emotions and impulses and urges emanate." Schwartz's work as a therapist taught him something different: each one of us has different parts or "sub-minds." "Remembering a time when you faced a dilemma, it's likely you heard one part saying, 'Go for it!' and another part saying, 'Don't you dare!' Because we just consider that to be a matter of having conflicted thoughts, we don't pay attention to the inner players behind the debate," he writes. Schwartz notes how the mono-mind paradigm has pathologized the presence of parts, and the person who has multiple personalities is viewed as "sick or damaged" as a result of trauma, which has fragmented their supposedly unitary mind. But really, these parts are protectors, here to help us survive in a traumatizing world. As such, there are "no bad parts."

Since starting somatic trauma therapy, I've been learning the language of parts to better understand how structural dissociation has impacted my life. In their book *The Haunted Self: Structural Dissociation and the Treatment of Chronic Traumatization*, the authors describe how when one is living in an environment that is chronically traumatizing, a way to cope with the uncertainty is to split into day child and night child. The day child makes sure to show up to school, get good grades, complete their homework. The night child keeps watch for danger. This is the landscape of structural dissociation, and it helped me understand how I was able to be so highly functional while living through ongoing daily trauma. For most of my life, I just figured that it was pure survival mode. I had no choice but to get good grades, raise my younger brother, care for my disabled father, work forty hours a week, and somehow have a social life. That I accomplished all of the above while struggling with drug addiction, high every day from as soon as I got to school, has not ceased to amaze me.

It was Janina Fisher's book *Transforming the Living Legacy of Trauma* that helped me understand how my brain managed these feats. Fisher explains that our brain is divided into two halves: The left side of the brain is the chief executive brain or, as Fisher calls it, the "going on with normal life" self, and the right side of the brain is the survival brain or the "traumatized part of the personality." In between the left and right sides is the corpus callosum, a thick nerve tract that enables communication and collaboration between the two. *Corpus callosum* is Latin for "tough body." Perhaps we could say that those of us living with complex trauma have a *corpus tener*: a body that is delicate or tender. Our delicate corpus makes structural dissociation more possible. Under chronic stress and trauma, a "survival-related splitting occurs" and the left- and right-brain sides begin to function independently of one another, "to allow the individual to do two things at once: to carry on as if nothing has happened and to prepare for the next threat—and the next and the next."

I see in Fisher's words a description of what happens during ugly sex: One part of us holds the desire for this connection, and the possibility of pleasure, while another part holds our repulsion, our fear, and our pain. Ugly sex requires a kind of splitting; or, put a different way, this splitting goes hand in hand with ugly sex. Ugly sex was all I knew throughout my adolescent and teen years, years ruled by structural dissociation. During sex, I had to ignore the fact that I was being used, that I was putting myself in danger in order to receive the contact of my skin against another's. Similarly, at school I had to ignore the bullying in order to get good grades, while another part of me remained on guard, waiting for the next threat to come. At home, I had to ignore that my father—the man who should have protected me—was another bully I had to hide from. I was structured by ambivalence. One part of me screamed for connection while another reached for protection. This dance between the desire for connection and protection is one of the hallmark signs of disorganized attachment.

Attachment theory was developed by John Bowlby, a British psychologist. During his time working with young children at Tavistock Institute in London in 1946, Bowlby found a direct correlation

between the delinquent behavior of the youths he studied and a sep-
aration event from their primary caregivers. Bowlby would go on to
argue that when caregivers are absent, emotionally unavailable, abusive, overbearing, or all of the above, children's core developmental
needs for emotional regulation and attunement, safety and security,
aren't met. These absences negatively impact how they will relate to
themselves and to the world.

In 1950, Bowlby returned as the director of the children's ward at
Tavistock and began work with Mary Ainsworth. By 1978, Ainsworth
would define three attachment styles: secure, avoidant/dismissive, and
anxious/preoccupied. Psychotherapist Jessica Fern, author of *Polysecure: Attachment, Trauma and Consensual Nonmonogamy*, explains
how those with an avoidant/dismissive style tended to have caregivers
who were "mostly unavailable, neglectful or absent," with a parenting
style that is "cold, distant, critical or highly focused on achievement
and appearance." The child in this environment learns that it's best to
not depend on others to meet their needs.

When these children become adults, they pride themselves on being self-sufficient and tend to distance themselves from others. On
the other hand, those who are anxious-preoccupied may have had
caregivers who expressed love but were inconsistent. They thus came
to fear abandonment. As adults, this fear results in "a disconnection
or loss of self through over-functioning and over-adapting in the relationship in an attempt to maintain and preserve the connection."
Self-sacrifice and disavowal of needs are the terrain of the anxious/
preoccupied.

For most of my adult-in-therapy life, I've assumed that I have an
anxious attachment style. I find myself in relationship after relationship with people who tend to pull away—those with avoidant attachment. They take two steps back and I run right after them. Hands
wrapped around their body. Begging them not to leave me. But after reading *Polysecure*, I learned that there's another attachment
style that I hadn't heard of, one defined in 1986 by psychologists
Mary Main and Judith Solomon: disorganized attachment, or the
fearful-avoidant style. Children who develop disorganized attachment vacillate between anxious and avoidant because they learned
that their caregivers were not safe. Main termed this response "fright

without solution." And it is here that I find myself. "The disorganized attachment style," explains Fern,

> is most commonly associated with trauma and it typically arises when a child experiences their attachment figure as scary, threatening or dangerous. When we are afraid, our attachment system gets activated to seek proximity to and comfort from our attachment figure, but what happens when our attachment figure is the person causing the threat? This puts the child in a paradoxical situation where their care-taker, who is supposed to be the source of their comfort and the solution to their fears, is actually the source of their fear instead.

Disorganized attachment shows up in families that have experienced lots of chaos. For me, this looked like the loss of my mom when I was eleven; my dad developing ALS just a few years later; our descent into poverty, which brought with it unstable housing and two winters without heat in our home. Disorganized attachment also develops when our caregiver is unpredictable, when we're unsure of whether we'll receive their love or their punishment. What do you do when the person who's supposed to comfort you is the person who is causing the harm in the first place? You vacillate between the desire to be close and the desire to pull away. These conflicting desires played a major part in shaping my sexual relationships.

When looking back at poems I wrote in my early twenties, I see my disorganized attachment captured. These poems were written for a class assignment, meant to represent the voices of secondary characters in novels that we'd read that term. But teenage me is written all over them.

"I LOVE YOU"

i let him kiss me; does he taste my emptiness?
i let him kiss me, knowing that it will never mean anything
but still it means everything.
yet i do not care. his kiss means nothing just as i mean
nothing.
and still i let him kiss me.
he looks at me and i say: it's okay. i will be okay.

how easily some words flow from my lips.
and so he continues to kiss me; his hands feel as though
they are floating down my body.
his caress is more that i can comprehend, and yet it should
mean nothing.
he looks at me and kisses me with such undeniable passion
that i commend him for being able to put on such a
production.
to produce it at will for my (dis)pleasure.
and i let him undress me.
he says that the pants are his and he's right.
they are his; mine were soaked in the rain.
i wish he would say that i was his as well, but kisses will
fall from his lips many times and those words will never
come.
he touches me and i shudder and yet i do not know why.
his touch means nothing to me. it is soft and yet coarse.
it should mean something and yet it means nothing.
he wants to kiss every part of my body and i let his lips
fix all of the words that exited his mouth not long ago.
i could not, would not, ever mean everything to him.
i could mean something, but being something means just as
much as nothing.
i want to be someone and yet the kisses fall from my lips
with far greater ease than those words ever could.
he gives me the passion that i desire but it is devoid of
sentiment.
his passion is a fire that turns to ice with such haste
that it burns my skin.
and yet i cannot tell him to stop kissing me.
i desire to be desired; even if i mean everything now and
nothing once he has had his pleasure.
i will allow myself to be his desire for this moment as
though this is my only chance to be wanted by another human
being.
we lie there after and i refuse to dress.
i need to be bare in front of him for a bit longer so that

he can see how he has not only stripped me of my clothing,
but of my self-worth as well.
or did i do that when i put on his pants, knowing that he
would soon take them off.
we wax sentimental, speaking words that neither of us
understand. words that require us to feel something that we
long since decided had no necessity.
i smile and laugh and pretend as though this meant nothing.
it scares me how easily i can lie to myself, lie to him.
and then i just lie here numb. naked. exposed. and nothing.
i just want you to see me as something.
we sleep next to one another and yet our bodies never
touch.
we cannot risk that level of intimacy; how hilarious that
thought.
and now, in this moment i am no longer a desire.
i am nothing.
and i knew i could be that all along.

Because of all of the gaps in memory, I had to create a story of myself. In this story, I have no clue just how traumatized I am. And yet, here in this poem, I can see how much I did know. That connection required me to sacrifice my self-worth: *i will allow myself to be his desire for this moment as though this is my only chance to be wanted by another human being.* That sex and emotional intimacy cannot exist simultaneously: *he gives me the passion that i desire but it is devoid of sentiment.* That I wanted intimacy, to be everything, but at the same time was so terrified of love, so comfortable in being nothing. That love is so dangerous that the words "I love you" can only exist in the poem's title: the only space in which those words can feel safe.

Reading this poem, I can see my disorganized attachment so clearly. It can be found here too:

"AN IDIOT'S HOBBY"

Words disjointed course through my veins
like melted plastic.

Tools made of metal dismember me,
Limb by limb
Until I lie in pieces on your floor.
Pain produced by sentiment of folly,
Drips from my veins in place of red
Until nothing but a sea surrounds me.
You clumsily put the pieces back together;
But you know not of their place
And you do not know yours.
The words that spilt from your lips:
Cancerous,
Tainted my blood.
It hurt so deeply I know not
What recourse to take.
So I pulled them apart;
Letter by letter.
Now I sit in a pool of alphabet soup and my own blood.
I bleed myself out in hopes that your words would be truer.
You, the master of words
And of Love,
What say you now?
Make sense of your words,
My pain,
And all that mess you left
When you said you loved me.

When I read these poems together, I see what happens when I get to hear the words that I so desire (i love you): It dismembers me, infects me, leaves me bleeding out on the floor. These words literally fragment me. I cannot hold myself together when faced with the intimacy that I so desperately desire. It is too much. My attachment wounding taught me that the things I wanted were inherently unsafe. And so I spent years and years of my life running from love, like the speaker in this last poem, and toward those who would provide a similar experience to what I grew up with, as the speaker in the first poem does. One part desires connection and another part desires to flee. This kind of ambivalence is common among those living with sexual trauma, structural dissociation, and disorganized attachment. Most of the sexual encounters I had as a teenager and young adult fall into the category of ugly sex. At the same time that I was enjoying the experience, I was also seeking escape. I wanted closeness. I wanted intimacy. And I was terrified of both.

Like the queer Greek poet Sappho, "I [didn't] know what I should do: two states of mind in me." I find much solace in Anne Carson's exploration of what Sappho meant when she called eros "bittersweet." In response to her own question, "What does the word mean?," Carson muses: "Eros seemed to Sappho at once an experience of pleasure and pain. Here is contradiction and perhaps paradox. To perceive this eros can split the mind in two." Desire is, Carson proclaims, "an ambivalent being, at once friend and enemy, who informs the erotic experience with emotional paradox."

Quoting Simone Weil, Carson offers this elucidation: "All our desires are contradictory, like the desire for food. I want the person I love to love me. If he is, however, totally devoted to me he does not exist any longer and I cease to love him. And as long as he is not totally devoted to me he does not love me enough. Hunger and repletion." Simply put, desire ceases to exist once we obtain what it is we've been seeking. Or, as Carson puts it, "Pleasure and pain at once register upon the lover, inasmuch as the desirability of the love object derives, in part, from its lack."

Trauma adds another layer to this ambivalence at the heart of desire, for trauma pits connection and protection against one another. I see my ugly sexual encounters as my attempt to hold both simultaneously. Each time I slept with another boy who wouldn't call me afterward, I was enacting the same dynamic that shaped my attachment. You could call this a pathology; or you could call it an attempt to move toward connection. Every time I had ugly sex, it was as though a part of me was saying, *Intimacy is possible. Intimacy is coming, I promise.* In a world that pathologizes the desire for ugly sex, these moments of being touched helped me imagine new forms of intimacy to come.

With this phrase, I am playing on the double meanings of come, as both a call to a future temporal moment, and as bodily fluid. I had ugly sex because I was hungry for connection. I consented because of skin hunger. I needed to accept whatever scraps of touch were offered to me, whether they came in the form of empty consent or ugly sex. If we take a harm-reduction approach here, we can see how these moments of intimacy, while sad and harmful in their own ways, filled a hole within me.

Yes, sometimes we must take what is on offer—even when what is on offer is so, so far from what we deserve. And, at the same time, I can't help but wonder: Must we write off these experiences in their entirety simply because they weren't what we had hoped and longed for? Isn't it true that, as Alok Vaid Menon has said, "You survive by finding beauty in impossible and bleak situations"? My dissertation committee once lovingly called me out for my desire for the reparative gesture. I get it. We must be careful to not silver-line experiences that were harmful or traumatizing. For such gestures erase the harm, the messiness, the ugliness, because they make us uncomfortable. I want to resist binary thinking, for it's not so simple as an either/or here: Either we label the experience as bad and discard it; or we find the reparative reading. For me, it has to be both/and. Both/and is the only gesture that will fully capture the nuances of my desire for ugly sex.

My ugly sexual encounters also served as a stepping stone to the intimacy I would come to experience later in my life—intimacy that was, to borrow the words of the late José Esteban Muñoz, always on the horizon. I learned how to let myself be touched physically—and, eventually, I learned that it was okay to be touched emotionally too. There will always be a part of me that wishes that I hadn't needed ugly sex as a survival strategy; and another part of me is grateful that I could find something, anything, to help me feel less alone. Desire is always so much more complicated than we'd like it to be. And, at the same time, it is this messiness and ambivalence that makes desire all the more magical.

As someone who has had a lot of ugly sex, I want to reimagine the forms that sexual intimacy can take. I want us, to borrow the words of Maggie Nelson, "to allow ourselves to be unafraid of the contaminations of ambivalence." If we can stop pathologizing acts of sexual intimacy that fail to live up to feminist standards, we can open ourselves up to imagining new forms of intimacy that enable us to be seen and celebrated in our ugliness.

In a keynote address for the Femmes of Color Symposium, disability justice advocate Mia Mingus argued for the political necessity of embracing the ugly.

> As the (generational) effects of global capitalism, genocide, violence, oppression and trauma settle into our bodies, we must build new understandings of bodies and gender that can reflect our histories and our resiliency, not our oppressor or our self-shame and loathing. We must shift from a politic of desirability and beauty to a politic of ugly and magnificence. That moves us closer to bodies and movements that disrupt, dismantle, disturb. Bodies and movements ready to throw down and create a different way for all of us, not just some of us.

Mingus wants us to see the power and magic of the ugly for "how it has shaped us and been exiled. . . . Seeing it for what it is: some of our greatest strength." And so she poses a series of questions for the audience:

> What would it mean if we were ugly? What would it mean if we didn't run from our own ugliness or each other's? What would it mean to acknowledge our ugliness for all it has given us, how it has shaped our brilliance and taught us about how we never want to make anyone else feel? What would it take for us to be able to risk being ugly, in whatever that means for us. What would happen if we stopped apologizing for our ugly, stopped being ashamed of it?

I'm not longer willing to be ashamed of the ugly sex I had—and for the ugly sex that I'm sure I'll have again, in the future. I am choosing to not run away from ugliness, which is another way of saying the ambivalence of my desires. Doing so allows me to live fully, for I'm refusing to turn away from myself and from others. This is what I see as being possible with the intimacy to come: more joy and less shame; more pleasure and less pain; more mystery and less fear. Ugly sex taught me that it's possible for us to get to this place in which we don't have to eradicate parts of our being in order to be loved, to be desired, to be touched. We can show up, just as we are, and know that we are deserving—even if some part of us isn't ready to believe it yet.

HYSTERIA'S GHOSTS

In the fall of 2017, I posted a photo to Instagram: "Trying to not panic by taking selfies so you can see what I look like as a cyborg. I think it's an okay look on me. I've been trying to find humor in this situation while also honoring how freaked out I feel." In the photograph, I'm tangled up in a mess of red, white, yellow, and blue wires. Censors are taped to my forehead, chin, and cheekbones. I look directly into the camera and place my right hand back behind my head, like a model posing. I smile ever so slightly.

I was spending the night in a sleep clinic in the hopes of finding out why I had been exhausted for months. That spring, after spending six months dealing with a string of seemingly disconnected illnesses—including a UTI, sinus infection, and kidney infection—I was beyond exhausted. I was sleeping ten to thirteen hours a night, napping throughout the day, and I got winded making dinner. After rounds of blood work came back normal, my doctor suggested I do a sleep study.

So, there I was, in the bizarre space of the sleep clinic, feeling like I was in an episode of *Star Trek: Deep Space 9*. Connected to a million different wires, I walked through the clinic to see identical rooms with the same gray walls, double bed, and IKEA bedspreads, and wondered if anyone else was processing the uncanniness I felt. I would spend the night here and part of the next day. If I needed to use the bathroom during the night, I would have to buzz a nurse to come and disconnect me. And when I had resumed my place in bed, a voice would come on through the intercom telling me to blink, open and close my mouth, and wiggle my toes before telling me to have a good sleep. The decision to take this photo and post it to Instagram was motivated, in part, by a desire to show the world just how bizarre my experience was. But it was also because I felt anxious and wanted to connect with others. And so I took a selfie.

Selfie has been defined by the *Oxford English Dictionary* as "a photograph that one has taken of oneself, typically one taken with a smartphone or a webcam and uploaded to a social media website." Scholars Theresa Senft and Nancy Baym developed the following definition to highlight the relationality at the heart of the selfie: "A selfie is a photographic object that initiates the transmission of human feeling in the form of a relationship . . . a gesture that can send (and is often intended to send) different messages to different individuals, communities, and audiences." In *Selfie Aesthetics: Seeing Trans Feminist Futures in Self-Representational Art,* Nicole Erin Morse makes a similar claim. For Morse, social relations are "at the heart of selfie production and selfie viewership . . . . Selfies can make us vulnerable to others and impose ethical demands on us." When I took my selfie in the sleep study, I knew that I was exposing myself to everyone who followed me. I was asking them to see me.

These relational definitions run counter to the cultural anxiety surrounding selfies, in which selfies are pathologized and labeled as narcissistic objects that represent an unhealthy need for validation—especially among teen girls, young women, and femmes. In an article for *Teen Vogue*, psychologist Jill Weber argues, "In my experience, girls who repeatedly post selfies struggle with low self-esteem," while a 2020 study published in the journal *Computers in Human Behavior* went so far as to proclaim that "grandiose narcissism is associated with taking and posting more selfies." These same detractors are quick to decry selfies as a form of low art, despite the fact that, as various critics have noted, artists have been creating self-portraits for hundreds of years. The claim that selfies are narcissistic or shallow is misogynistic and demonstrates a narrow understanding of online culture. As Morse explains, "The stories we tell about selfies reinforce that there is something feminized, embarrassing, and even repulsive about the entire process of taking, sharing, and seeing selfies."

I also can't help but note that there is a fundamental misreading of narcissism in these hot takes. In Greek mythology, it is prophesized that Narcissus will live a long life so long as he never recognizes himself. In Ovid's telling, Narcissus is a beautiful man who rejects everyone who loves him. The gods punish Narcissus for his cruelty by making him fall in love with his own reflection. Day after day he stared at his reflection in the stream, until one day he is so exhausted that he falls into the stream and drowns. This story has been read by Freud and others as a warning against excessive self-love. But they've missed something crucial in the story.

In *The Selfishness of Others: An Essay on the Fear of Narcissism*, cultural critic Kristin Dombeck returns to the story of Narcissus in order to highlight how the cultural understanding of narcissism as purely self-interest is, in fact, a misreading of Ovid's story: "The prophecy was not that Narcissus would love himself, but that he would *know* himself; the curse was not that he would love himself, but that he would fail 'in that great love.'" And so when Narcissus looks at his reflection in the water, he sees someone entirely other, and it is that image that he falls in love with. It is time, then, for us to abandon the claim that selfies are narcissistic.

Forums like Instagram—in which the selfie has become a ubiquitous staple—have provided a vital platform for connection, where articulating the "I" vis-à-vis the selfie requires what Erin Wunker calls "a wager of vulnerability" as you watch the likes and comments come in—or not come in. Selfies often include a story about how the person is feeling that day, touching on a topic that the selfie-taker has been struggling with. Selfies can be a form of visual diary or life writing. In this sense, the selfie can be understood as a vulnerable act in which the subject asks, "Who will see this? How many people will like it?" We ask these questions not with narcissism; rather, we feel that all-too-human need to be witnessed, to be seen, to be understood by another. In this way, selfies are used as "a tool for being, becoming, and relating"; they express "an intersubjective, mutual act of recognition: 'I see you showing me you.'"

The images that I'm interested in, taken in beds and bathtubs, hospitals and treatment centers, create a community of care between the selfie taker and those who follow them. They also expand the archive into the present. Sickness selfies draw attention to—and challenge—the long history of pathologizing the mental and physical health of girls, women, and femmes that began with the work on hysterics in nineteenth-century France. These selfies reveal how this history is not over. Rather, it is alive and well in the treatment of chronic illness and autoimmune diseases today. I also see these images participating in what Allyson Nadia Field calls the "speculative archive" by filling in the gaps in history, offering images and stories that are absent from the public record. I see this particularly in the bathtub selfie, which is haunted by the history of hydrotherapy treatments.

Sickness selfies occupy a queer temporality in which we are simultaneously looking backward toward the past, forward toward the viewer, and toward the future we dream of. Speculative archives, Morse argues, "produce new histories that become the conditions of possibility for liberatory futures." For me, the selfie is an act of caring for the individual as well as an act of care for the community. Given that being sick can lead to feeling isolated, as we are unable to leave our houses and sometimes our beds, this act of making the chronically ill self visible fosters connection—with those who are sick and those who are not.

☾

In a talk at Harvard University, author Meghan O'Rourke argued, "If every age has its representative poorly understood and highly symbolic disease, ours is autoimmunity." O'Rourke—who was diagnosed with late-stage Lyme disease in 2012—notes that "in a normal immune response, the body creates antibodies and white blood cells to fight off viruses and bacteria." Autoimmunity, then, is what occurs when the body's immune system mistakenly attacks the body's own tissues and is no longer able to recognize the difference between self and nonself. The cells fail to tolerate the very tissues that they are meant to protect.

Autoimmune diseases tend to be invisible—meaning that the symptoms are not as obvious as, say, a cough when you have a cold—and are much harder to diagnose. Symptoms often include fatigue, brain fog, headaches, or other forms of bodily pain in the muscles or joints. This invisibility makes it all too easy to assume that autoimmune diseases are rare. According to the American Autoimmune Related Diseases Association (AARDA), there are eighty to a hundred different autoimmune disorders. Among some of the more commonly known diseases are type 1 diabetes, lupus, endometriosis, multiple sclerosis, and amyotrophic lateral sclerosis, otherwise known as ALS or Lou Gehrig's disease (the same disease my father died of).

Despite these numbers, Anne Elizabeth Moore, author of *Body Horror: Capitalism, Fear, Misogyny, Jokes*, notes that "the National Institutes of Health (NIH) funded autoimmune research at a measly $850 million in 2016, a drop from 2012's $867 million, since which time diagnoses of individual autoimmune diseases rose between 2.5 percent and 6 percent a year, depending on the condition." If autoimmune diseases are becoming increasingly more common (or, at least, more commonly diagnosed) then why is the funding for research on the decline? Moore's *Body Horror* offers one possible answer: misogyny. And Moore isn't the only one to make this claim. In the 1970s manifesto *Complaints and Disorders: The Sexual Politics of Sickness*, Barbara Ehrenreich and Deirdre English proclaim: "The medical system is also strategic to women's oppression. Medical science has been one of the most powerful sources of sexist ideology in our culture."

This history must be acknowledged, especially given that most people diagnosed with autoimmune diseases are women. While autoimmune diseases impact 20 percent of the population in the United States, according to AARDA 75 percent of those diagnosed with autoimmune diseases are women. To translate those percentages into numbers, if around 50 million people live with autoimmune diseases, women make up 37.5 million of them. Journalist Maya Dusenbery notes how "women are twice as likely to have autoimmune diseases, many of which bring with them persistent pain." Dusenbery also explains, "More than half of all American women have at least one chronic health condition, and women are more likely than men to have multiple chronic problems. What's more, prevalence rates of many of the conditions that disproportionately affect women—from autoimmune disease to Alzheimer's—are increasing."

Chronic illnesses are largely invisible: There are often no visible markers of the disease, and so those who suffer can walk through the world looking "normal." The invisibility of chronic illness, coupled with the gender disparity between those impacted by these diseases, has real stakes. In a 2015 essay for *The Atlantic*, "How Doctors Take Women's Pain Less Seriously," Joe Fassler recounts how his wife Rachel arrived at the emergency room in excruciating pain only to have her pain dismissed by ER doctors and misdiagnosed as kidney stones. Eventually, a different doctor came on rotation and realized that Rachel was experiencing ovarian torsion. Fassler goes on to detail how things might have been different if he were the one in pain, not Rachel: "Men wait an average of 49 minutes before receiving an analgesic for acute abdominal pain. Women wait an average of 65 minutes for the same thing." What makes Rachel's case special is that she had her husband there to help advocate for her, and that he would later recount this story in writing for the entire world to read. And fourteen hours after she showed up in the emergency room, Rachel was wheeled into surgery. Rachel survived the ordeal, but as her husband notes, "Rachel's physical scars are healing, and she can go on the long runs she loves, but she's still grappling with the psychic toll—what she calls 'the trauma of not being seen.'"

There are benefits to being seen: quick diagnosis, and efficient and adequate treatment. But being chronically ill is a sort of double-edged sword. On the one hand, being able to pass as healthy has certain benefits, and many would prefer to not disclose their illness out of fear that it could make it difficult, for example, to land that job they want. And yet, on the other hand, looking "healthy" provides doctors and other medical health professionals with a rationale for not taking women's pain seriously. In a 2015 essay for *The Toast*, author Esmé Weijun Wang recounts how she lost her medical insurance after a private investigator followed her around and noted in his report: "Observation indicated that the subject was seen *laughing and smiling* while conversing with the employee who rang up the subject's latte. No grimacing or hobbled movement was noted." What Wang's account highlights is the way that able-bodied society has certain expectations of the sick body—what she should look like, how she should move—and those expectations can dictate the care that the subject receives.

In her book *Fantasies of Identification: Disability, Gender, Race*, philosopher Ellen Samuels provides a useful framework for understanding the incredulity that the chronically ill are forced to confront again and again. Building on Michel Foucault's concept of biopolitics, which explains how the state works to control the bodies of its subjects, Samuels coins a new term: biocertification. For Samuels, biocertification "describes the many forms of government documents that purport to authenticate a person's social identity through biology" and "materializes the modern belief that only science can reliably determine the truths of identity and generally claims to offer a simple, verifiable, and concrete solution to questions of identity."

In other words, if a doctor is unable to certify your symptoms by way of a diagnosis, your symptoms must not be real. This dismissal is justified, according to Samuels, by "the overmastering fantasy of modern disability identification," which claims that "disability is a knowable, obvious, and unchanging category." Anything that confounds the doctor's understanding—usually because it is not visibly marked, or because it refuses to be static, as is the case with so many chronic illnesses and autoimmune diseases—will not receive biocertification. And without these medical documents, those who are sick will find it difficult, if not impossible, to receive the government support they need.

The sickness selfie is a different form of medical document, one that stands in opposition to the state-sanctioned forms of biocertification. Every time I take—and then post—a sickness selfie, I take the legitimization of my lived experience into my own hands. But these photographs are so much more than that. In these images, I wish to speak to those who're sick in the present, as well as to those sick women of the past: Jean-Martin Charcot's hysterics who lived at the Salpêtrière Hospital in France in the mid- to late 1800s.

Located in Paris, the Salpêtrière was a gun factory that was transformed into a hospice for poor women under the order of Louis XIV in 1656. By 1690, three thousand women—made up of prostitutes, the mentally ill, and other deviant women—occupied the Salpêtrière and became, to borrow the words of Georges Didi-Huberman, "the city of incurable women." Toward the end of the eighteenth century, the hospital underwent a reform led by Phillipe Pinel, the chief physician at the Salpêtrière as of 1794. It would take another seventy years before Jean-Martin Charcot, a neurologist and professor of anatomical pathology, began his work at the Salpêtrière in 1862. For

Charcot, the Salpêtrière was "a kind of living pathological museum," and it was there that he worked to understand the root cause of what became known as hysteria.

Today's woman in pain finds herself being treated like the hysterics of the nineteenth and twentieth centuries: dismissed as irrational, treated as pathological, and labeled hysterical.

☾

The word *hysteria* existed long before Charcot. Its first usage can be found in Hippocrates's thirty-fifth aphorism, written in 400 BCE. But as Georges Didi-Huberman notes in *Invention of Hysteria: Charcot and the Photographic Iconography of the Salpêtrière*, it was Charcot who transformed hysteria into a pathology. For Charcot and others who followed him, including Sigmund Freud, hysteria came to describe a series of seemingly disconnected symptoms that disproportionately impacted women. According to Elaine Showalter, Charcot believed that "hysteria was an inherited disease of the nervous system that could be triggered by emotional or physical trauma in vulnerable men or women." Didi-Huberman explains that Charcot's goal was to codify the expressions of the hysterical women into a "recordable state of signification." In other words, Charcot wished to create a taxonomy of the madwoman, as if to say: "Here's what this sickness looks like." And that's exactly what he did.

Every week at the Salpêtrière, Charcot would give an informal lecture on Tuesday morning and a more formal prepared lecture on Friday afternoon. Those in the audience were varied and included students and physicians as well as artists, actors, socialites, and politicians. The lectures were so famous that the hospital became a tourist destination. As scholar Jonathan Marshall shares: "The Salpêtrière itself featured prominently in the newspaper articles and even tourist guidebooks" of the time. While the audience was diverse, the lectures were not open to the public, and those who wished to attend needed a formal invitation. Why were so many interested in the weekly lectures of a neurologist? The reason: Charcot would bring his patients up onstage and have them act out their symptoms.

There was performance upon the stage, as well as in the photographs that made the Salpêtrière famous. Taken between 1875 and

1880 by intern and photographer P. Régnard, the photographs found in the *Iconographie photographique de la Salpêtrière* document approximately twenty patients, notably all women. As Didi-Huberman notes, "Men did not enter the Salpêtrière as patients until June 21, 1881" when the outpatient clinic opened. And it was "not until 1888 that one could contemplate the photographed traits of a hysterical man." Alongside these photographs are descriptions of each patient's pathology, written by Charcot and his associates, including the *Iconographie*'s author Désiré-Magloire Bourneville and Charcot's assistant Paul Richer. They believed that there was much to gain from a visual representation of what they saw taking place in their sessions with the hysterical patients. And so they turned to photography to serve as record, and therefore evidence, of pathology.

Charcot's weekly lectures and photographs resulted in much fame for the doctor, fame that he wouldn't have been able to achieve without his most photographed subject: Louise Augustine Gleizes. Augustine was hospitalized on October 21, 1875, when she was fifteen, and diagnosed with hystero-epilepsy. In the *Iconographie* Augustine is described as though she is a scientific specimen: "Tall, well-developed (neck a bit thick, ample breasts, underarms and pubis covered with hair), with a determined tone and bearing, temperamental, noisy. No longer behaving in the least like a child, she looks almost like a full-grown woman, and yet she has never menstruated. She was admitted for paralysis of sensation in the right arm and attacks of severe hysteria, preceded by pains in the lower right abdomen." Not a girl ("no longer behaving in the least like a child") and not quite a woman ("she looks *almost* like a full-grown woman"), Bourneville is confounded by Augustine's adolescent state. As he catalogs her symptoms, he notes that the abdominal pain can cause Augustine to pass out completely.

Augustine's fits made her one of the Salpêtrière's ideal subjects for study. She was a "living work of art," "a masterpiece" because of how her symptoms manifested. It is noted in the *Iconographie* that Augustine's "poses or passionate attitudes have the most regularity" and Didi-Huberman proclaims Augustine as "one of the great stars." Their praise of Augustine comes from the fact that her attacks were punctuated by periods of repose, enabling the photographer the time they needed to capture her gestures on camera.

Didi-Huberman describes Augustine's temporal progression as "the sort of dramaturgical cutting of her symptoms into acts, scenes, and tableaux." I can't help but think of how one of the tenets of being a successful fashion model is that you allow the photographer just enough time to capture your pose before moving onto the next movement. Today, Augustine would have earned the title of supermodel.

Paul Richer explains that her poses and passions, "correspond mainly to two events of her existence. She was a victim of the first when she was ten years old. It was terrible for her and marked her entry into life. The second event, on the contrary, was the source of much pleasure, which she did not try to conceal." In the second volume of the *Iconographie*, Bourneville fills in the blanks left by Richer. In a section marked "further information," Bourneville describes the first event.

Around the age of ten, Augustine lived in a religious boarding school in La Ferté-sous-Jouarre. She was free to roam about as she pleased, and so she would go out for walks in the country, where it is said that she'd let men embrace her in exchange for candy. While out, she'd often visit the wife of a painter named Jules. Jules was prone to getting drunk and physically assaulting his wife, and Augustine was often a witness to these attacks. One day, it is reported that Jules tried to kiss Augustine and was violent with her. And this was, obviously, quite a traumatizing event.

The second traumatic event: Her mother's lover, also Augustine's employer, rapes her at age thirteen. Bourneville explains how "C . . ., after making her all sorts of dazzling promises and giving her pretty dresses, etc., seeing that she would not give in, threatened her with a razor. Taking advantage of her fright, he forced her to drink some liqueur, undressed her, threw her on the bed and consummated relations." The following day Augustine falls ill, vomiting and experiencing stomach pains, which a physician attributes to the start of menstruation without even examining Augustine. A few days later, Augustine falls into a hysterical fit upon seeing "the green eyes of a cat looking at her; when she cried out, her mother arrived to find her utterly terrified and bleeding from her nose. Then the *attacks* broke out." Augustine's parents placed her as a servant at an old lady's house. What transpired between this event and Augustine's admittance into the Salpêtrière is unknown, but she would stay in the hospital for five months.

During this time, Bourneville would record numerous outbursts or "fits" as they were called. In a rather disturbing transcription of Augustine's speech during one of her hysterical attacks she asks: "What do you know about medicine?" before proclaiming,

> "I don't want to feel you near me! . . . I won't uncross my legs! . . .
> Oh! You really did hurt me . . . No, you won't manage! . . . Help! . . .
> Leave me alone. . . . It's impossible. . . . You don't want to anymore?
> Again! . . . Get rid of that snake you have in your pants! . . . You
> wanted me to sin before you, but you had already sinned."

It is unclear who the "you" is in Augustine's speech. Without any context, it at first appears that she could be speaking to Bourneville himself. But then one starts to get the sense that the identity of "you" has changed. "Get rid of that snake in your pants!" she cries out, thus making one wonder if Augustine is now back in the past and is speaking to the man who raped her. Asti Hustvedt fills in the gaps, explaining that Augustine's rapist, Mr. C., "had actually sat in on Charcot's classes in the hope of catching a glimpse of the girl he had assaulted. On two separate occasions he watched her from the audience. . . . Several days later, when she was not hallucinating, Augustine told Bourneville that the second time he came, she had spoken to him and threated to denounce him if he ever returned."

Bourneville, tasked with discerning whether this story was a case of hysterical fabulation, decides to believe Augustine because of the memory's coherency. Bourneville recognizes that Augustine's symptoms were tied to her traumatic past, and he "understood perfectly that childhood trauma explains the 'conversion' that is hysteria." And yet, if he believes in Augustine's account, why does it end up in "further information," thus turning one of Augustine's traumas into a parenthetical aside? As I read the translation of this scene in Didi-Huberman's text, I also can't help but wonder: Why has it taken him more than sixty pages to get here only to refer to it as "a detour"? Didi-Huberman evokes a different meaning of "detour": It is not just to change direction, but also to turn away. Much like Freud, those at the Salpêtrière did not want to acknowledge that the root cause of hysteria was sexual assault.

☾

There's another archive I'm interested in tracing: the bathtub selfie. I've posted many of these since becoming sick, as a way to feel like a babe while tending to my chronically ill body. In the caption to my last bathtub selfie, I describe how, "In these moments [of pain], it can be hard to find myself attractive. My body feels like my mortal enemy. But when I take a selfie, I reframe my relationship with my body from one of shame to one of celebration. To me, this photo says 'Yes, I may be sick. But I am still desirable.' I will no longer hold onto the belief that sickness marks me as undesirable or as undeserving of care." This selfie extends beyond me and to the viewer: "I want to reach out to other sick babes and let them know that they're not alone as they soak their aching bodies in hot water and salt. I want to touch you too—literally and metaphorically—so that none of us have to feel that our bodies, and the care we offer them, need to be kept hidden."

While I'd originally shared this photo to help others feel less alone, what I discovered is that *I was not alone*. There were many others sliding into or out of baths at the same moment: "About to get in the bath to ease my Lupus joint/nerve pain. I think I'll take some photos while I'm there!"; "I'm just home from soaking my fatigued and aching body at hot pools ♥"; "I love this (and I'm literally reading this in the bath) ♥"; "Seriously in the bathtub right now because of a terrible flare, feeling so ugly and unworthy of care, and your words were what popped up when I opened instagram. You wrote this for me. Thank you." As we sit alone in our bathtubs, we're all bathing together. There's something so beautifully queer and intimate about this.

When I posted this photo, another commenter asked if I'd read Abi Palmer's book *Sanatorium*. Palmer brings together memoir and poetry to document her time at a thermal water-based rehabilitation center in Budapest and her time back at home in London as she attempts to use an inflatable blue bathtub to help mitigate the pain of psoriatic arthritis and Ehlers-Danlos syndrome. Over the span of a month, Palmer receives three therapies a day, including underwater and above-water massages, and underwater gymnastics. In between, "you go and lie in the sulphurous water, which is meant to be really healing." Floating, for Palmer, "eases physical pain because you have reminded your body what it is like to live without it" and "opens up a world in which I can move with relative ease, where gravity becomes less of an obstacle and where I can see, think, and feel with a clarity I do not experience on land. The downside," she continues, "is that I have to return to a waterless space."

Hydrotherapy has been a popular mode of treating physical pain and illness (both mental and physical) for centuries, but its use within medicine was popularized by doctors in the eighteenth and nineteenth centuries to treat everything from nightmares to leprosy, inflammation, and gout. As professor Ian Bradley explains, gout "covered a multitude of conditions, including what would now be diagnosed as rheumatism, arthritis, irritable bowel syndrome, diverticular disease, chronic gastroenteritis and myalgic encephalomyelitis/chronic fatigue syndrome." Gout, it is worth noting, "was regarded as a disease of the affluent," and so it is not surprising that those who frequented the waters at Bath, and other famous spas, were those of the upper class.

While those at the spas would be prescribed to drink and bathe in the water, those locked up in asylums had a decidedly different experience. The Royal College of Physicians of Edinburgh describes how "at the other end of the scale from the luxurious spas was the medicinal use of bathing in madhouses—plunges into cold bathing being used alongside purges, vomiting, and restraints in an attempt to treat patients. One example was known as 'the surprise,' and it consisted of a coffin with holes drilled in the lid, where the patient was fastened before being lowered into water." Patients might be wrapped up in wet towels and forced to remain bound for hours, sometimes days at a time. Others would be put into a bath and kept there by restraints for days, and could only leave to use the bathroom. High-pressure jets might also be used while patients were strapped down, unable to escape.

Baths were not the only form of hydrotherapy. In an essay for *The Atlantic*, "Showering Has a Dark, Violent History," Sarah Zhang describes how, "In the early nineteenth century, physicians designed the first manufactured showers for the purpose of curing the insane. Sustained falls of cold water were prescribed to cool hot, inflamed brains, and to instill fear to tame impetuous wills. By the middle of the century, showers had appeared in both asylums and prisons." Another form of "treatment" was the plunge bath. A physician in the *Journal of the American Medical Association* wrote in 1896 that

> the plunge bath was formerly and sometimes is now substituted for the cold shower. . . . A violent and excited patient is forcibly taken by his legs and plunged head foremost into an ordinary swimming bath. He is not permitted the use of his limbs when in the water, but is detained there, or taken out and plunged again into the bath, until the required effect of tranquility is produced.

Hydrotherapy became a "form of therapeutic discipline," and water became a weapon.

☾

Hydrotherapy was one of the many popular treatments for hysterics. Moriz Rosenthal and Leopold Putzel's 1879 *A Clinical Treatise on the Diseases of the Nervous System* argues that "baths play an important part in the treatment of hysteria," and that "hydrotherapeutic treatment continued perseveringly for a long time, diminishes the extreme impressionability of hysterical patients, strengthens them, and increases their power of resistance to irritating influences." One of the most common forms of hydrotherapy for upper-class hysterical women was the pelvic douche, a "treatment [that] involved aiming a powerful jet of water at a woman's inner thighs and genitals," causing a hysterical paroxysm to occur in under four minutes. Having reached climax, those who received the pelvic douche left "feeling extreme relief from hysteria and felt as if they had been drinking champagne." Those in asylums, on the other hand, had their hydrotherapy treatments limited to cold showers and prolonged baths.

Nanette Leroux, an eighteen-year-old peasant girl from France, was an exception to the rule. After falling ill in the summer of 1822, Nanette received treatment at the luxurious Aix-les-Bains when she became the charity patient of its medical director, Antoine Despine. In her comprehensive study of this case history, *Hysteria Complicated by Ecstasy: The Case of Nanette Leroux*, scholar Jan Goldstein recounts the patient's symptoms as follows: "convulsions, lethargy, and an episodic presentation of the rigid, immobile posture that physicians of the era called catalepsy—a stubborn muscular contraction that fixed the arms, legs, and other body parts, statuelike, in the positions they happened to be occupying when the symptom took hold." Also among her list of symptoms were the loss of speech and "episodes of the *transport des sens*, a migration of sensory capability from the organs in which it is physiologically lodged to other parts of the body." Nanette would receive three diagnoses from Despine: catalepsy, hysteria, and ecstasy.

Unlike the hysterics who would come after her, the origin of Nanette's symptoms was no great mystery. Nanette recounts being repeatedly frightened by "an evil person, a rural policeman (*garde champêtre*), who on several occasions tried to offend her modesty." Nanette does not provide much detail on what exactly happened with the policeman named Peclet, though there is a reference in the manuscript of Nanette's case that calls his act "*attentat à la pudeur*—both a vernacular term and a technical legal one that in the Napoleonic Penal Code referred indiscriminately to a whole gamut of sexual behaviors, from exhibitionism to attempted (but unconsummated) rape." The closest we get to finding out what happened comes from one of Nanette's somnambulic reenactments of what the doctors call the "Peclet scene": "She sees him coming, hurls reproaches at him, wants to escape. He runs to attack her, solicits her, offering 3 louis, then 6, then 12, then 25—all without success. He sets his dog on her, draws his sword, threatens her. She gets angry and extremely agitated; she taunts him. Returning home out of breath, she is scolded by her mother, to whom she dares not confide her secret, and ends up weeping bitter tears." Despite Nanette repeating this scene, in every detail, eight times, Despine labels her performance as imaginary.

While the doctor dismisses Nanette's reenactments, he does believe that her encounter with Peclet is the source of her trauma. Goldstein, recounting the manuscript, describes how "Peclet so terrified the girl that her agitated mental state had strong physiological sequelae; it tightened the nerves in her sensory organs and disequilibrated the electrical fluid in her nervous system, thus bringing on her cataleptic symptoms." To add insult to injury, Nanette experiences a second psychic trauma: "The adults in her life had failed her: they had made no attempt to punish or even reprimand Peclet after she informed them of his vile conduct toward her. Thus she found herself caught between a wish to speak out and an implicit social pressure to remain silent and passive, to behave in a manner befitting a traditional peasant girl." Like the hysterics that come after her, Nanette lives under rape culture, another kind of trauma, one that gets lodged in the body that will attempt to speak the unspeakable through a whole host of seemingly disconnected symptoms.

As if that isn't enough trauma for Nanette to deal with, she too is subjected to being put on display for the public. We're told, "As Nanette embarked on the career of a nervous patient, 1820s-style, a crowd of onlookers, many of them laypeople, usually assembled to view the doctor's treatment of her. . . . A flock of eager spectators almost always surrounded him." During her first shower, Nanette makes it clear that she does not want more than two observers present: Despine and a female attendant. The "Scottish shower" had just been introduced at Aix the year prior to Nanette's arrival and would soon become a popular mode of hydrotherapy for treating nervous patients—one that has since been adopted at spas and wellness centers around the world.

At the time of Nanette's treatment, the Scottish shower involves sitting naked in a tub of hot water while a stream of cold water is directed against one part of the body. Despite the deeply vulnerable nature of this treatment, Despine ignores Nanette's injunction and allows other members of the public to slip into the consulting room in the hope that hot water will induce lethargy and dull her senses. Nanette "immediately protested his act of bad faith by beating the water with her fists and emitting shrill cries."

It's not shocking to me that Nanette would devise her own Scottish shower at home five months later. While still under the care of Despine for another two years, Nanette's trips to Aix would be punctuated by time spent at home in her native village of Trévigny, under the care of an older male friend named Maillard. Goldstein tells us how Nanette "gained a measure of mastery over the Scottish shower that, at Despine's hands, had so much upset her. She 'had a little Scottish shower of her own invention set up and took one almost every day.' This self-prescribed version of Despine's celebrated treatment proved more efficacious than the genuine article; it successfully curtailed the spontaneous reappearance of her crises." By drawing her own baths, and creating her own rituals, Nanette takes control of her illness and her sexuality and cures herself of her ailments. Unfortunately, Nanette's symptoms return a year later, after she is married and is four months into her pregnancy.

It feels important to name that it is Nanette's lower-class status that justifies her public objectification. Had she or Augustine been members of the middle or upper classes, there is no way that their families would have consented to such a spectacle. Similar to Nanette, Palmer is able to access the hydrotherapy treatments she received in Budapest thanks to outside funding: "In 2017 I received an Arts Council England grant to complete research for my book *Sanatorium*. Writing a book was the only way I could think of funding a much-needed visit to a water-based physiotherapy rehabilitation programme."

In an essay for *The Guardian*, "Wellness is a seductive lie—and it is changing how we treat illness," Palmer talks about how class stratification determines who can access wellness. While at the rehabilitation center, Palmer is surrounded by affluent women who

had the means to lean into the sense of luxury, transforming medical intervention into something akin to a cruise. They traveled across the world, meeting up with friends to 'take the waters' in a host of healing locations. They didn't have to juggle working or childcare. Although their conditions were—like mine—all forms of inflammatory arthritis, through retiring early and attending regular private treatment, they had managed to completely avoid use of the immuno-suppressants, opiates and mobility equipment that I require to function. As we floated on our backs in the mineral-rich water, I noticed that many of the spa's most glamorous inhabitants were fond of repeating a particular phrase: "I deserve this."

Palmer's visit to an NHS inpatient physical rehabilitation program in the years prior stands in stark contrast: "Unlike the sanatorium, NHS rehab is not glamorous. I shared a ward with 16 women. At night, people would wake each other up with cries of pain. Where the affluent women in the sanatorium talked about deserving their health, many people in the NHS system talked about deserving the more punishing aspects of their long-term conditions. They worried about the ways that they might have contributed to their illnesses." Poor women's relationship to sickness was to blame themselves, while for women of the middle and upper classes, to borrow the words of Barbara Ehrenreich and Deirdre English, "being sick was fashionable."

In *Complaints and Disorders: The Sexual Politics of Sickness*, Ehrenreich and English note how "upper- and upper-middle-class women were 'sick'; working-class women were 'sickening.'" For affluent women, sickness was a romantic pathos. For poor women, sickness was a pathology. In Palmer's differing descriptions of the sanatorium and the NHS facility, it is clear that this belief still holds weight today, embodied in the lack of funding and access for the poor who find themselves sick.

And so we take to our bathtubs at home in the hopes of finding relief. I've always loved baths because I love the water. But when fibro came into my life, baths became a form of survival. During the first four years of my illness, I couldn't afford naturopaths, supplements, tinctures, massage therapy, or other forms of holistic medicine that might have enabled me to experience some relief. All I had was my bathtub. I'd buy the cheapest bag of Epsom salts I could find, fill my tub with steaming hot water, and sit for as long as possible while the inflammation eased. Baths became a daily ritual, my crip poor femme way of healing myself. They were also a tool to help me return to my body on days when dissociation had totally taken over. I'd sit with my knees against my chest, pool water into my hands, lift them up, and watch the water fall: a reminder that I still had agency at a time when I felt totally disembodied and hopeless. The bath became a sacred container.

Being in the bath reminds me that "water is both common and in the commons." In their essay "Water as Protagonist," the After Globalism Writing Group writes that "water stands as the symbol and vehicle for inequality, vulnerability, racism, labor, land-based relationality, and capitalist infrastructure . . . the great mediator and equalizer. . . . Water levels." Given water's ability "to overcome structures of thought that seek to divide and classify the messy realities of lived and shared environments," I see the bathtub as a site of the commons, one that I can occupy at the same time as so many other chronically ill, traumatized humans, regardless of our class positions. While "water is the foundation, the magical liquid that sustains chemical relations of life on Earth," the bathtub is the site that supports my healing, that makes life, as I know it, possible.

☾

While we may sit in our bathtubs alone, we're not as isolated as we may feel. What bathtub selfies have revealed to me is that we're never the only one in the bath. After the publication of Palmer's *Sanatorium*, the book's publisher, Penned in the Margins, made an Instagram post with the caption: "Where are you reading Sanatorium? We've found the bath to be the perfect spot! Send us your #bathtubselfie." On Palmer's Instagram there's a highlight called Bath Babes, featuring photos from readers of *Sanatorium* in or around their bathtubs with Palmer's book. In one photograph, @haganartist sits in the bathtub naked, prosthetic leg exposed, while *Sanatorium* is positioned to cover the rest of their naked body. In another, @subversivegayaesthetic poses alongside @martha_again, both clothed in off-white. Each model holds a dried rose, framing *Sanatorium*, as @martha_again rests her chin sensually against the book. I see these selfies, as well as my own, as participants in the speculative archive along with Nanette's story. It's as though we're reclaiming the bathtub as a site of pleasure, connection, and possibility.

Sickness selfies remind us of our interdependence and interconnectedness in a late capitalist landscape that wants us to be isolated and alone. In an interview with *Tin House*, Porochista Khakpour, author of the memoir *Sick* writes: "Nothing I feel is more deadly than the isolation we especially experience in the West. I truly believe we are pack animals and we need each other, much more than we want to admit." And so we must form new modes of kinship and affiliation. I'm reminded here of Alyson Patsavas's discussion of leakiness: "When we recognize the leakiness of pain, we can begin to conceptualize bodies, desires, and experiences (pain, shared, and otherwise) within systems of connectivity. My experience of living with pain leaks onto those around me in a way that cannot be contained by the boundary of my body or my experience."

Leak, from the Middle English *leken*: "to let water in or out." Synonym: spill. Sickness leaks and spills like water: "I am so full of sickness," Palmer writes in *Sanatorium*, "it swells my feet. I can't fasten my boots. Sickness spills out of my shoes and forms droplets on the pavement, following me around. You can always trace me, through forests and corridors and under arches. It's impossible to get lost under all this sickness." These images of sickness leave traces, connect us to one another, and can help us imagine a politics of care. The invisible illness and the invisible women and femmes who suffer are made present as they invite a world of strangers into their most intimate and fragile moments.

These images bring the sick out of hiding, enabling them to take control of the objects—cameras, bathtubs—that were once used to pathologize and dehumanize. The sickness selfie marks a desire to connect with the world outside of the bedroom, the hospital, the bathroom, or the other spaces that the sick body is confined to. The ideology of ableism, a crucial component of the neoliberal world, focuses on what the sick cannot do; because they're too weak to get out of bed, they cannot hold down a job and cannot possibly live full lives. But when we untether the good life from the productive drive of late capitalism, we can turn our focus to caring for one another and for seeing what is possible when all of our bodies—sick or healthy—are seen as sites of potentiality rather than sites of pathology.

FEMME4FEMME INTIMACY

"So what's your dissertation about?" he asks me, lying on his bed, wearing a black lacy thong.

"It's about trauma and chronic illness and intimacy and queer sexuality," I respond, doing my best to give my Cliffs Notes version.

"Are you gonna write about this?"—and by "this" he means us, two strangers, both of us femmes, one nonbinary, the other gender-fluid, having sex during the COVID-19 pandemic.

I laugh, "Yeah, actually, I am."

"Good," he tells me, a smile across his face.

☾

It's late August 2020, seven months into the pandemic. I'm in Toronto for a few weeks to support one of my best friends as they have top surgery. I knew that returning home during the pandemic would look different from the last trip I took back in December, just a few months before the World Health Organization declared COVID-19 a global pandemic and cities across the world began to shut down. There would be no hugging. No touching. Losses that I would feel deeply within my touch-oriented friendships. But we were committed to figuring it out, not wanting to pass up the opportunity to be together after seven months apart.

The trickiest part of my stay is figuring out how to navigate hookups. In Calgary, where I'd been living the last year, the queer community is small, and the queer polyamory community is even smaller. I want to make the most of my time here, and so I create a Tinder profile: "Polyam femme witch/switch, cancer sun, sag rising, aries moon. Super into talking about feelings, transformative justice, and the queer utopia. Looking for playful makeout sessions, sexual chemistry, kink super welcome. Am in Toronto until the end of Aug and would love to navigate COVID connection with consent and care."

I quickly matched with Jamie. I immediately thought he was beautiful, with his long, curly black hair, dark brown eyes, and nails painted a sparkly black. But it was the presence of the word *femme* in his bio that made me excited to swipe right. We exchanged Instagrams and then quickly started texting. As we discussed a time to meet up and see if the chemistry was there, he offered to send me some nudes, and I enthusiastically said yes. The next day I woke up to a number of photos of Jamie in various stages of undress. In my favorites, he is wearing fishnets and a thong. In another, there is a jeweled butt plug in his ass. I send him some of me in lacy lingerie.

In between nudes, we discuss our boundaries and what we need to feel safe.

"You don't mind being around someone smoking weed do you?" he asks.

I pause and reflect on this question. I knew he smoked weed because in many of his Tinder pictures there's a joint in his mouth. In the past, this would've been a deal breaker for me.

"It's something I can be around," I text back, "but just for full disclosure, I've been sober from drugs for ten years. Addiction was something I really struggled with and so I tend to not spend time around folks who're smoking weed. But given the circumstances I think it'll be fine."

I hit send and then nervously compose a follow-up message: "Hope that's okay—always feels a bit vulnerable to disclose that."

I first got high when I was fourteen. I smoked at the park near my house, with the boys who dated popular girls and hung out with me in secret. When I return to the diaries I kept when I was thirteen and fourteen, I find poems where I write of unrequited love: "But your love goes to that of another; you are her world, you are her lover. You hold her, you kiss her, you are in love. I will wait for the day for you to love me." I used to think that my longing to be loved by those who couldn't or wouldn't love me didn't start until after my mother's death. Either I didn't keep a diary before the age of twelve, or they didn't make it in the eviction from our home.

One day, I'm going through old report cards that my mom kept, and I find a poem that I wrote. There's no date, but the penmanship tells me that I must have been eight or nine. I'm charmed by the title "heart bet"—clearly a misspelling and yet it perfectly captures the wager that is intimacy.

> When your heart bet's like thunder open eye and see your heart bet for love. Open your eye and see the man that you love like you love like crasy. Give him a big kiss. Then tell him that you love him. Over years and years you tell him that you want to marryed but love stoped's there so stop rint there the love is gone he doesn't love you any more kiss your love goodbye.

For my thirty-sixth birthday, I ask my friends and loved ones to read things they wrote as kids, and I surprise them all with a rendition of this poem, accompanied by my friend's banjo. It is meant to be playful, but I also want to retain the sense of sadness I felt upon finding this poem: proof that my desire to be loved by another predated my mother's death. I don't know what to do with this information, as it gives a new beginning to the story of my attachment wounding.

Maybe it's the case that I've always been needy. In her book *White Magic*, Elissa Washuta, a fellow Taurus north node, writes that "what we Taurus north node people want is to merge with another person; what we need is to stop feeding our power to another." Washuta goes on to quote Jan Spiller's *Astrology of the Soul*: "The first step toward self-acceptance for Taurus north node people is to acknowledge that there is a needy person inside and to take personal responsibility for fulfilling those needs."

The website Astrology Owl offers another explanation: "The North Node in Taurus is helping you achieve the sense of self-worth you feel you have been denied." I think about how my south node is in Scorpio in my twelfth house, where Pluto also lives. My past is the realm of the ineffable. An underworld of ghosts and spectral wounds that need healing. It makes sense that I'm needy. I have spent lifetimes attached to ghosts. Now, I am hungry for bodies that are of this world.

Or maybe my attachment wounding has something to do with the fact that Chiron, the planet of the wounded healer, is in Gemini in my seventh house of committed partnerships. I once read somewhere astrologer Chani Nicholas's description of those with this placement: "Your bruises include moments where you find yourself searching, again, for your twin—where you doubt, even for a minute, your own wholeness." Chiron is conjunct Venus in my chart, meaning that I will find beauty in pain, that I will let myself be hurt again and again in the name of love. You can call it the fate of the stars, or the fate of being a human being trying to love under the cisheteropatriarchy. In reality, it's both.

Before boys started to use me, I was already an object in my own home: surrogate mom after my mom's death, expected to do all the housework and provide all the care, not seen or loved as the human being I was. As my dad's illness progressed, I'd be expected to do more: help him eat, bathe him, complete whatever tasks he'd told friends he'd do for them. There were so many moments where I wanted to tell him *I'm your daughter, remember?* The drugs I used weren't just a response to the rape. They were a response to my life. Sex, care, intimacy, and substances became inextricably linked. I needed the substances to access connection. Or, to pretend that what I was being offered could be called care.

I feel like I'm being given the opportunity to untether sexual intimacy and drugs from my trauma. With Jamie, this will be the first time I'm allowing myself to be with someone who uses substances since I got sober at age twenty-four. The last time I did this, I ended up getting high again. And while I no longer feel that same urge, I worry that being around drugs will trigger a trauma response.

As if anticipating my fear, Jamie asks me "Does the smell of weed trigger you?"

I feel my body sighing at his question, a sign that I feel within my window of tolerance.

"I'm not sure. But my body isn't freaking out at the idea, so I think that's a good sign :)."

"I get smell linked to trauma all too well" he texts back. "I also have visual scars from interpersonal issues from the past so trauma hasn't been hard for me to shy away from."

The capacity to name their traumas is one of the many reasons I find myself surrounded by femmes. Without knowing the details, we accept from the start that trauma lives within our bodies. It isn't something that we have to hide from one another.

After sharing little details about our trauma histories—he doesn't know his birth parents, and both of mine are dead—I suggest that we talk about how we're practicing harm reduction while hooking up. It feels easy to transition from talking about our trauma to our forthcoming intimacy.

"I basically ask people how they protect themselves from the outside and if it is equal to or greater than mine it checks out. Not tooooo sure what else to do. Also have sanitizer when I walk in."

I share some of the precautions I'm taking during the pandemic—socially distanced hangs with pals, only sleeping with one person at a time outside of my partnership. "I have a compromised immune system, so I have to be super careful."

We talk about who's in our bubble and he tells me that he'll let me know if he hooks up with anyone else in between seeing me so that we can wait a few days before hooking up again. Even with all of the precautions, we both know that it's a risk to fuck. And at the same time, if this is the way that the world is going to be for the foreseeable future, we need to figure out how to access the pleasure of sex and intimacy in the meantime.

Many people I know in the polyamory community have been talking about harm reduction approaches to sex. In her *Radical Love Letters* series, my friend and fellow activist and academic Raechel Anne Jolie reflects on how "abstinence-like models of remedy," which promote only interacting with those in your household, end up privileging "not just people who had physical homes in which to live, but very specifically, monogamous people who live with their partners/bio-families." Raechel goes on to argue: "It behooves us to pause when we are told that protecting human life must simultaneously uphold systems that harm us. . . . We have to think critically when the onus of stopping a pandemic falls to individuals and their actions rather than structural forms of care and support."

Alongside questioning whose care is privileged, I can't help but wonder: Whose pleasure is privileged? The people who are the most concerned about protecting those most vulnerable to COVID-19 (immunocompromised folks, the working-class poor, homeless, the incarcerated, and those who are Black, Indigenous, and people of color) are also the ones asking the questions that Raechel poses:

> Can we keep each other safe and also keep joy alive? Can we both make responsible individual decisions that protect the most vulnerable among us, and also direct our ire toward the State rather than toward our friends who have decided to consensually hang out with other friends without masks? Can we concede that a quick, masked hug between two consenting adults may be something toward which our bodies begin to urgently move? Can we draw on the spirit of our queer ancestors who knew that connection is all at once dangerous, life-giving, and also impossible to withhold?

I read Raechel's questions and my body says *yes, yes, yes.* If anyone can imagine these possibilities, it's femmes.

Historically, femme identity has been understood as being the counterpart to butch lesbian identity. Sadly, without the butch lesbian, the queer femme is all too often misread as straight: an act that has become known as "femme erasure." The irony of the internalized misogyny inherent in this misreading—that as a femme, you can only be read as queer in relation to someone who is masculine presenting—has been taken up by queer femmes with the hashtag #Femme4Femme, which works to draw attention to the ways that femmes desire bodies other than those that are masculine of center.

In her essay "A Modest Proposal for a Fair Trade Emotional Labor Economy (Centered by Disabled, Femme of Color, Working-Class/

Poor Genius)," Leah Lakshmi Piepzna-Samarasinha offers another definition that really resonates with me:

> Femme: a person who has one of a million kinds of queer femme or feminine genders. Part of a multiverse of femme-gendered people, who have histories and communities in every culture since the dawn of time. Often complicated remixes that break away from white, able-bodied, upper-middle-class cis femininity, remixing it to harken to fat or working class or Black or brown or trans or nonbinary or disabled or sex worker or other genders of femme to grant strength, vulnerability, and power to the person embodying them.

Because of the ways that refusal is written into femme identity, femmes face erasure and rampant femmephobia from feminists and queers who believe that to be feminine is to consign yourself to the gendered expectations of the patriarchy. I'm reminded of Piepzna-Samarasinha's proclamation: "Forget femme invisibility; the thing most femmes I know are impacted by is the lack of femme respect"— an impact heightened for trans women and nonbinary femmes of color.

I want to name that as a white nonbinary femme, I can embrace my femme identity with much greater ease than trans and gender-nonconforming femmes of color. According to Advocates for Trans Equality, seven months into 2020 the total number of murders of transgender people surpassed the total for 2019, with twenty-eight dead, the majority of whom are Black trans women. By the end of the year, forty-seven trans people had been murdered. Their names are Dustin Parker, Alexa Neulisa Luciano Ruiz, Yampi Méndez Arocho, Scott/Scottlyn Devore, Monika Diamond, Lexi, Johanna Metzger, Penélope Díaz Ramírez, Layla Pelaez Sánchez, Serena Angelique Velázquez Ramos, Nina Pop, Helle Jae O'Regan, Tony McDade, Dominique "Rem'mie" Fells, Riah Milton, Jayne Thompson, Selena Reyes Hernandez, Brayla Stone, Merci Mack, Shaki Peters, Bree "Nuk" Black, Summer Taylor, Draya McCarty, Tatiana Hall, Marilyn Cazares, Tiffany Harris, Queasha D. Hardy, Brian "Egypt" Powers, Aja Raquell Rhone-Spears, Lea Rayshon Daye, Kee Sam,

Aerrion Burnett, Mia Green, Michelle Michellyn Ramos Vargas, Felycya Harris, Brooklyn Deshuna, Sara Blackwood, Angel Unique, Fendi Mon'ezah Armstrong, Yunieski Carey Herrera, Asia Jynaé Foster, Chae'Meshia Simms, Skylar Heath, Kimberly Susan Fial, Jaheim Pugh, Courtney Eshay Key, and Alexandria Winchester.

That there was a rise in the deaths of trans women at the same time as a global pandemic and the Black Lives Matter Revolution is no coincidence. Femmes are the original agitators. It was Marsha P. Johnson and Silvia Rivera who threw the first bricks at Stonewall and initiated the queer revolution in 1969. And it is Black femmes who're leading the BLM movement.

It's vital to recognize how the continued violence against femmes and lack of respect is, for Piepzna-Samarasinha, informed by the belief that femininity and femmeness is "weak, less than, not as smart or competent, 'hysterical,' 'too much,' and not as worthy of praise or respect." To be femme (and feminine) is to be sick: "hysterical" and "too much." And so Piepzna-Samarasinha will go on to write in her essay "Two or Three Things I Know for Sure About Femmes and Suicide": "Being perceived as too much can kill you." It is this logic of pathologization that informs femmephobia. Femmes are the original hysterics. Or perhaps another way of saying this is: hysterics are always already femme.

When I talk about being femme, it's "a gender experience that is never tied to biological sex." Femmeness can be located in gender expression (the donning of nail polish and lipstick and floral prints) but it is also a gender identity and thus might refuse to be easily indexed. Femmeness does not need to be tethered to gender, sex, or sexuality. Rather, as nonbinary femmes like Alok Vaid Menon have shown me, femmeness is a way to exist in a world without gender. To be femme is to refuse the cisheteropatriarchy's valorization of the individual and independence. What femmes recognize is the power of interdependence: that we need one another in order to live. If the future is femme, which I believe it is, then it is full of pleasure and possibility. Femmes are the ultimate dreamers of care and intimacy.

It's not surprising to me that my fellow femmes actively crafted templates for intimacy in the midst of a global pandemic. Because femmes are always already sick, we understand that our mental health is inextricably linked to our physical health, and so in staying away from those with whom we practice intimacy, pleasure, and care, we're putting our bodyminds at risk. And so, I return to Raechel's final question: "Can we draw on the spirit of our queer ancestors who knew that connection is all at once dangerous, life-giving, and also impossible to withhold?"

☾

I arrive at Jamie's place the night after we meet. I'm anxious. And not because I know that we're about to have sex. In between my legs, just below my crotch, is an eruption of red spots. Eczema. Since birth I've been haunted by dry skin that transforms into a rash at the blink of an eye. Atopic dermatitis. You can see it in my baby photos: cheeks aflame. As a preteen, it'd flare up conveniently the day before picture day, just above my lip. Waves of shame would come over me as I prepared myself for yet another rashy yearbook photo.

None of that would prepare me for the ways that eczema would take over my arms and legs after I began high school. I'd wake up in the morning with swollen red blisters, oozing and inflamed, all down the insides of my elbows, the insides of my calves, and the backs of my knees. As a young girl full of hormones, and who equated sex with love, the worst part of my eczema wasn't the pain or the constant itch: it was the shame and fear I felt whenever I thought about my legs being exposed during sex. I'd turn off the lights and take extra precautions by removing my pants underneath the blanket. I masked my shame with coyness, and it worked. But I was always dreading the moment when my red, pussing legs would be revealed.

I could never find a pattern for my flare-ups. Dermatologists have long understood the link between stress and eczema outbreaks. But what if your whole life is under constant stress? What do you do then? Doctors still aren't sure what causes eczema, but recent research is showing that there is a connection between the parasympathetic nervous system and atopic dermatitis. Polyvagal Theory, developed by psychologist Stephen Porges, has demonstrated how our autonomic nervous system functions through the sympathetic nervous system (SNS) and the parasympathetic nervous system (PNS). Our SNS controls our fight-or-flight response. Our PNS controls our ventral vagal system, which is our optimal state of engagement, and our dorsal vagal system, which controls our freeze and submit responses. When you live with trauma, your SNS and PNS are under chronic stress, and chronic stress causes autonomic imbalance, greater sensitization, and triggers the massive histamine release associated with atopic dermatitis inflammation.

Given that the most traumatic years of my life happened between ages eleven and twenty-one, I can see why these years were also riddled with flare-up after flare-up. If I couldn't talk about and process my mother's death when I was eleven, or the rape that happened the summer before high school and the slut-shaming that came after, or the years of having my needs and identity erased because all that mattered was my father and brother, then my body would speak it for me.

The etymology of the word *eczema* confirms my suspicion that these red rashes are inextricably linked to my trauma. Eczema: *something thrown out by heat*. Trauma as heat. Eczema as that which is thrown out of the body, externalizing that which is internal.

Perhaps my eczema was my body's way of saying, *Don't do it. You'll only get hurt.* What if those eczema outbreaks were my body's way of telling me that there was just too much trauma around sex and intimacy. What if my red oozing skin was a somatic attempt to keep me from repeating the same pattern: get high, have sex, be abandoned, abandon yourself. Or maybe it was like a shield. A protective barrier between the vulnerability of my soft flesh and the other person's body. *I'm not that fourteen-year-old anymore,* I try to tell my trauma responses. *This time can be different. You can have connection without abandoning yourself.*

I stand here at Jamie's front door, aware of the red, itchy pain between my legs. I worry about how he'll respond when all is revealed but tell myself that he won't notice. And if he does, it won't matter.

He opens the door in a robe, and I can see the hint of a black lacy bra underneath. Eventually, as we undress one another, I can see the care and pleasure he took in getting ready for me. He moves his body as femmes often do. Wrapping his legs around mine, he pushes his ass up into the air so that I can observe his soft brown skin next to black lace. When he fucks me, my legs wide open and up in the air, he moves his hands alongside the inside of my thighs, overtop of my eczema, and keeps fucking. In this moment, I feel how queerness makes it possible for us to find pleasure in loving our sick and traumatized bodies.

Afterward, sweaty and out of breath, he is the little spoon. I trace my fingers over his skin, and he shivers. As we're lying there wrapped up in each other, he dozes off. I must have been falling asleep too because I suddenly awaken: his arms and legs start to spasm, contract, and then relax. They go through the same motions again and again. I feel him move his shoulders and hear the bones crunch and crack underneath the skin. Then he shoots up. Awakened by his own body.

"Does that always happen when you sleep?" I ask.

"Yeah. Used to be way worse. Sleep paralysis. Eventually it stopped freaking me out."

I want to ask him more questions, but then he's asleep again. As I lay there beside him, I think of the hysterics at the Salpêtrière Hospital. In the photographs, you see their bodies in various states of contraction and contortion. Their bodies trying to speak the trauma that their mouths cannot. I understand this all too well. Eczema. Fibromyalgia. My body attempting to speak the unspeakable. I'm learning how important it is to listen. I will not gaslight myself as Freud once did with his hysterics. I lie there, letting his body communicate with me. I want him to know that I'm listening.

We continued to see each other many times over the next two weeks. One day I show up wearing a black lace bodysuit, and Jamie takes photos of me. I have a hard time finding myself sexy in photographs. But with Jamie behind the camera, his hands reaching out to move my head back, I find that I'm excited to see the results. Then he joins me. Our legs—mine bare, his in black pantyhose—contort and twist together, and we transform trauma into pleasure and intimacy.

Back at home, I tell my therapist about Jamie. In recounting my experiences, I realize that not once during our time together did I get triggered. Not by the pot smoke (which was copious). Not by hooking up (also copious). According to my therapist, this is stage three of trauma work: future templates, or integration and living without dissociation. In trauma recovery, stage one is finding stabilization (me, starting somatic therapy after spending the summer of 2017 in a near constant state of dissociation). Stage two is reprocessing (four years of weekly therapy later, and we still haven't touched all of my trauma, but I know that we've reprocessed a lot). In stage three, you start to use the new neural pathways you've created, and instead of getting triggered by a smell, event, scenario, your frontal cortex knows that this time is different.

I ask my therapist how this is possible—*How did I manage to do this on my own?*—and she tells me that it's not so much the memories themselves that need to be reprocessed, but the stories and beliefs attached to them. I think back on all of the work we've done so far: the trauma of my mother's death and all of the emotional abuse and neglect I suffered under my father. I now know that all parts of me are deserving of love. That I am loveable. It becomes clear that these same stories drove me, in the wake of being raped, to seek out the love of so many adolescent boys. In offering them my body, I was hoping to affirm that I was loveable.

We've only just started to return to those memories, which are, really, just fragments of memories. But that doesn't matter. Because I know that the story attached to these traumas isn't true. This is how I find myself doing something that I used to do, something attached to so much trauma, without dissociating: fucking someone I don't know, during an eczema outbreak, pot smoke around me. Instead, my adult self tells my trauma responses that this time is different, that they don't need to protect me. Without knowing it, I've reprocessed and integrated years of traumatic memories. This is the magic of Femme4Femme intimacy.

SUMMER 2021

I come back into my bedroom and Emily is standing, looking at the bed.

"Ummmm, so I just saw a cockroach," they tell me.

"On the bed?"

"Yeah . . ."

We pull out our phones and shine our flashlights until we find it: underneath the mattress, clinging to the bed frame. I scan around me for something I can use to kill it before it scuttles off. It looks like my phone is the weapon of choice. Emily holds up the mattress and in one fell swoop, the roach is dead.

"Wow, I'm impressed," they tell me when I come back into the room after cleaning the remains of the roach off my phone.

"To be honest, I am too." I've never been the one to kill bugs. But in this moment, I'm the service top in this relationship.

"Did that just kill the mood?" I ask, moving closer to Emily.

We'd just moved upstairs after making out on the couch. Tonight is take two. The first time we had sex, we just weren't in synch. Mouths and hands moving too fast. And it didn't help that I was dissociating. It wasn't that the sex was bad. It was ugly sex. I could tell that some part of me was turned on even as another part of me fled the room.

As I walked home afterward, the laugh track known as my shame spiral cued itself up, with one question on repeat: *Am I broken?* This was not the first time this question had plagued me, but I'd been asking myself this question more frequently since a therapy session a few months back. I was trying to make sense of how, once again, I'd found myself in a platonic partnership when I'd been looking for someone I could fuck *and* talk about my feelings with.

"Maybe there's a part of you that wants that, and another part of you that believes that's not possible to have a relationship with emotional intimacy and sexual connection," my therapist proposed.

My stomach dropped. I knew that she'd hit on something.

Since then, we've been working with my different "parts." Parts language became popularized by a method of therapy called Internal Family Systems (IFS), Janina Fisher's "mindfulness of parts" approach—which combines an understanding of structural dissociation with somatics, IFS, attachment theory, polyvagal theory, and neuroscience. It has transformed my healing. Drawing on split-brain theory and the structural dissociation model, Fisher explains how those of us who live in chronically traumatizing environments, where trauma remains unresolved, handle this stress through splitting our brains into a "going on with normal life" part and a "traumatized part of the personality."

For some of us, primary splitting isn't enough to keep us safe, and secondary splitting occurs. Here, the traumatized part of the personality splits into subparts, each with their own personalities, behaviors, and beliefs. These parts are called fight, flight, freeze, attach-cry, and submit. Fight keeps us alive through hypervigilance, judgment, mistrust, control, and self-destructive behaviors. Flight keeps us safe by creating distance from others, often relying on addictive behaviors such as substance use, gambling, and disordered eating to help us escape our reality. Submit believes that shame, self-hatred, self-sacrifice, fawning, and caregiving support our survival, and is ready to activate chronic pain flareups and other symptoms of illness to keep us in a state of collapse. Freeze protects us through dissociation and panic attacks. And attach-cry supports our survival by ensuring that we'll never be abandoned, accepting the scraps of connection and intimacy that others throw our way. This is the landscape of my structural dissociation.

I appreciate how Janina Fisher describes splitting as a utopian process:

> To get up each morning and face death, abandonment, assaults, or imprisonment requires somehow disowning the horror and the fear left from the day before and the dread of what is to come. Disowning "the other one" inside is a survival response: the overwhelming feelings are no longer ours; that shame does not belong to us but to "[them]"; the white-hot rage and violent impulses certainly aren't "me." By disowning our traumatized parts and/or "not me" self-states, by disconnecting from them emotionally or losing consciousness of them via dissociation, we preserve our hearts and souls from growing as bitter as our circumstances. We hold out hope for the future and we keep going.

Fisher believes that we need to reframe so-called "self-destructive behaviors": "Unsafe behaviors historically labeled 'self-destructive' can be better understood as a desperate attempt to survive, a way to tolerate shame, rage, and fear, to inhibit flashbacks and nightmares, or to use endogenous and exogenous substances to regulate a traumatized nervous system." Fisher's depathologization of trauma and dissociative splitting via utopian longing feels like a queer, crip, femme reimagining to me.

This splitting into parts saved me, at a cost. I can see how my freeze part helped me dissociate during sex after I was raped. My attach-cry part needed whatever scraps of intimacy and connection it could get, and that included having sex with whatever random boy showed me a modicum of attention. My flight part also participated, always ensuring that we were high during sex. Together, they helped me access connection. But in doing so, I learned that it wasn't possible to experience safety and connection at the same time. I'd always have to sacrifice one for the other. "When we disown needs that can't be met or feelings that are unacceptable," Fisher writes, "we protect ourselves from unbearable disappointment or punishment. . . . One way to accomplish this challenging task is to split the sense of desperate needing and the refusal to need anything between two parts: one part that actively seeks proximity, comfort, or needs-meeting and one that just as actively pushes others away or keeps a hypervigilant, suspicious distance."

I can see how this splitting played out during my adolescence and into early adulthood. I was starved for connection and sought it out from whomever might give it to me. On the rare occasions when someone expressed their desire to be in a relationship with me, I'd find myself repulsed and would pull away. To my trauma brain, safety equaled only getting the scraps. Fisher notes, "The discussion of safety is another topic that can trigger parts' survival responses. Some parts might feel confused or frightened by the word 'safety,' having been told they were 'safe' when they were not." This response to intimacy is disorganized.

I think about all of the relationships I had as a teenager and young adult. The few that weren't abusive, that offered safety and connection, never lasted long. For my nervous system, anything that wasn't cold and withholding was experienced as too much.

I return to this question again: What is the origin of my attachment wounding? Kathy Kain and Stephen Terrell, authors of *Nurturing Resilience: Helping Clients Move Forward from Developmental Trauma*, explain how, when disorganized attachment was discovered, "the research ultimately concluded that unresolved trauma and loss in a parent's life is the best predictor of disorganized attachment between parent and child." They note that

Epigenetically, disorganized attachment can be passed on for generations. The parents' limited capacity to regulate their responses can look like anger toward the infant/child—and may in fact manifest as anger toward the child—while the child has no coping skills to help him tolerate the scary parent. He is instead constantly on the lookout or preparing for another outburst, attack, or scary moment, and is rarely able to let his guard down.

I think about my father. At the age of two, his mother left him and his brother with my grandfather, never to return again. The following year, my grandfather remarried. My father's stepmom was an austere woman whom one would be hard-pressed to describe as compassionate or maternal. She felt that her new stepsons were a burden and focused her energy on the two daughters she'd have with my grandfather. My dad used to regale my brother and me with stories of being chased by my grandmother with a wooden spoon or a belt. He laughed as he told these stories—a defense mechanism he'd learned to distance himself from the realization that he'd been abused.

While I remember my father as being deeply loving when I was a child, my mother's death broke something in him. I can only imagine that her death was felt by his nervous system as abandonment, a repetition of what he had experienced as a two-year-old. To defend himself, he became cold, withholding, punitive. It didn't help that after my mother's death, he began to develop ALS, or Lou Gehrig's disease. I remember him sharing with me that his doctor thought that the disease might have been brought on by the grief and trauma of my mother's death. I believe that doctor was right. And there was more to it than that. A lifetime of living with the impacts of early trauma played a part too.

His disorganized attachment helped set the blueprint for how I'd come to understand love as inherently unsafe. Describing the impact of disorganized attachment, Fisher writes: "Because closeness and safety are intertwined when we are dependent for survival on caregivers, the implicit message is: 'It isn't safe to depend. It isn't safe to get too close or to love those closest to you.'" Subsisting on scraps of affection was the safest thing, and this belief has structured my intimate relationships for most of my life.

Fisher translates attachment theory into parts language. For her, disorganized attachment "reflects the relationship between a proximity-seeking attach part and a hypervigilant, protective fight part. . . . The submit part also frequently serves the needs and goals of the attach part by trying to please those whose connection the attach part seeks [and] avoid displeasing potential attachment figures." Again and again, my submit part ignored the cries of my fight part, helping me offer up my body to any person who'd take me. Intimacy and connection became inextricably linked to sex and drugs. If sex couldn't happen without the absence of safety and self-regard, then neither could connection in any of its forms. If I wanted intimacy, if I wanted to feel like I belonged, then I needed to leave my boundaries and desires at the door. I became an absent-presence in these encounters. I'd dissociate during sex again and again, because to be present in the moment would be too much for my nervous system to handle. And so I came to learn that it wasn't possible to have emotional intimacy, care, connection, *and* sex. They were their own islands, and I'd move between them, wanting but never believing that there was a place where I could have both.

☾

Back in Emily's bedroom after our first date, I can see that my nervous system is living in the past. Emily's darkened basement bedroom reminds my trauma brain of past sites from my teenage years, where young boys moved too fast, too soon, never once looking me in the eyes. I need to bring my parts up to speed, show them that they no longer need to protect me. Each time I feel myself leaving my body, I try to return. *Look at the tattoos on your body. You didn't have those when you were a teenager. You're here. You're safe now.*

When I arrived in Toronto this summer, I wasn't sure if I'd be able to get on dating apps again. *Maybe I'm too messy and in process*, I told myself. But I decided to open up Feeld, an app for folks who're nonmonogamous. An experiment in curiosity, I told myself, to see who's out there. And then I came across Emily's profile. Emily is a poet, PhD candidate, and "top-leaning switchy bitch." We've known each other for years. I'd often see Emily at a reading; the summer before I moved to Calgary, I asked them to read at a femme picnic I was organizing with a friend. I loved how they describe "being-femme" as "a nourishing, even healing, way of being in the world." Swoon.

I'd always thought they were cute and smart and super talented. But it never crossed my mind to explore anything further. Until this year.

The day after our first date, I reread their bio and decide that I don't want to give up on this connection. I messaged Emily:

"Was wondering if we could take a walk Friday evening so that I can share some vulnerable feels/needs around sex. The TLDR is that I'm processing a lot of sexual trauma stuff in therapy right now and could tell that my nervous system was activated when we were having sex. Which meant that it was hard for me to be present. I'd love to chat about some ways that we could work together to co-regulate my nervous system if we wanna continue to have some sexy times while I'm here."

I waited anxiously for their response.

"yes of course!" Emily replied. "i wd love to go for a walk and in all honesty i was not feeling particularly present either and im sorry if that energy rubbed off on you [literally]. we were both sent to our respective polyvagal VAGAS casinos to gamble with our AFFECT. would love to chat more about this//thank you for presenting this opportunity to do so!!!!!!! you literally are so heckn cute n cool thanks for letting me get close to ya xoxoxoxo"

On our first date, we did what two trauma bbs do: we talked about polyvagal theory.

Emily calls their vagus nerve the "vagas casino" and I can't help but think of heart bet. What is intimacy if not an act of gambling with one's affect as we confront our own non-sovereignty—and our trauma—in the face of the other.

Before we meet again, I sit down with my journal and I write. And then, across from Emily in Dufferin Grove Park on Friday for our second date, I read my notes, and they listen:

- I find it really challenging to talk about sex without having a freeze response
  - a partner asking me what I want can be really activating
  - And so at first, what feels supportive is being asked "would you like X" because then I can answer
  - eventually, as I feel safer, I'm quite verbal + enjoy dirty talk + can be more assertive verbally

- Moving quickly (from fast kisses to moving from making out to sex) can be quite activating
  - slow(er) kisses + spending more time in all activities helps me feel safe
  - I also just really enjoy lingering + luxuriating in sexual activities
- Eye contact can feel hard but keeping my eyes closed can also activate dissociation.
  - Being prompted to open my eyes is helpful. This can look like just saying "Hey" and that'll bring me back to the room.
  - I need to know that you want me to be present with you.

When I'm done, I feel the grief swell up within me. From the time I was raped through my early twenties, I was never present during sex. The boys I slept with didn't care about me. I was just a body to them. That was the only part of my presence that mattered. My lack of presence was also self-preservation. Because if I was, I'd have to grapple with the grief of my rape, and all of the nonconsensual experiences that followed it. In repeating the pattern of my rape, I could normalize it and transform it into something else. Something that I could control.

I don't share all of this with Emily in this moment. And I know that I don't have to.

"I'm trying to put to memory everything you just shared there," they tell me. "I don't want to forget it."

"Would you like to take a picture of my notes?"

"Wow, I mean that'd be great but I also get if that's super vulnerable."

"I mean, I share all of this stuff in my writing, so I'm not really worried about what you could do with it. Plus I love that you want to remember."

As they pull out their phone and capture my words, I'm so deeply moved by the softness and care of this act, this commitment to remembering.

Later that night, when they walk me home, we stop to kiss in front of the house I'm staying in, and it is everything I want. Slow.

Soft. The perfect amount of tongue. My body does a little dance afterward. Maybe I'm not so broken after all. Maybe I just need to feel safe. To know that I can share what happens inside of me with another human and see them show up to make some co-regulation magic happen.

When we grow up in homes with neglectful or overbearing caregivers, we do not learn how to regulate our nervous systems. "Regulation is the term used to describe our ability to manage our emotional state, to calm ourselves during times of heightened emotion—when we become fearful, deeply sad, angry, or frustrated," Kain and Terrell explain. As infants, we have no idea how to regulate our emotions and rely entirely on our caregivers to help us co-regulate. If an infant hears a loud noise and gets startled, they'll seek safety from their caregiver, who will hopefully come over, pick them up as they cry, and make soothing noises to calm them.

When we're children, we may run into our parents' room in the night, crying about a monster under our bed. If we're lucky, a parent will take our hand, walk us back to our room, and search for the monster. If we're not lucky, they'll tell us that there's no such thing as monsters and to go back to sleep. These consistent acts of co-regulation support the development of self-regulation. Kain and Terrell note that healthy attachment and bonding "allow us to develop the early ability to self-regulate our systems and trust the shared experience of co-regulation and connectedness." That is to say, if you've experienced anxious, avoidant, or disorganized attachment, your regulation skills will likely be underdeveloped.

One of the impacts of a low capacity for regulation is the development of a false window of tolerance. In his book *The Developing Mind*, psychologist Dan Siegel coined the term *window of tolerance* to describe the state in which our nervous system is regulated. From our window of tolerance, or what polyvagal theory would call ventral vagal activation, we can access feelings of safety, connection, and self-regard. When we're outside of our window, either in a state of hyperarousal (fight and flight) or hypoarousal (submit/collapse and freeze), our nervous system is dysregulated, and it can be very challenging to recognize the markers of safety, to experience connection (with yourself or others), and to feel a sense of self-regard.

And so we develop our own coping mechanisms, which give us the false sense of being in our window of tolerance. This is what's called a "faux window of tolerance." We might feel like we're okay when in actuality we're in a state of collapse and we've mistaken numbing for regulation. We might turn to substances to help us regulate states of hyperarousal, and we come to believe that being high is being regulated. The faux window requires the use of what Kain and Terrell call "defensive accommodations": "behaviors such as self-harm, eating disorders, compulsive behaviors—anything that substitutes for regulation, or anything that helps support a sense of control, safety, or connection." For Fisher, these defensive accommodations are "survival resources":

> The most common error made by professionals and lay people alike in understanding high risk behavior is the automatic assumption that self-harm, suicidality, eating disorders, and substance abuse are destruction-seeking rather than relief-seeking. . . . At the heart of all self-destructive behavior is a simple fact: hurting the body, starving it, planning its annihilation, or compulsively engaging in addictive behavior result in welcome relief from physical and emotional pain.

These defensive accommodations, similar to dissociative splitting, are a means of survival. While it may look like we're barreling toward annihilation, we're in fact desperately seeking to live.

Each time I got high, it's as though I was saying *I want to exist, but the world is so unbearable.* I'd put myself in danger again and again, whether with drugs, unprotected sex, or both, not because I was all death drive; rather, I wanted nothing more than to move toward pleasure, to escape the pain of my mother's death, my rape, my father's abuse, our poverty, the slut-shaming, the bullying. I wanted something so much better than the reality I was given. And drugs and sex offered me that. But living in a chronic state of dysregulation has also come with its costs: physiological, behavioral, emotional, and relational. Memory loss, fear of abandonment, abusive relationships, the inability to feel my feelings, let alone speak them to another, and chronic pain.

The fact that Emily also lives with complex trauma and chronic illness helps me open up, turn toward them rather than running away. After our evening in the park, I experience a few days of calm before my parts are activated again. I recount my spiraling thoughts to my therapist: "Now that this conversation has gone well, it's like my parts are moving the goalposts. Now they're telling me that Emily won't be interested in a relationship with me. That they'll only want sex. Or if they do want more, my no drugs boundary will be a deal breaker. And it's not even like that's a problem for my adult self. I can handle that disappointment. But I'm feeling some pretty major activation from attach-cry, who wants this connection, and my inner critic who feels like it's stupid to hold out hope for anything more."

"It sounds like your inner critic fight part wants to keep the status quo of disappointment that it knows so well. And maybe it's doing this in order to protect attach-cry from getting hurt again. Does this part of you know that you can tolerate disappointment now?" she asks me.

I check in with my body, feeling the tension in the chest, the bracing. "I don't think so."

"How about we go to the meeting place? And maybe we can see if fight will trust adult self a bit more?"

I close my eyes and find myself on the beach. I see attach-cry, fight, and adult self are all present. Fight is standing in front of attach-cry, protecting them.

My therapist switches over and starts talking to my parts.

"Fight part, can you see that adult self is there and that they want to help attach-cry too? Do you think that you could step back and let adult self protect attach-cry?"

"They are suspicious, but said that they'll try. There's like a brick wall there, on the beach. Maybe they can stand behind that and keep watch?"

"That sounds like a great plan. Thanks fight. Now attach-cry, do you see adult self there?"

I nod.

"What would you like from adult self right now?"

"To be held."

"Of course. And adult self, can you hold attach-cry?"

I say yes, and as I do, I can see my adult self embrace this much younger part of me. Fight part looks on from behind the brick wall, still unsure about this arrangement, but wanting to trust.

"What your parts need right now," my therapist tells me, "isn't reassurance about your external relationships. What they need is to know that no matter what, their internal relationship with you is solid. Once they feel that, they won't keep moving the goalposts on you because external intimacy won't feel so scary anymore."

"Right. That makes so much sense. Internal intimacy is what they want. My parts are looking for the adult that they didn't have when I was younger."

I think of all of the times that I cried when a boy broke up with me, and my dad's cold responses: *These guys aren't worth crying over. These relationships won't matter when you're older. Just get over it.* All I wanted was for him to hold me and tell me *I know this hurts right now. I'm sorry that they didn't see how amazing you are or couldn't handle it.*

I recently watched the film with Gabor Maté, *The Wisdom of Trauma*, and can't stop returning to these words: "Children don't get traumatized because they get hurt. They get traumatized because they're alone with that hurt." Child, teenager, adult. We all need others. And that absence, especially when we're wounded, is the trauma. I didn't have the adult I needed back then. Now, that adult can be me.

☾

"How're you feeling?" Emily asks me, lying on their stomach, face turned toward me.

We've just had the most incredible sex, both of us present. This time, I'm able to open my eyes as I ride on top of them. And I can see them looking back at me. We smile, and then I close my eyes—not out of a need to dissociate, but because I want to connect with the sensations happening inside of me. The feeling of their cock against my g-spot.

I've spent so much of my life disconnected from my body. The first time my therapist asks me to locate a feeling in my body, I'm silent. "I'm sorry, what?" I'd thought that I was so connected to my body, but turns out I was unskilled at interoception.

Kain and Terrell explain that "interoception is the process by which we notice our internal state. We evaluate a combination of sensations and perceptions of physical processes to assess our interior milieu and decipher what it's telling us about what we are feeling, how we are, and even who we are." One example of interoception in action is feeling your eyelids get heavy and knowing that you're tired. Interoception helps us understand our experience of self in relation to others, whether we're safe or not, and "whether an external event or person is pleasurable, exciting, or threatening."

Growing up in a chronically unsafe home, with a father who was supposed to be my source of love and life, but who threatened me, neglected me, or was unable to attune to me, means that my interoception does not work as it should. I came to learn that the people that should be safe are not. And so the world itself was inherently unsafe, even in those rare moments that I'd find myself in the presence of safety. Because safety can only be fleeting. Soon, the other shoe will drop, something horrible will happen, and my world will come crashing down all around me.

Without accurate interoception, everything and everyone is dangerous. It's not shocking to me that difficulty with interoception has been linked to anxiety disorders and addiction. Interoceptive sensitivity is a major contributing factor to anxiety and paranoia. I remember all the years I spent terrified of the sounds I'd hear in my house when I was the only one home. A creak meant, *There's someone in the house. Someone bad. You must get out.* Substances helped dull my interoceptive sensitivity. Instead of feeling like everything was dangerous, everything—including acts that were actually quite dangerous—felt safe. My worries and paranoid thoughts would vanish.

As a result, I lack what Kain and Turrell call a safety map:

> Clients who lack a 'safety map' are primarily tuned to danger. They have well-developed filters and somatic narratives about what danger is and what it means—because danger has been an imperative in their lives—but they often have a somewhat limited ability to recognize safety, either within their interoceptive self-communication, or in the perception of their external environments.

I think of that first time with Emily, floating above my own body, unable to tell that this experience was safe, that I wasn't in danger.

Our ability to distinguish between threat and danger depends on three things according to Kain and Terrell: consistent access to a feeling of safety (*After my mother's death, all sense of safety would vanish*); attuned caregivers who can help us assess the difference between threat and safety and help us regulate our responses (*My father was the threat, and so I had no one to help me make this assessment*); and "coherent feedback from our social groups about how we ought to categorize our experiences" (*After I was raped, and the rumors about me spread, my friends abandoned me. Everything, therefore, was a threat*).

I wouldn't understand what safe, consensual sex was until my early twenties, almost a decade after the rape. At that time I started seeing someone who asked if he could kiss me, who asked if he could touch me. He wanted me to be present with him. And so I learned, slowly, how to return to my body, and I experienced my first orgasms.

"I'm amazing," I tell Emily as I trace my fingers along one of their tattoos, where the word *eros* repeats and overlaps with itself, and the word *sore* emerges. A poetic embodiment of ugly sex, I think to myself with delight.

"Before I saw the cockroach I was looking at your notes on my phone," Emily said. "But I wasn't able to read through them all, and so I just wanted to make sure that felt good for you."

My notes. The ones I shared in the park. I nuzzle my head into the nook of their armpit.

As I kiss Emily's chest hair, I tell them, "You did great. That was great." And I mean it. I can feel my clit still throbbing from the multiple orgasms they gave me, the sensation of their cock inside of me as we lie side by side. I play with Emily's earring, kiss their cheek, and I'm truly present. My body understands this feeling: we're safe.

I get up to pee, and when I step into the bathroom I see it: another cockroach. When I was a kid, my family and I used to take vacations in South Carolina. One day we were in a shopping mall and went to use the bathroom in Sears. I must have been no older than eight or nine, feet hovering off the floor while sitting on the toilet. For whatever reason I looked down, and under the wall of the bathroom stall I see a giant cockroach, larger than my hand, making its way toward my stall. I scream and run out of the bathroom, forever terrified of these bugs. After moving to Toronto, I'd hear stories of friends who'd lived in roach-infested apartments, and I'd pray that never happened to me.

Now, in this bathroom, I look at the roach. This one is writhing on its back, clearly in the process of dying. I find myself pleased and horrified that my sex with Emily has been bookended by cockroaches. I'm no longer afraid. I grab some toilet paper, pick it up, and flush it down the toilet, along with Emily's cum.

THEN, NOW, AND FOREVER

"What is broken in me, Varia? Why am I spiraling?"

Earlier that day, I'd reached out to one of my besties, Varia, for some support. I'd found myself tapped back in an old obsession: the desire to fix the emotionally unavailable boy who just told me he thinks we should just be friends.

I'd been seeing Jasper for a month, and things had been feeling super easy. We were having amazing T4T sex, made each other laugh a lot, and never ran out of things to talk about. I wasn't sure if we'd be compatible in a long-term kind of way, but I was excited to find out. I thought the feeling was mutual, and so I was shocked when he told me that he was only having friend vibes.

Under normal circumstances, the end of a month-long casual connection would not have felt so all-consuming. But the past few months of my life had felt like the Tower card in tarot: everything crumbling all around me. I had just launched a Kickstarter to fund the writing of this book when I found out that there was an Instagram account seeking to deplatform me; and I'd just ended a four-year-long partnership after realizing that I really needed to be with a queer and trans human. So this definitely wasn't an ideal time to be starting a new relationship. And yet, here I was, consumed by this desire to show Jasper that his lack of romantic feels was really just his body not knowing what secure attachment could feel like, and I would be the one to help him work through his attachment trauma.

Varia asks me if I really want her to answer my question: Why am I obsessing over this human?

"Yes, yes I do."

"You're going through a major period of transformation in your life, some might even say a crisis. In order to not focus on all of this change, which is terrifying for your nervous system, your trauma brain has created a distraction. Do you really want to help this human work through his insecure attachment? Is that something you have the energy for right now?"

"Adult me doesn't," I respond. "But wow, some other part of me sure does."

"Whenever I become fixated on something or someone external to me, that's a sign that I need to be turning my attention inwards. You've just ended a long-term relationship and are going to be moving to a new city. You need time to grieve and to focus on yourself."

The resistance that I feel throughout my body at Varia's advice tells me that she's hit on something. When I'd talked to other friends about what happened with Jasper, they'd asked me, "Do you really want to be with someone who isn't ready to be with you?" To which my attachment trauma screamed *YESSSSSSSS*. But what I'd really needed to hear was, "Are you ready to be with someone who hasn't healed their attachment wounds?" Suddenly I could feel the obsessive thoughts dissipate.

Later that night, my friend Quail reads my chart for me. I'd reached out to them to figure out what was happening astrologically. There had to be some cosmic force at play to justify all the chaos and upheaval in my life. I also wanted their insight into my attachment wounding.

"Venus is the planet that gets described as the mother and usually correlates to our early adolescence. How old were you when your mother died?" Quail asks me.

"Eleven."

"Right, and so you lost your mom right around the time that you started thinking about romantic relationships. The fact that Chiron is in your descendent means that you look outwards rather than inwards. You're focused on others outside of yourself," they tell me. "My guess is that you'd identify as having disorganized attachment. You're going to experience lots of disappointment."

Here I am, faced with two connections ending. All I want is to love deeply and be loved deeply. And I'm terrified that I'll never find that kind of love. That I'll always be searching.

It's in these moments that I turn to my two best friends, fellow femmes Varia and Natalie. Not just for support. But for reminders that I've found the kind of love that I long for in my relationships with the two of them.

In her zine *Soft Femme*, my friend and fellow femme Andi Schwartz describes femmeships as something different from friendships with other femmes: "I understand femme connections as politically significant friendships that take the form of political alliances and communities of care." For Andi, "there is something distinctly femme about forming and valuing connections with others. In our masculinist, binary-obsessed society, independence is prized, while interdependence is seen as weak. Our desire for connection is called 'crazy' and 'needy.'" And yet, "to be femme is to rely on each other."

It is through these femmeships that I learned what secure attachment is. Jessica Fern describes people with secure attachment as experiencing

> a healthy sense of self and seeing themselves and their partners in a positive light. Their interpersonal experiences are deeply informed by their knowledge that they can ask for what they need and people will typically listen and willingly respond. . . . A child with a secure attachment style will likely grow up into an adult who feels worthy of love and seeks to create meaningful, healthy relationships with people who are physically and emotionally available. [They're] comfortable with intimacy, closeness and their need or desire for others. They don't fear losing their sense of self or being engulfed by the relationship. . . . Securely attached people experience relational object constancy, which is the ability to trust in and maintain an emotional bond with people even during physical and emotional separation.

These experiences were uncharted land to me prior to meeting Natalie and Varia in my early twenties. I hated myself, was terrified of asking for what I needed, and felt totally unworthy of love. I sought out human after human who could not be emotionally available. And

I certainly had never felt object constancy; my life, and my relationships, had been built on the tumultuous foundations of insecure attachment. Chaos and turmoil were all I knew, and I sought them out again and again, especially when my relationships were going smoothly. I now understand all the reasons why I needed to repeat this cycle.

Our experiences with our caregivers impact us at a neurobiological level and shape when and how our reward circuits release dopamine and oxytocin. Journalist Katherine Wu explains: "Dopamine, produced by the hypothalamus, is a particularly well-publicized player in the brain's reward pathway—it's released when we do things that feel good to us" and comes into play when we're attracted to another person. Alongside the release of dopamine is norepinephrine, which "may sound familiar because it plays a large role in the fight or flight response, which kicks into high gear when we're stressed and keeps us alert. These chemicals make us giddy, energetic, and euphoric, even leading to decreased appetite and insomnia—which means you actually can be so 'in love' that you can't eat and can't sleep." Dopamine releases oxytocin aka "the love drug" and, if our understanding of love has been shaped by insecure attachment, both of these chemicals can push us toward humans who will not give us the love that we actually desire.

Attachment shapes attraction, romance, love, and intimacy. "Kids who are securely attached to their adult caregivers will, as adults, most likely attach securely to their romantic partners, and kids who are insecurely attached to their adult caregivers will, as adults, most likely attach insecurely to their romantic partners," writes Emily Nagoski in *Come as You Are*.

If we grew up experiencing insecure attachment, then our reward circuits are hardwired to release dopamine and oxytocin when we receive the hard-earned rewards of insecure relationships. If you're anxiously attached, the reward is your partner turning toward you. If you're avoidantly attached, the reward is distance from your partner. And if you have disorganized attachment, proximity and distance can each be their own rewards. For us insecurely attached humans, secure attachment will not feel as good to us because of how our reward circuits are oriented. We may find ourselves thinking, *This can't be love because I'm not feeling all of these intense emotions that usually release these reward chemicals that make me feel good, while also paradoxically making me feel bad.* Intimacy becomes a high-stakes risk—one that I sought out again and again.

Me, forever falling for boys who couldn't fully commit; who were scared of intimacy; and who withheld the depths of their emotional landscape from me. This chase, and the brief moments of intimacy I'd sometimes obtain, produced dopamine hits that were tethered to the insecure forms of attachment I grew up with.

When we finally experience our first taste of secure attachment, our nervous system freaks out. Because new equals unsafe. Our nervous system will then decide how to respond. Do we fight? Do we flee? Do we freeze? Do we submit? While all of those options will feel very appealing, we actually need to do the scariest thing possible and be with the discomfort so that we can move through it. We need to open ourselves up to the experience of safety. Which is a lot easier said than done when our survival physiology is oriented toward protection and away from connection. But I know that it's possible, because I've experienced it. Varia and Natalie opened the door to a new world of relational intimacy that I had dreamed of but never thought was possible.

☾

One of the amazing things about our brains is their neuroplasticity. Not having secure attachment in our developmental years doesn't have to haunt us for all of our lives. We can rewire our neural pathways through earned secure attachment. That I learned how to build secure attachment through my femmeships is not a coincidence. Earned secure attachment is a femme superpower because of what's required: the desire to attune oneself to the other; a commitment to deeply listening to another's story, which means holding space for their trauma and their pain; compassion and reverence for all that the other has done to survive; an understanding that caring for each other should always be consensual and reciprocal, and never framed as an obligation; and the capacity to meet vulnerability with softness.

I recall all the times that I called Natalie when I was home alone and heard a noise in the house. Since I was a teenager, I'd been terrified of being the victim of a home invasion. After seeing the movie *Red Dragon* when I was seventeen, I slept in a spare bed in my dad's room. My father never asked me why I needed to do this. At the time, I felt grateful for his silence. I knew that if I told him about the stories keeping me up at night, he'd think I was crazy. And yet, his silence about my bedtime needs meant that he never asked me if I was okay, if perhaps I needed help. In hindsight I recognize that his silence was his own survival strategy. As a single father who was beginning to experience the early signs of Lou Gehrig's disease, raising two kids on his own was more than enough work. The last thing he needed was a child who believed that their whole family would be murdered in the middle of the night.

With Natalie, I got to practice giving voice to this fear: "I think there's someone upstairs. I mean . . . I know that there's no one upstairs, but . . ." Never once did she tell me that I was being crazy or irrational. "Okay, I'll be right over and we can go upstairs together." And if she couldn't come over, she'd stay on the phone with me until I was sure I was safe.

Years of therapy later, I'll come to realize that my fear of empty houses was just a stand-in for a fear buried much deeper: the fear that my world would fall apart again, just as it did when my mother died. The killer I was so afraid of was a stand-in for my father. My disorganized attachment led me into his bedroom each night to sleep in that spare bed, just a few feet away from the man I was terrified of. In the end, I was the one who cared for myself night after night until I was able to return to my own bed once again.

I think back to those nights when my fear of empty houses would lead me to call Natalie. This time, I spoke my fears out loud: "I'll always be abandoned. Nothing good can stay. There must be something wrong with me. I don't deserve to be happy." And she turned to me, with all of the softness and care and compassion that had been missing for so many years in my life, and told me, "I can see why you'd be afraid of that. But that's not going to happen this time. I'm not going anywhere." With these words, Natalie gave me the missing experience I'd longed for growing up.

The *missing experience* is a term I learned in a class on the evolution of somatic psychology with Kekuni Minton. Within each nervous system state—play, joy, depression; fight, flight, freeze, submit, attach-cry—there is a missing experience that shapes our beliefs, emotions, sensations, movement. These missing experiences can include: a positive belief, the processing of an emotion, missing attachment experiences, resources that weren't there, individuation and differentiation from our caregivers, and the enactment of defensive responses that didn't happen during the original trauma. The stories that we create about ourselves and the beliefs that we hold emerge out of the missing experience: *It's not okay to be sad; I must always take care of others; I am undeserving of love; the trauma isn't over.*

With Natalie, I replaced the negative belief "I must be crazy for thinking that there's a killer in the house" with "I am deserving of care—regardless of whether or not my thoughts are rational." Instead of staying frozen in dissociation, intrusive thoughts, and panic, until I can eventually self-soothe my way out of them, I now get to experience the co-regulating presence of someone who loves me, and I complete the stress cycle. Giving one another the missing experience feels like a femme tool because it requires us to be soft with each other as we refuse to pathologize our inner landscapes.

I've had similar experiences with Varia. The previous summer, while visiting Toronto, we went to Lake Ontario for a swim. When we got there in the morning, the beach was empty. As the day went on, and the beach became more populated, two young men and their dog sat nearby. Varia and I were deep in conversation when I felt myself starting to dissociate. The men had lit a joint and as the smell drifted over to us, I felt like I'd been taken back in time. I couldn't figure out what had triggered this or what was even happening in my nervous system. Varia noticed that I was no longer feeling present and suggested that we pack up and go. All I could do was nod.

We walked back to the car with our arms linked through each other's. Eventually, words came back to me. "Wow, as soon as I smelled weed, a part of me recognized how similar they looked to the boys I hung out with at the park where I was raped. Their clothes, the beers they were drinking, the joint in their hand."

"I figured that might have been what happened," Varia responds. "Is there anything else you need right now to feel safe?"

"Just knowing that we could leave, and that you initiated that when I totally shut down, really helped," I told her.

Getting up and leaving wasn't an option I'd had access to in the past. My ability to make different choices now, with the support of one of my best friends, is a profoundly healing experience. This is Femme4Femme intimacy.

☾

We're sitting in a darkened corner of a wine bar in Toronto's Little Italy in the days between Christmas and New Years. Varia is in her signature leopard print and bright red lipstick. Natalie blends masculine and feminine together with her tomboy femme ensemble of skinny jeans, printed blouse, and eyebrow pencil. And I've selected one of my many '90s floral print dresses. As we all arrive, we ooh and ahh over each other's sartorial choices.

We've come to exchange presents, but really we've come to celebrate each other and the fact that this is our tenth holiday season together. It doesn't take long before Natalie suggests that we go around and share our reflections on each person's growth over the last year. And it takes even less time before we're holding each other's hands, crying and laughing simultaneously.

"It's like we're in an episode of *Baroness von Sketch*," Varia jokes through tears.

Three femmes, sitting around a table, telling each other how much we love one another while detailing each other's emotional and psychic growth between sips of bougie wine. And we wouldn't have it any other way. We've seen each other through so many romantic and sexual relationships. The one constant is our connection. We all trust that truth: that our Femme4Femme4Femme love is forever.

I've read so many scholars' writings on queer temporality, and I find myself wanting a femme understanding of time. Instead of thinking about the past and the future, as is the focus of most queer discussions of time I've encountered, I want to think about duration. For me, femme temporality is invested in forever—but not in the "till death do us part" kind of way that has been romanticized by the cisheteronormative couple formation. Forever marks an intended duration, one's intention to be in relation for as long as is possible.

I am reminded of Billy-Ray Belcourt's words in his poetry collection *This Wound Is a World*: "the body is an assemblage, a mass of everyone who's ever moved us, for better or for worse." Foreverness, here, is less about pledging to be a physical presence in each other's lives forever. Instead, it is about honoring, in our hearts, the ways in which our love leaves imprints, ephemeral traces that never go away. Forever as in the Donna Lewis lyrics "I love you always forever. Near and far closer together. Everywhere I will be with you" but without the "everything I will do for you" because we've all been working hard on letting go of our codependent tendencies. Our forever is built on the soil of earned secure attachment.

Femme temporality also holds space for the foreverness of trauma. In the online healing spaces where I circulate, I see how so many are invested in a narrative of healing that results in *I am healed*. Past tense. Healing journey over. I'm not the only one to reject this narrative. In her essay "Not Over It, Not Fixed, and Living a Life Worth Living: Towards an Anti-Ableist Vision of Survivorhood," Leah Lakshmi Piepzna-Samarasinha explains the dangers of believing in this past tense capital-H Healed:

> The idea that survivorhood is a thing to "fix" or "cure," to get over, and that the cure is not only possible and easy but the only desirable option, is as common as breath. It's a concept that has deep roots in ableist ideas that when there's something wrong, there's either cured or broken and nothing in between, and certainly nothing valuable in inhabiting a bodymind that's disabled in any way. It's also an idea that's seductive to survivors. We want the pain, the trauma of surviving sexual abuse or assault to be over. Who wouldn't?

When we hold space for the fact that our trauma will always be with us, that there may be a foreverness to healing, then we can move away from the shame that we're "not healed yet" and toward celebrating all the ways that we have survived, thanks to our brilliant trauma brains. These "survivor skills," as Piepzna-Samarasinha calls them, enable us "to imagine survivor futures where we are *thriving* but not *cured*."

Within a femme temporality, we accept that our trauma will be with us forever. But its impacts on our bodyminds will ebb and flow like water. "Long after internal attachment bonds have been established," Janina Fisher writes, "clients and their trauma-related parts may still periodically suffer distress, still be vulnerable to depression and anxiety, and even have destructive impulses. But earned secure attachment provides a stable base that enables individuals to tolerate grief, loss, betrayal, and other stressful normal life experiences."

This is where I am right now. I have securely attached relationships *and* I am still experiencing panic attacks, intrusive thoughts, and old attachment patterns. I'm not sure if they'll ever stop happening. But when they happen now, they do not derail me for hours, days, weeks, months. There is a foreverness to my trauma, yet the duration of my symptoms has shifted. I come back into my window of tolerance more quickly and with greater ease because I've learned how to tend to these scared parts of myself. My femmeships taught me how.

Within Femme4Femme intimacies, I do not need to be over my trauma. I do not need to "evolve" into some human who is Fully-Healed™. I get to be forever messy, forever traumatized, forever moving toward the queer utopia of my dreams. And I get to do that with the humans who love me, with the humans who're also invested in a soft femme future.

SOFT MAGIC

I'm sitting across from my therapist—a Gestalt practitioner who reminds me of my mother with her fiery red hair. She's asked me to speak to my anxiety, to tell it how I feel. I turn to the pillow beside me. "I don't like you. I wish you would go away. You make life so difficult. Why won't you leave me alone?" Then comes the switch: she asks me to change roles. Stepping into my anxiety, I respond: "I'm so sorry for hurting you. It's not my intention. I hate that you're in pain. I'm sorry."

After the exercise, my therapist offers me an analogy that fundamentally transforms my relationship with my anxiety: "If a child cries out in the middle of the night, screaming about a monster under their bed, what would you do? Would you tell them that monsters don't exist? Or would you take the child's hand and validate their fear? Would you search the room until they felt sure the monster was gone and, even if it wasn't, let them know that you were there to protect them?" She then asks me to imagine taking this approach with myself. What might happen if I turned this care inward?

A decade later I come back to these questions again and again when I spiral into shame or self-hatred—in moments when I'm being unkind to my inner child. Being hard on myself wasn't actually serving me. It wasn't making my anxiety go away. In fact, it was making my anxiety worse. I needed to soften. In softening, I found a roadmap for my healing. I reoriented myself to the world.

My internalized hardness was, of course, a survival strategy. When my father told me to stop crying, when my brother told me that he didn't care if I was hurt, I began to believe that my softness was a problem. I came to believe that my needs were too much. I was too much. To avoid the rejection I felt when I cried out and no one held my hand, I became my own worst critic. If I kept my feelings to myself, I kept myself safe from rejection.

And so, when paranoia gripped me during my seventeenth year, and the monster came, I told no one that I was convinced a killer would break into our house in the middle of the night and kill everyone. Looking back, I realize that what I'd done was some pretty serious reparenting work. In the absence of my father's care, I cared for myself. Lying in my childhood bed, with my father asleep just a few feet away, I held my scared inner child and told her that we'd be okay. Eventually, she believed me. In being soft with myself, the fear dissipated. I don't know how else to describe this experience: It was magic.

☾

In the summer of 2017, dissociation and chronic pain entered my life with a force. I'd sleep fourteen hours a night, nap throughout the day, and when I awoke, I felt as though I was in a cloud, hanging above myself, always on the verge of tears. The constant dissociation made it impossible to string sentences together. As a writer, I felt totally lost, disconnected from myself in myriad ways.

I fell in love with stories at a very young age—a love nurtured by my mother—and had been reconnecting with my love for writing when chronic pain struck. My chronic pain and complex trauma are deeply interconnected: the former a manifestation of the latter. Not being able to write, to tell stories, only amplified the sense of fragmentation that trauma brings with it. I needed a new way to tell a story. I found it in tarot.

I'd purchased my first deck on the winter solstice in 2014, the night that my now ex-partner of four years was on a plane moving halfway across the world. I performed a ritual with a dear friend to mark that moment of grief. After that night, my tarot deck sat collecting dust in my bedroom. Three years later, on days where the pain wasn't debilitating, I'd slowly walk to my favorite park in Toronto, my tarot deck and journal in my backpack. As I sat on the grass and pulled cards, I felt a sense of calm come over me. It was a kind of magic.

When our trauma responses are activated, we enter a state of dysregulation. Our sympathetic nervous system (fight or flight) or our parasympathetic dorsal vagal (collapse or freeze) has taken over. We are living in the past. We are not present in our bodies because we're too busy trying to defend against the perception of danger. We don't understand that the danger is long over, that we're safe now. Each time I pulled a tarot card, I was activating my ventral vagal nerve, the part of our nervous system that enables us to occupy the present and feel a sense of safety. The fact that we can change our nervous systems by self-regulating is total magic. It's an alchemical process in which we transform terror into safety, isolation into connection, shame into compassion. Prior to starting somatic trauma work in my mid-thirties, I couldn't have imagined that this transformation was possible; that one day, I would feel connected to my body's rhythms and needs. But I was already doing this work through tarot, tethering myself to story, bringing myself back to the present.

Reading tarot mirrors the work of healing from trauma. Each time you pull cards from the tarot deck and lay them before you, you construct a story. At first, the story in front of you might not make any sense. But you work with those pieces. You take the meaning and significance of each card, look at their placements in relation to one another, and you begin to construct the narrative. Just as with a novel, you don't have to believe that the story is true for the cards to resonate with you. You take the significance and let it guide you. I understand now that tarot was helping me return to my window of tolerance, helping me root down into myself and bring the storyteller in me to the surface. In between the cards, there are gaps: connections that need to be made. But you don't need to construct a full and complete story in order to access the healing magic of tarot.

Since Sigmund Freud, mental health professionals have believed that the way to heal trauma is to construct a narrative of what happened and share that narrative with another. Beginning in the 1980s, trauma specialists such as Judith Herman have been advocating for a different approach: one rooted in somatics and the body. The more we learn about how trauma impacts our neurophysiology, the clearer it becomes that a narrative approach to trauma work can often cause more harm than good. With a somatic approach, we recognize that trauma lives in our bodies, and thus we must work from our bodies if we're going to heal from trauma. We are "little somatic beings," to borrow the words of somatic practitioner Staci K. Haines. Haines explains that trauma gets transformed into "somatic narratives" that get stored in our brain's emotional and somatic memory bank and do not make it to our chronological memory storage. This is why fragmented memory is a common symptom of living with trauma.

I've long resisted the impulse of so many nonfiction writers to fill in all the gaps you can with facts. To do so feels like a betrayal. And now I understand why. My mind chose what to remember, what to repress, and it will let me know when I'm ready to remember the pieces that are missing. For now, I craft my own story out of the fragments, and parts of me that I didn't know existed come alive.

☾

It's been five years since I started seeing a somatic therapist for complex trauma and chronic pain. During this time, I've come to see many affinities between witchcraft and somatics, between witches and those of us living with trauma. Historically, the traumatized subject has been given the label of hysteric. The relationship between hysterics and witches has a long lineage. Barbara Ehrenreich and Deirdre English's *Witches, Midwives, and Nurses* maps out the connections between these two groups by looking at the ways that they have been abused by the medical system. Hysterics were grossly mistreated and misdiagnosed by doctors and psychoanalysts, most famously Jean-Martin Charcot and Sigmund Freud. And witches, some of the original healers, were cast out of the world of medicine with the emergence of the male-dominated medical profession in the nineteenth century.

Hysterics, like witches, were in need of containment and control. Instead of being locked in jails and tortured into submission or death, as the witches were, hysterics were locked up in asylums and tortured by way of forced treatments, including hypnosis, lobotomy, and later, pharmaceuticals. Freud himself noted the connection between witches and hysterics. In a letter to psychoanalyst Wilhelm Fliess, Freud wrote:

> What would you say, by the way, if I told you that all of my brand new prehistory of hysteria is already known and was published a hundred times over, though several centuries ago? Do you remember that I always said that the medieval theory of possession held by the ecclesiastical courts was identical with our theory of a foreign body and the splitting of consciousness? But why did the devil who took possession of the poor things invariably abuse them sexually and in a loathsome manner? Why are their confessions under torture so like the communications made by my patients in psychic treatment? Sometime soon I must delve into the literature on this subject.

I read the histories of hysterics and witches and see myself in both. I'm a hysteric and a witch. I'm thus not surprised that somatic therapy has played such an integral role in my healing.

I recently took a human I was dating to my favorite tree in Toronto's Trinity Bellwoods Park.

"I'd come to this tree again and again in the summer of 2017," I say "lying underneath it for hours. Sometimes with a book in hand. Other times just staring up at the leaves."

"Do you want to lie down under the tree with me?" they ask—and so we do.

As we look up at the leaves, I tell them, "One of the reasons that trees are so soothing for our nervous systems is because leaves are fractals, just like our brain. I love the idea that our brain recognizes affinity with trees, and this connection soothes us, brings us back to our bodies."

Andrea Glik, somatic therapist and creator of the popular Instagram account @somaticwitch, explains the connections between witchcraft and somatic work to me in an interview:

> I think somatic work is always witchy because it connects us to our bodies; it's not this very cold, clinical, patriarchal idea of healing that

happens in your brain and not in your body. A lot of somatic practitioners are women and queer people, and a lot of witches are also
those things. When you're doing witchcraft, you're in your body.
When you're connecting with your body you're also connecting with
your ancestors and the planet.

This sense of interdependence present in somatic work and witchcraft is echoed by another somatic practitioner and witch, Nik
Border, who describes how both somatics and witchcraft "rely on
relationship as the hub for all life/death/rebirth." For Border, "relationships are the bridges and connections within an interdependent
web." They go on to explain:

> I believe somatics and witchcraft are ways of engaging with the worlds
> inside and outside of us while creating entirely new landscapes that
> can hold what we are emerging into. Where we can acknowledge our
> pain and envision new relationships to it without bypassing the real-
> ity of what this suffering has meant for our multiple bodies.

Witchcraft and somatics bring us back to our bodies; they help us
soften so that we can foster forms of relationality where we show
up as our full selves, trauma and all. Somatic therapy, and generative
somatics in particular—a branch of somatic therapy that brings a
politicized lens to understanding how trauma is caused by systemic
oppression—is a form of soft magic.

☾

In her book *White Magic*, Elissa Washuta, member of the Cowlitz
Indian Tribe, writes: "I google spells to take the PTSD out of me.
But is that what I want? To stop my brain from thrashing against
the wickedness America stuffed inside? I need to get better and I'm
out of ideas. I arrange the candles, and I pray." Noting the ways in
which her trauma is caused by settler colonialism, Washuta reflects
on how it's impossible to fully heal from trauma unless we heal the
world we live in: "Every day, the universe reminds me that, yes, I
am safe now, but I am in America. I could be gouged out again."
Today, the reclamation of witchcraft as a form of healing is a deeply

political act and one central to those living with chronic illness and complex trauma, the manifestation of a sick world that takes up residence in the body.

These chronically ill and traumatized femmes have long recognized that witchcraft is a practice of healing our bodyminds. And in this moment when the world is literally on fire, we need witches to heal the world we live in before it's gone forever. Bri Luna, creator of the popular website The Hoodwitch, defines the practice of being a witch as follows: "The power to boldly and unapologetically embrace nature, heal yourself, and heal your community." This statement from Luna echoes the concerns of those within the healing justice and disability justice movements, which place interdependence and collective care at the forefront. The power of the collective is an integral aspect of reclaiming witchcraft and is vital to crip, mad, and sick political action.

Philosopher Silvia Federici explains that one of the most threatening aspects of the witch is her ability to foster and maintain community. In branding the witch as a criminal figure who caused harm, the state worked to turn women against one another, effectively broke down any attempts at community building and political action, and ensured that women were no longer able to pass down the wisdom they carried regarding healing. I'm also struck by the ways in which the state effectively impoverished these women—both financially and relationally. In severing the ties between witches, capitalism followed the lead of colonialism, which had been stripping Indigenous communities of their traditions and forms of knowledge, ensuring that these witches and healers could no longer pass on their wisdom of herbs, medicines, and spells.

Witches are revolutionaries, and so too are somatic practitioners. Both figures say no to the pathologizing frameworks of the medical industrial complex. Johanna Hedva, another witch and human living with complex trauma and chronic illness, proclaims, "You don't need to be fixed, my queens, it's the world that needs fixing." One way to heal this world is through magic. In her essay, "Trash-Magic: Signs and Rituals for the Unwanted," Maranda Elizabeth asks: "What would it feel like to imagine we are destroying capitalism with each spell we cast? Destroying capitalism with each candle we light, each breath we breathe? To know it's crumbling, to know we'll survive and build new worlds?"

Softness is a political positioning that rejects the hardness and grittiness of neoliberalism. In her essay "The Cultural Politics of Softness" Andi Schwartz describes softness as "a general orientation to the world that foregrounds vulnerability, emotionality, and earnestness." Making the link between softness, trauma, and healing, Andi writes: "Softness is not 'showing up' as a temporary, band-aid solution for superficial pain, it is showing up, hoping to transform others and the entire socio-political terrain with our radical honesty and vulnerability. In its queer and feminist context, softness is the place from which we can build better political principles, the place from which we can build a better world."

Andi's words remind me of Staci K. Haines's book *The Politics of Trauma*. Haines is one of the cofounders of generative somatics, a field of therapeutic work for trauma survivors that helps us be in better relation with our bodies, or soma, as that is where trauma lives. "Embodiment," writes Haines, "encourages us to keep growing, to move toward more aliveness and possibility, to both soften and enliven." Where generative somatics departs from other somatic practices is in its belief that we need to heal individual trauma and collective trauma. This requires a social analysis of trauma that takes into consideration the ways in which trauma is caused by systemic oppression. It is not just individuals that need healing, but whole communities—and given the impact of climate change on our planet, the world needs healing too.

Within generative somatics, Haines explains that healing begins with these questions: "What do you want? What do you value? What do you long for? What is yearning to heal? What do you want to be possible for your community or for the world?" These are "questions of possibility" that orient our bodies toward change. Healing from trauma is a queer utopian project that honors softness, vulnerability, desire, longing, magic, and interdependence.

In my largely queer community filled with trauma BBs and sick babes, we understand the power of softness and the radical potential of interdependence for building the queer utopia that we may never see but need to imagine. Softness isn't just an aesthetic; it's a political orientation toward the world that believes in our collective ability to heal. I'm a soft person. Softness is my path toward liberation.

☽

I'm a small child, standing in front of a table of crystals and stones. My mother is beside me. I pick up a piece of amethyst with a sense of awe and reverence. This sliver is all that remains of this memory, which was buried deep within me until I started to explore the power of my intuition a few years ago. One of the most difficult things about losing a parent is those moments when you recognize a shared affinity. I'll never be able to ask her why we were looking at crystals: "Is it because you're a witch too?"

I keep a photo of her at my altar, taken many years before I was born. She's in the woods. It's fall and the leaves are bright orange and red and yellow. She's found an abandoned car, rusted from all the years that it's lived in the woods. In the photo, she's posing beside it, a branch of leaves obscuring parts of her face. There's something magical about this old relic. She knows it. And I know it too.

In all of the photographs of my mom, I'm struck by her softness. In every photo, she's smiling. Radiating. I imagine running my fingers through her hair. How soft it would feel to the touch. I try to remember what it felt like when she held me in her arms. The trace of her existence can only be captured in photographs and my imagination. But I know that she is the one guiding me toward soft magic.

What does it mean to embody softness as a tool for resistance, liberation, and transformation? I ask this question because the world we live in is not soft. Under capitalism and colonialism and the cisheteropatriarchy, we've been taught that the only way to be, if we want to succeed, is to be strong, tough, gritty. Growing up, I saw this script play out in my father's inability to hold me when I cried, in the way my brother's trauma could only be expressed through rage, in our collective inability, as a family, to name just how hard it was to live in poverty. There was no softness in my home, and its absence became another form of trauma I'd have to reckon with.

The more work I do to heal my trauma, the more I embrace my softness. My softness enables me to be compassionate. My softness helps me foster supportive relationships with others. My softness enables me to better care for myself and for others. Given all the trauma I have to push through in order to be soft, my ability to do so is pretty fucking magical. I have taken something I was taught to see as weakness and I have transformed it: being soft is one of my greatest strengths.

Soft magic is a term I started using in 2019 to describe the process of healing our trauma, which is truly one of the witchiest practices there is. Soft magic is a somatic practice that helps us soften our bodyminds so that we can show up as our full selves, trauma and all. Soft magic is a practice of healing that shows us that our bodies can be sites of safety and power. Through soft magic, we're reminded that the natural world is sacred, that our interdependence must be honored through reciprocity rather than extraction, through mutual aid rather than charity.

Soft magic is a politics and a set of practices that enable us to heal ourselves and our world: compassionate accountability, vulnerability, curiosity, community care, and collaboration. Extending care toward others is magic. Opening ourselves up to accepting care from others and extending care toward ourselves is even more magical because in my experience it's so much fucking harder.

Vulnerability is perhaps the most terrifying of these practices. Whenever we foster an intimate bond with another, we become deeply vulnerable because we've opened our heart—and in so doing, we've opened ourselves to the possibility that another person might hurt us. We're no longer just an "I" with all of our sovereignty. We're an "I and you" and a "we." Being vulnerable means loosening our grip on the need for control and opening ourselves up to being hurt by another.

As we move away from control and step into vulnerability, we show our trauma brains that no matter what happens, we can hold the hurt that may come. When we recognize our own capacity for vulnerability, we begin the practice of undefending our hearts so that we can sit with the discomfort that vulnerability brings with it. In this way, I'm reminded of the Strength card in the tarot, in which a figure dressed in a white gown gently pets the lion standing at their feet. This card asks us: How can we welcome the lion that scares us and learn to become their friend? Vulnerability is a form of soft magic because it enables us to transform the fear of being hurt into the joy of fostering intimacy.

Soft magic is recognizing that we've all caused harm and that we're all still deserving of compassion. It can be much easier to extend compassion toward others and much more challenging to offer it to ourselves. The truth is: We have and will hurt others, just as we have and will hurt ourselves. The question is: Can we be accountable? The prison-industrial complex has taught us that the only person who deserves compassion is the person who's been harmed. Under this logic, the person who caused harm should be punished, shamed, exiled, locked away. No need for compassion. Purity culture on the left fails to hold space for the fact that we're all still unlearning the forms of systemic oppression that live within us.

Transformative justice helps us see that no one heals when we punish, shame, and withhold care and compassion. We can take accountability for the harm we caused, and we can receive and extend compassion toward ourselves. Compassionate accountability, as an alternative to punishment and shame, enables us all to move toward healing. Compassion is soft magic because it turns shame into accountability and harm into healing.

Each time we extend care toward others and toward ourselves, we cast a spell. Each time we open ourselves up to interdependence, we cast a spell. Each time we choose compassionate accountability over shame-filled punishment because we know that we all have the capacity to fuck up and have fucked up and will fuck up again, we cast a spell. Each time we are terrified and yet still say yes to vulnerability, we cast a spell. This work of being with ourselves and with others is magical. It is soft magic.

☾

I have always felt that stories held a kind of special magic. Growing up, I was always reading. After my mother's death, I'd lie upstairs on my bed, reading *The Baby-Sitters Club* books, while my dad and brother watched horror films downstairs. Eventually, I'd begin a PhD in English literature at the University of Toronto. During my qualifying exams, I realized that all of the books I'd planned to write about in my dissertation involved girls whose mothers were missing or dead. Without knowing it, I'd be grieving the loss of my mother through literature. In Roland Barthes's *Mourning Diary*, he writes, "For me, at this point in my life (when maman is dead) I was recognized (by books)." I have found myself having this same experience of recognition, again and again throughout my life.

Recently, I found myself in the story of Inanna, the Sumerian goddess and Queen of Heaven, and her twin sister Ereshkigal, Queen of the Underworld. My friend and brilliant astrologer Quail Pepper recounted the story in their class Venus in the Underworld. They noted how their version of this story differs from readings that are more commonly known, and for reasons I'll share later, I prefer Quail's version and offer it here.

Ereshkigal is born first, and thus should be favored by her father. But Inanna is more beautiful than her sister, and so she is the one chosen again and again to receive the teachings of her father. Traumatized by the lack of his love, Ereshkigal finds her own kingdom in the Underworld, and she separates herself from her family, retreating, Quail tells us, "into the company of ghosts."

Years later, Ereshkigal's husband dies. Overwhelmed by grief, she closes the doors to the Underworld and will not let anyone in. It just so happens that this death occurs at the same moment that Inanna has been married. One's gain mirrors another's loss. Inanna ventures into the Underworld to speak with her sister and be with her in her grief. At each of the seven gates, she must sacrifice a piece of clothing, until she arrives at her sister naked and unadorned, just as the dead must arrive at the Underworld. In all of her rage and grief, not just at her husband's death, but at a life of childhood trauma, Ereshkigal kills her sister and throws her body onto a meat hook, and Inanna hangs there for days. Ereshkigal, overwhelmed by the grief of her husband's death, and now her sister's, sits wailing beside her sister's body.

Ninshubur, Inanna's servant and messenger, realizes that something must be wrong. She goes to the god of the sun and the god of the moon to ask for their help, and they both deny her. It is Enke, the god of water, wisdom, healing, and possibility, who will help save Inanna by creating two little genderless mourners out of the dirt under his fingernails. These tiny mourners sneak into the Underworld unnoticed, eventually reaching a weeping Ereshkigal. They sit beside Ereshkigal and join her in mourning. Ereshkigal hears their cries, picks them up in her hand, and is so moved by their fellow feeling that she grants them a wish: to revive her sister. In their collective grief, Ereshkigal softens, and some healing is made possible. Before Inanna can return to earth, she must choose someone to replace her in the Underworld, and it is decided that her husband will spend half of the year with Ereshkigal in the Underworld, and the other half of the year with Inanna on earth.

I can't help but notice that there is something witchy about Ereshkigal and this story. Scholar Diane Wolkstein argues as much when she writes that Ereshkigal "can be considered the prototype of a witch," and yet I am troubled by the definition of a witch that she offers: "unloving, unloved, abandoned, instinctual, and full of rage, greed, and desperate loneliness." Perhaps another way of saying this is that witches live with trauma. In order to heal, they need to not be left alone and naked in the Underworld. We all need tiny mourners to sit beside us in our grief and our rage, to help us feel less alone.

I love Quail's telling so much more than others that have been offered, which usually frame Ereshkigal as an evil and spiteful woman craving sexual satisfaction. Inanna, on the other hand, is either perfect or selfish and egotistical—classic misogyny. We're never given the backstory for the tension between Inanna and Ereshkigal. The closest we get are Ereshkigal's words in the later Neo-Assyrian story of "Nergal and Ereshkigal": "Since I, thy daughter, was young, I have not known the play of maidens, I have not known the frolic of young girls." Wolkstein describes Ereshkigal as "this underground goddess, whose realm is dry and dark, whose husband Gugalanna is dead, who has no protective or caring mother, father, or brother (that we know of), who wears no clothes and whose childhood is lost." Quail's retelling fills in the gaps. We understand the trauma that Ereshkigal experienced from her father repeatedly telling her that she was ugly, and thus unwanted, always abandoned in favor of her sister.

Jungian readings of the story argue that Inanna's journey into the underworld represents a human's quest for wholeness, which can only be accomplished when we're vulnerable and naked in front of our shadow self. If this is the case, then the only person who truly matters in the story is Inanna, and Ereshkigal is ignored once more and reduced to a plot device. In Quail's retelling, there is a sense of mutuality between Inanna and Ereshkigal. Quail explains how the relationship between the sisters represents "the deep grief that our shadow selves are experiencing" for "when our bright self gets something, the corresponding experience is that shadow self often loses something."

Their words remind me of the day child and night child of structural dissociation. In their book *The Haunted Self: Structural Dissociation and the Treatment of Chronic Traumatization*, Ellert R. S. Nijenhuis, Kathy Steele, and Onno van der Hart begin with an epigraph from Marilyn Van Derbur that reads: "Without realizing it, I fought to keep my two worlds separated. Without ever knowing why, I made sure, whenever possible, that nothing passed between the compartmentalization I had created between the day child and the night child." The authors of *The Haunted Self* will use this metaphor of the day child and the night child to explain the state of primary splitting within the structural dissociation model.

I've spent the last five years in therapy learning how to foster more collaboration between these two children that live within me. This is a process of internal mutuality. And it's made all the more complex by the fact that the day child and night child are not alone. There are many other parts that want my attention. It's my job to show them that I want to foster relationships with them that are built on mutuality and collaboration. Together, we can find new ways to keep me safe, and to let go of the old coping mechanisms that no longer support me.

When I think about Inanna and Ereshkigal through the lens of structural dissociation, what I recognize is that every time I move toward the love I want, every time I choose to value myself, every time I say *I'm not willing to sacrifice this*, my parts lose something: their control over my actions, which once kept me safe, and their sense of being needed. It's my job to show them that they're still very much needed.

We need our Ereshkigals as much as our Inannas. We must help them learn how to be in conversation with one another, how to love one another, and how to work with, rather than against, one another. Echoing this sentiment, astrologer Chani Nicholas recounts the story of these twin sisters in her newsletter: "The parts of self that have been given the worst jobs need help if they are to have their own rebirth. When we dignify them with an acknowledgment, we return them to their valuable state. . . . All aspects of myself are restorable if I take a trip to visit them and acknowledge all they've tried to do to keep me from harm. All parts of myself want to be known."

I do not want a story of these sisters in which Inanna transforms and Ereshkigal is reduced to a plot device. The day child and night child are equally important to our survival. In healing, we're not getting rid of our parts; we're learning to collaborate with them so that they can be reborn. We're not sacrificing the needs of one part in order to meet the needs of another; we're finding a third path so that everyone's needs are met. No one part is left alone to grieve these changes. Just like the tiny mourners, we cry together. Our healing is a process of grieving. Grief and trauma are the mirror to love and healing. In honoring our grief and our trauma, they begin to soften.

What I've learnt through many years of therapy is that underneath trauma is grief. Grief for what we should have had access to but were denied. Grief for all of the selves we could have been had we received the love and care that we deserved, if [insert bad thing] hadn't happened to us. Grief is perhaps the most terrifying emotion for those of us living with trauma because we had no one to support us with our grief when the original trauma(s) happened. And so we repressed the grief, buried it deep down within us. Anytime my therapist tried to help me be present with my grief, I'd freeze. It was as though I was standing in between two panes of glass, and if I moved ever so slightly, if I tried to let just a little bit of grief in, the glass would shatter and grief would flood me until I was left drowning in my own tears.

And yet, in order to heal, we must grieve. As part of the grieving process, we have to let all parts of us know that it's safe now. An adult self is here and isn't going anywhere. We can feel the grief just a little bit at a time, so that it won't overwhelm us. Alone in the Underworld, Ereshkigal opened the door to her grief, and it came flooding out. Like a hysteric, "her hair swirls about her head like leeks" and she wails

"Ohhhhh! Oh! My inside! Oh! Oh! My belly! Oh! Ohhhh! My back! Ah! Ah! My heart!" It is too much for her to bear on her own.

I get it. I spent most of my life overwhelmed by grief and anger and shame and longing and loneliness. My night child taught me how to dissociate from these unbearable feelings: drugs, sex, more drugs, more sex. How different life might have been, in the wake of my mother's death, if my father could have sat down beside me and my brother, and together we welcomed our tears and our grief.

Healing cannot happen entirely in isolation. We must let others in, if we're so lucky to have those in our life willing to venture to the Underworld to grieve alongside us. I did not have any tiny mourners as a child. But I have them now. In 2016, on the eve of the twentieth anniversary of my mother's death, and just a week away from Samhain, the pagan holiday focused on remembering our ancestors and the dead, I invited my dearest humans to a grief ritual on Toronto Island.

It didn't matter that no one had ever met my mother. I asked each person to bring a quotation to share. Something about mothers or grief or any words that they felt like sharing—each offering their own small eulogy. They brought two copies: one for me to keep, and another to be put in the fire together. "Fire," we were told by the funeral officiant I'd hired, "teaches us about transformation as the paper turns to heat, light, smoke, and ash. Fire symbolizes purification as what is no longer needed is cleared away, making room for what comes next. Let the transformation of the pieces of paper in the fire activate the quotes and encourage Margeaux's release and healing."

Next, we did a ritual with water. Earlier that week I'd found a vessel: a ceramic cup with lines of purple, orange, blue, and gold splattered haphazardly across it—reminding me of my mother's love for bright colors. I'd walk to the lake and fill this cup with water, and each person would take a turn pouring the water from my vessel into another cup. The water was meant to signify my tears—all that I'd shed before and all that I'd come to release in the days, weeks, and years to come. In transferring my tears from one cup to another, each person was a participant in my grief. Later, I'd use that water to nourish a plant that would grow in the vessel. And so my tears would sustain another living being—just as the tears of the tiny mourners made by Enke nourished Ereshkigal and moved her toward healing.

☽

I'm sitting on my floor arranging the sixty affirmation cards in front of me. In less than two weeks, I'll be staging my first installation, *Soft Magic*, for the #CripRitual exhibition at Tangled Arts + Disability, a gallery in downtown Toronto. On their website, the curators of #CripRitual explain how "Disabled, crip, d/Deaf, Mad, and Sick people face a lot of barriers and stigma. One way that we deal with these barriers is through rituals. Rituals can be things that we do to create accessibility, mark important moments, or to be in community with others who have similar experiences." For my installation, I have created a space with three stations, each representing a different ritual that has supported me in moments when complex trauma has been overwhelming. I name them ANCHOR, AFFIRM, CONTAIN.

Within the world of trauma healing, there's a lot of emphasis on the practice of grounding, which is when we move out of states of nervous system activation by feeling the ground underneath us. In my experience, grounding often feels inaccessible. Anchoring, on the other hand, doesn't require us to fully come back into contact with the ground. When I imagine a ship's anchor, I think about how the ship floats above on the water, knowing that the anchor is keeping it safe and connected to the seafloor beneath. In their tarot practice, teacher Lindsay Mack explains,

> Anchoring is when we intentionally develop a root system of safety around a practice, or a tool—the breath, a certain person, deity, phrase or mantra, prayer, scent, etc.—so that we can call upon it in moments of distress. Anchors help us to stay in our center when the inner storms rage. They can act as a foundation in moments when we feel that the bottom has dropped out of our lives, an experience and feeling that is shared by many trauma survivors.

For Mack, a tarot card can become an anchor. My altar in my bedroom is filled with anchors: ceramic cats, tarot cards, crystals, tinctures, sacred objects from my mother. Every morning, as I pull a fresh pair of underwear out of my dresser drawer, I encounter their magic. So few objects from my childhood remain. These gifts from my mother—my bronzed baby shoes, a figurine of a girl with long blond hair with the number ten marked in front of her, clearly a gift for my tenth birthday—are some of the most magical objects I own. They're reminders that I was loved, cared for, deemed worthy of remembering at various stages in my life until that love and care stopped abruptly a year later when my mother died. I feel her living in each of these objects at my altar; they are talismans, her offerings of protection.

It would be all too easy to label the objects at my altars as inanimate, as lacking animacy. Jane Bennett seeks to disrupt the argument that inanimate objects lack vitality in her book *Vibrant Matter*. For Bennett, objects have the power to act upon us and direct our actions—a kind of "thing-power" as she calls it: "the curious ability of inanimate things to animate, to act, to produce effects dramatic and subtle." I'm reminded of Mel Chen's words in their book *Animacies*, in which they explore "how matter that is considered insensate, immobile, deathly, or otherwise 'wrong' animates cultural life in important ways." I'm particularly struck by Chen's proclamation that animacy—or, in Bennett's words, vibrant matter—has the capacity to "rewrite conditions of intimacy, engendering different communalisms."

At my altar, human, animal, spirit, and nonhuman objects overlap and commune: a photograph of my mother and me; various ceramic cats; crystals; candles. Each with their own important magic. It is my hope that my ALTAR station can create other conditions for intimacy: between myself and those viewing it; between them and the objects gathered there; between all of us.

The next station, AFFIRM, features sixty collaged affirmation cards, strung across a wall by string lights. I began to make affirmation cards in 2018, a year after starting somatic therapy. Making these cards enabled me to activate my ventral vagal nerve. Any creative practice will do this. Before making them myself, I'd found a lot of self-soothing potential through affirmation cards, but their messages didn't quite fit with my values, politics, and identity: *You're so resilient. This too shall pass. It will all be okay.*

I'm a queer sick and disabled femme deeply committed to social justice work, and I wanted to see affirmations that reflected the ways in which trauma impacts us on individual and collective levels.

I wanted to see affirmations that addressed how systemic oppression causes and exacerbates trauma. I also wanted to acknowledge that when we heal ourselves, we heal the world we live in. Committing ourselves to our healing work is a personal and political act. And so I sat down and created the affirmations I wanted to see: *Your boundaries are sacred. Your fear is valid. It's okay if it's not okay.*

At this station, viewers are invited to submit their fears to me, and in exchange they will receive a ritual connected to one of the affirmation cards. At the end of the exhibition in April, I gathered all of these fears and held a public ritual for everyone who submitted. Together, we thanked our fears for all that they've done to protect us, and we released them. Reading through all of the fears that people have submitted, I saw the fear of abandonment coming up again and again, the fear of never finding someone who'd love you and all your messy parts, the fear that you'll never heal from your relational wounds. I know these fears all too well.

I look back at a list I'd made, titled "things i'm afraid of":

1. I'll be alone forever
2. Everyone I love will realize I'm a horrible person and abandon me
3. If I do find love, something horrible will happen
4. Someone will abduct, rape, and murder me
5. Someone will break into my home, rape, and murder me
6. I'll always live with chronic pain
7. I made up my trauma
8. I experienced trauma(s) I can't remember
9. Everyone will hate my installation
10. No one will participate in the affirmation ritual
11. I'll get sick and die young just like my mom
12. I'll never be a successful writer
13. I'll live in poverty forever
14. No one actually wants to be my friend
15. My needs are too much
16. Heights
17. Spiders. All bugs really
18. Rats and mice

19. Vomiting in public
20. Going for intakes
21. I'll be broken and inconsolable when my cats die
22. I'll always live with intrusive thoughts
23. Being pushed onto the subway tracks
24. Being hit by a car when riding my bike
25. Being hit by a car when walking
26. Being in a fatal car accident
27. I'll never experience secure attachment again
28. I'll never have emotional and sexual connection in the same relationship
29. I'm doomed to repeat the patterns of behavior that I want to let go of
30. I'll relapse and overdose
31. I'll cause irreparable harm to others
32. I'm broken
33. You'll read this list and think that I'm super fucked up
34. You'll read this list and find me insufferable
35. You won't read this list at all

To protect ourselves from the things that scare us, we make up stories: Our fear of abandonment becomes "I'll always be abandoned." In this way, we create self-fulfilling prophecies. And I say that not in the sense of "you make your own reality," because that kind of spiritual bypassing ignores the reality of the world around us and places the onus of achievement solely upon the individual.

What I've been learning is how, when old beliefs come up, my trauma brain immediately starts to find selective data to prove that those beliefs are true. If we find evidence for the beliefs that were ingrained in us by caregivers, loved ones, or the world, then we don't have to grieve the heartbreak of never being fully loved. Our beliefs become a method of controlling the world around us. They help us armor up. It's as though if I can predict what will happen, it won't hurt as much. The funny/annoying thing that I've learned is that prediction doesn't actually protect me from disappointment when the thing I'm afraid of happening actually happens. It still fucking hurts.

As someone who has lived most of their life gripped by fear in the form of intrusive thoughts, panic attacks, dissociation—the tools fear uses to keep us from feeling the pain of our trauma—I've longed to be free from fear. But the more I tried to cut fear out of my life, the louder it screamed. The goal, I learned, wasn't to be free from fear; the goal was to learn how to listen to, be present with, and collaborate with my fear.

Unfortunately, it's hard to take this approach in a world that has labeled fear as a weakness, something to hide, something to overcome. If we don't feel fear, then we don't need others to comfort us. I think about how, as a child, if I woke up in the night terrified, I'd run into my parents' room and they'd comfort me. I honored the fear; I sought out connection. Later, after my mom's death, when intrusive thoughts took over my life, I didn't tell anyone. I pretended I was fine (except, of course, for the fact that I slept in a spare bed in my dad's room for months). I knew that things were different. If I named the fear now, my father would dismiss me. It would take until my early twenties before I expressed my fears to another person again. This time, my best friend. And each time I did, she showed up and validated my fears. In this way, my fear was the catalyst for moving toward connection.

We think that the first thing that happens when we're afraid is that we go into fight or flight mode. But that's not true. First, we look for connection: Is there someone here to protect me, comfort me, validate me, care for me? In the absence of a caring other, our sympathetic fight or flight is activated. And when fight or flight aren't options, a different state of fear takes over: tonic immobilization. We freeze. We play dead. Fear becomes a permanent state rather than a fleeting emotion that we move through. The antidote to fear is connection, interdependence, care from another. I hope that in these affirmation cards I've made, folks will find the experiences they were denied. Affirmation is the missing experience that I want to offer to others and to myself as well.

The hard truth is that the only person we can ever truly depend on is ourselves. For those of us who grew up as caregivers in our homes, always placing others before ourselves, this truth can feel like heartbreak. And yet it has freed and empowered me in ways I couldn't imagine. When I stop responsibilizing others to soothe me, and I turn toward myself for that care, I heal the younger parts of me that never had a safe and stable adult to trust. I get to be that adult for myself. This is what so many call the act of reparenting.

I want to provide participants with a strategy for reparenting their inner little ones, for holding themselves in moments of fear. And so I create the final station of the installation: CONTAIN. At this station is a video of me, in bed, surrounded by pillows and covered by my weighted blanket. One of my cats comes to join me, as I sit, hands over my heart, and breathe. Throughout the installation are various pillows that folks can sit with if they wish to join me in the practice of container building.

Early on in trauma therapy, I learned about the power of the "container": a space within ourselves where we can go to feel safe when we're triggered, a space that enables us to feel held. Staci K. Haines explains how humans have three core needs: safety, belonging, and dignity. Trauma can be caused by any of these three needs being threatened or unmet. In my own healing, restoring my dignity and sense of belonging has been challenging, but not nearly as hard as restoring a felt sense of safety. Because the reality is that we live in an inherently unsafe world, and the more marginalized identities we inhabit, the more dangerous the world is. I recognize that I can't control the world. But what I have learned is that no matter what the world does to me, I can always return to a sense of internal safety by creating my own little container.

I love looking up the history of words in the dictionary: container: *con (hold)* + *tain (together)*. What I see in this word's etymology is that we don't need to do this work alone. We can hold trauma together, a collective act of care that reminds us of how much we need and deserve connection. Container building is a kind of world building. A sacred practice of interconnectedness and care, in which we all work toward building a world big enough for us all to be cared for in the ways that we so deserve.

☾

My unconscious has also been calling on Medusa as a talisman. In the classical telling of the myth of Medusa, Medusa is cursed by Athena after being seduced by Poseidon in one of Athena's temples. The goddess is jealous, and so to ensure that Medusa has no more suitors, she turns her hair into a thousand snakes and curses her with a stare that turns men into stone. In a workshop, astrologer Renee Stills offers a feminist retelling: Medusa is raped by Poseidon, and Athena wishes to protect her from future harm. Snakes and stone turn into shields against rape culture.

Over the past three months, my dreamscape has been haunted by the boys and men of my past. Night after night a new one emerges. First, an ex-partner whom I was with for almost four years. Then, boys I went to high school with, the ones who made fun of me when we hung out with our friends, but would later try to coerce me into having sex with them. The latest boy to push himself up from the watery depths of my unconscious is the boy who raped me when I was fourteen—taking my virginity with him.

I woke up one morning from a dream about him. I went down a Facebook rabbit hole when I typed in his name and sat, frozen, staring at his profile picture. I can see that he's moved out of the suburbs we grew up in and into Toronto, the city that I lived in for fifteen years before moving out west. *I could have run into him. What if I had run into him?* I doubt that he'd recognize or even remember me. I feel my heart break at the realization that someone who could mark your life so violently could live without a trace of you marking them.

In the dream, I'm walking down Bloor Street in Toronto when it becomes clear that someone is following me. As I walk faster, he starts yelling. I see a man standing outside his car on the street and beg him to unlock the doors so I can climb in. I beg him to drive away but he won't. He wants to confront the man chasing me. The two men fight but I don't remember who wins and who loses because suddenly I'm at a school to give a talk. I keep turning around to look at the back of my legs, covered in one giant purple welt from being slammed against the concrete road. Perhaps this happened during the altercation on Bloor Street but I have no memory. Just the welt. The body keeps the score, I think to myself, and laugh at just how literally my unconscious has manifested this metaphor. Every time I see a new person, I show them the welt and they cringe, ask if I'm okay. "Yes, yes, it's fine," I reply. But is it?

As happens in dreams, I'm suddenly transported to a new location: a farmhouse. The man is coming for me again. I look to the right and see a fence of barbed wire. I want to jump over it and run into the field, but I know that I'm too short to clear it. The man catches me and places his hands tightly around my throat. As he strangles me, I look at my friend and with my eyes I plead with her to get her father from inside the house. But she is frozen in place. No one will save me. I'll have to save myself. Just as I have done again and again throughout my life. And so I go limp, play dead. I try to convince him that he's won. I'm dead now.

Then I'm at the Pickering Town Centre, the mall back in the suburb where I grew up and where I was raped. I have a dress to return. It's clear that there is something more urgent occupying my mind. I'm waiting for him to text. It's his turn. He's the one who hurt me. I pull out my phone to see if he's tried calling—he hasn't—and put the phone back in my bag. I will not be the one to reach out. This time, I feel empowered. I am aware of my desirability. If he wants me (which he does) then he will contact me. I'm no longer waiting to hear back from boys who choose to ignore my existence when it pleases them. I know now that they don't deserve me. *I am a gift. I am a gift. I am a gift.*

These words come to me during a workshop for the upcoming eclipses. The facilitator has asked us to connect to the line that runs from your mouth into your pelvis and genitals. "What's emerging?" they ask. And this is what I write: *"You don't deserve me. I am a gift." Pushing them away from me: "It's so fucked up that you would use me—use anyone—for your pleasure. How the fuck can you do this? No. I will not put your cock in my mouth. What the fuck is wrong with you?! How could you go and tell people that we had sex when what actually happened is you got a fourteen-year-old girl—barely fourteen—high and then you took her into the woods, took her pants off, and put your unprotected cock inside of her. Why don't you tell them that?! I am done with you. You will not take anything from me again! You were so mean to me! And I took it because I was so sad and lonely and needed connection. But I won't take that anymore. I am done."*

In writing these words, I have given myself the missing experience. I am finally getting to say all of the things that I never got to say before—things that were not only impossible to utter, but that I couldn't even conceive of saying. Now, things are different. I'm not that young girl anymore. I'm an adult human who knows their worth. This dream has given me the opportunity to rewrite the story of my trauma.

Despite this achievement, I spend the day dysregulated, dissociative. In the evening, my best friend comes over to celebrate the new moon and to prepare for the eclipse portal that has just opened. I tell her about my day, about what I've been processing, and she suggests that we make some art together. Sitting on the floor, I draw Medusa. In that workshop, I'm told that Algol, the fixed star known as "the demon star," is conjunct with Taurus and this north node eclipse. Algol takes its name from the Arabic word meaning *demon's head* and is thus associated with Medusa.

Medusa feels like a protector that's come to show me that I may not have had the power to participate then—but I do now. And so I draw my own Medusa, eyes closed, smile on her face. Underneath her I write the words *I am a gift.* It is as though she is uttering these words so that I do not forget them. That night, I go to sleep and do not dream of the boys of my past. In the morning when I awaken, I feel that something has moved through me. Old patterns have emerged for resolution. I'm no longer beholden to these boys and men and their desires. It's as though I've stepped into the abyss of my own powers. I'm the one in control of the story this time. I can turn these boys and men to stone. Magic.

"I was thinking we could do a ritual together at the river. And take some cute photos of us together for our altars."

When I receive this text from my friend Sam, I respond "YESSSSSSSSSS." It's that day after the eclipse portal has closed. Eclipses occur when the moon moves between the sun and earth, thus blocking the light of the sun from reaching earth and casting a shadow on earth. Eclipses bring to the surface all that has been blocked by the light, all that we have disavowed. Old wounds may reemerge. We may find that parts of ourselves that we do not love are calling out for our attention. This is a time for reflection and rest.

This eclipse portal opened on April 30, with a solar eclipse in Taurus, and closed with a lunar eclipse in Scorpio on May 16. Days before the portal doors opened, I saw my therapist, who reminded me that she'd be away at a training the following week, and so we'd see each other again in two weeks. "No problem," I told her. "I'm feeling great." Two nights later, I have the dream about my rapist. Annoyingly, I am not surprised at the timing. Looks like I'll have to move through this activation on my own.

This is a potent time for me. It is my nodal return. The lunar nodes of the moon are divided into the north node, which represents your destiny in this life, and the south node, which marks your past lives and karmic conditioning. All of the eclipses this year will happen in Taurus and Scorpio, my natal north node and south node. Taurus and Scorpio rule over our attachments—material, emotional, and psychic—and the psychology of our hungers and our repulsions. And so it makes sense that this eclipse portal brought old attachment wounds up to the surface. Old patterns emerge for resolution. I will be uncovering the ghosts that haunt my past, and reckoning with the lessons that my past selves failed to learn, while also cultivating a sense of stability and security in my day-to-day life. I will learn to advocate for and express my power. NBD.

When Sam proposes this ritual, I know exactly what I want to do: I'll release the fears that folks submitted as part of my installation. And with them, I'll release some old stories and beliefs that continue to haunt me: that I do not deserve love; that I'll never find the love I'm searching for; that I'll always be the person who is alone.

At the river, we each write down what we want to release, as well as what we want to welcome in. *I do not need to give myself away. I am so deserving of love. I am a gift. I will no longer abandon myself. I haven't found my person, yet. I do not need to change to be lovable. What happened to me wasn't okay. I don't need to hide from the pain anymore.* I tuck those new beliefs into my journal and walk up to the river with close to one hundred slips of paper in my hands. I offer them to the water with gratitude. *Thank you for always protecting us*, I whisper. The water will tend to these fears now.

Of course, letting go of old beliefs is never as simple as a singular act. It is a practice. Imagine that you walk across a field to get to school every day. Intuitively, your body will take the same path each time. It takes a while before the grass, once standing, succumbs to the weight of your feet. Eventually, the grass vanishes, and a dirt path takes its place. The more you walk that path, the bigger and deeper the path becomes. Let's say one day, after all these years, you decide that you want to create a new path. For the first couple of days, you remember your intention to walk this new path. But on the fourth day, you find yourself back in your old path and you're not sure why. Muscle memory. Despite your desire to create a new path, your brain is wired toward the familiar.

When I think about healing all of the trauma I hold around sexuality and intimacy and love, it's like a pathway I've taken for more than twenty years of my life, both literally and figuratively. As our brains develop, we create neural pathways that tell us how to act—and these pathways attach themselves to stories. Story follows state, after all. The great news about our brains is that their plasticity makes it possible to create new neural pathways throughout our life. If I'm working with twenty years of conditioning, then it's going to take a lot longer than I'd like to see those changes really stick. Sometimes I feel deeply frustrated by this reality. And then I remind myself that I'm practicing something new. It will take time, but with practice, I will see things start to shift. And I have. Our brain's neuroplasticity is another kind of magic.

As I let go of these fears, I'm telling a different story about myself. I no longer have to believe the story that shaped my life: that I am undeserving of love. Sam's presence with me attests to the fact that I am deeply, deeply lovable. After we've both said goodbye to our fears and beliefs, I grab my Polaroid camera and we start to position ourselves for a selfie, an awkward achievement when you're standing on a beach of rocks. As we prepare, two twenty-something femmes are walking onto the beach, and one of them offers to take our photograph. Another magical moment.

Feeling weirdly shy about asking them to take a second photo, Sam and I decide to take that selfie anyways. When I get home, I look at both of the photos, and my favorite is the one that the stranger took of us.

I text Sam a photograph of both images. "I'm not sure the selfie photo was a winner lol."

"Really??? I like that one the most I think!" Sam texts back.

It's perfect. We will each keep the photo that we love.

At my altar, this photograph is a reminder that I'm able to heal from the wounds that have afflicted me. With Medusa watching me from across the room, I get to offer myself the security and protection that I didn't have growing up. Each day, I am coming into my authority more and more, reclaiming my voice, while also honoring the people I've been and who I've shapeshifted into in order to survive.

The week that the eclipse portal ends, and I do this ritual with my friend, my therapist is back. I tell her about the dream and the work I've done. I feel like I should be proud, but instead I am engulfed by shame, and my body is in one of the worst pain flares I've experienced in years.

"Sometimes, to get out of a bad situation, we have to put ourselves in another bad situation," she tells me.

These words open something up in me. I take a deep breath and feel my body expand.

"What just happened there?" she asks me.

"I just felt compassion for myself."

Again, I'm reminded of the power of soft magic. I do not need to carry this shame anymore. I can alchemize shame into compassion.

"Look at where you are now. Look at how far you've come."

It's true. The person I am now was once unimaginable. If that's not magic, I don't know what is.

QUEER WOUNDS; OR WHAT
WE OWE EACH OTHER

So far, I have been talking about the harm and violence I have experienced at the hands of straight cis boys and men. I wanted to write a book about the ways in which queers living with chronic illness and trauma can foster forms of intimacy that support our healing and enable us to thrive in the face of oppression. We need these stories. And, at the same time, we also need stories about the pain we can and do cause one another, of the harm and violence we enact and the wounds we create. Then, hopefully, we can try to heal. "We will all mess up and make terrible mistakes," writes transformative justice activist Mia Mingus. "We will all hurt people we love and care about at some point. We will all have our time on the chopping block."

Harm, abuse, and violence aren't the exclusive domain of cisheternormativity; they happen in queer relationships too because we have all grown up in this toxic world. And yet, not very many of these stories are out there—and I understand why. Earlier in this book, I shared Melissa Febos's thoughts on why there are so few depictions of bad queer sex. She explains, "This is in part because there are so many fewer descriptions of queer sex overall, but it is also due to the phenomenon of image management that often occurs in representation of marginalized communities." Despite the fact that "all of us queers know that not all of our sex is healthy and satisfying," we are beholden to policing by "our own communities to represent our sex in an idealized way."

The same holds true for our relationships. We do not want to name the harm and violence that occur in our interpersonal intimacies and in our communities because of the fear that such truths will be weaponized against us by those who seek to destroy our ways of loving one another. In an interview with *AnOther Magazine*, author Carmen Maria Machado is asked about her memoir of domestic lesbian abuse, *In the Dream House*. To the question, "Why do you think we read so little about queer people who experience this kind of abuse?" Machado responds:

> Queerness and abuse are both subjects that are typically thought of as shameful and not worth committing to the page or the archive. I think there's also a pressure that queer people feel to kind of "perform virtue." Because we're constantly fighting for rights of various kinds, there's this desire to be, like, "Look how good I am. Queer relationships are great—they're just as great as straight relationships!"

If queer relationships are as great as straight ones, then they are also capable of replicating the same kinds of violence. Machado resists the tendency to only represent the good queer relationship: "I enter into the archive that domestic abuse between partners who share a gender identity is both possible and not uncommon. . . . I speak into the silence. I toss the stone of my own story into a vast crevice; measure the emptiness by its small sound."

There has been much conflation between the words harm, disagreement, conflict, and abuse, so it feels important to offer some definitions. The organization Spring Up defines disagreement as "a lack of consensus or agreement, there is a difference of opinion," whereas conflict is "a disagreement stemming from deeply-rooted opposing wants and needs." In my conflict workshops, I define conflict as a disagreement in which something we care about has been threatened (and that threat can be perceived or real). We might disagree on which contestant on *RuPaul's Drag Race* should win; we might get into conflict if my best friend is one of the contestants and you are one of the judges who thinks they should go home.

As philosopher and writer Sarah Schulman has so famously put it in her controversial book of the same name: conflict is not abuse.

There are competing definitions of abuse out there, so I have gathered a few that resonate with me. For somatic practitioner and author Kai Cheng Thom, abuse "is the misuse of power to cross someone else's boundaries." Similarly, in her book *We Will Not Cancel Us*, adrienne maree brown defines abuse as "behaviors (physical, emotional, economic, sexual, and many more) intended to gain, exert, and maintain power over another person or in a group."

Abuse tactics include gaslighting, coercion, manipulation, neglect, isolation, denial, minimization, and leveraging one's power over another with less power. Conflict and abuse can and do cause harm. For brown, harm is "the suffering, loss, pain, and impact that can occur both in conflict and in instances of abuse, as well as in misunderstandings steeped in differences of life experience, opinion, or need." For Spring Up, "harm is when the actions of a person (or people) or system(s) has a negative impact on a person (or people) that creates unmet needs and obligations. This is often an abuse of power." What differentiates hurt from harm is that hurt is short-term pain and it doesn't result in long-term damage. Harm, on the other hand, can impact our sense of safety, belonging, and self-worth.

As humans, we all have core needs. In addition to our basic needs for food, shelter, mobility, resources, and education, Staci K. Haines includes safety, belonging, and dignity. "We are tracking for safety, adapting to belong, and organizing ourselves to find dignity," writes Haines. We feel safe when we have access to our material needs. But safety isn't limited to the material realm, and includes emotional, spiritual, and relational safety: "Safety gets created when your agency, your interdependence, and your autonomy are affirmed. Emotional and relational safety is created when people acknowledge and support your emotional life, your empathy, and your capacity to act on your own behalf, as well as on behalf of others." We feel safe not only when our material needs are met, but when we can feel "secure and vulnerable, authentic and without fear that this vulnerability will be used against [us]." In situations of harm and abuse, our safety can be threatened in all of these ways.

Equally important is our need to belong—our survival literally depends on it. In the early days of human experience, you survived by being a part of a group. If you didn't agree with the group, you risked being ostracized and alone. It became advantageous to adapt your behavior and avoid rejection. The website GoodTherapy writes, "Those who were able to avoid further rejection were more likely to survive, while those who did not find rejection to be particularly painful may not have corrected the offending behavior, making them less likely to survive. In this way, humans may have evolved to experience rejection as painful." These days, one can survive much more easily if they're alone and isolated. But humans still need to feel a sense of belonging and connection with others; isolation, abandonment, not being seen, heard, or respected, all of these experiences can be quite traumatic. "We need to be part of the pack" writes Haines. We need to know that we belong.

Finally, we have a core need for dignity. Haines offers this definition: "Dignity is our inherent value and worth as human beings. Dignity is a sense of worthiness. . . . Everyone is born with it. Everyone needs it." Haines explains, "We want to be of value, to live as inherently worthy, to not question our right to exist." Due to trauma and systemic oppression, so many of us do not have a strong sense of our own self-worth because we've been taught that who we are is wrong, bad, shameful. Shame moves us away from connection and toward protection. Author Shirley Davis describes how, "when faced with shame, the brain reacts as if it were facing physical danger, and activates the sympathetic nervous system generating the flight/fight/freeze response." Experiencing high amounts of shame early on in our lives, American educator Dr. John Bradshaw writes, "can result in permanently dysregulated autonomic functioning and a heightened sense of vulnerability to others." And when we're dysregulated, we shut ourselves off from curiosity, compassion, and connection—all of which are needed for accountability and transformation to occur.

When harm happens—for instance, when my partner yells at me—I find it useful to ask myself: What core needs have been threatened here? Most often, it's that they're not feeling seen by me. I ask this question because I don't believe that there are "bad" people out there who actively and intentionally want to harm others. We are all capable of causing harm, of enacting violence—especially when under threat. What I do believe is that people are hurt and afraid and are often responding from a place of trauma. When we act from a place of protection, rather than connection, we can inadvertently cause harm. And if we don't address the harm when it starts, harm can escalate into violence and abuse.

Violence never starts with violence. Its story begins with something much smaller: a hurtful comment, a microaggression, a crossed boundary, a failure to acknowledge how our actions impact others. As Kai Cheng Thom notes in her essay on queer harm and violence, "Chronicle of a Rape Foretold":

> As a community, we have a tendency to respond only to harm that is extreme and has been explicitly named for us, whereas we ignore the subtler ways in which harm occurs and intensifies. We do not understand how harmful relationships develop or how they progress; we do not recognize the early signs of violence or practice strategies that might help us end it before tragedy or trauma strikes. We do not become actively aware of harmful individuals until after they have already hurt someone so badly that it seems there is no option but to drive them out of community.

If we want to prevent violence from occurring and to stop disposing of those in our queer community who cause harm, we must get at the root of why that harm has occurred and pay attention to those smaller more quotidian moments of harm that take place along the way.

I'm grateful for the writing on queer intimate partner violence that does exist out there—we need to understand and be accountable for the emotional, sexual, and physical abuse that can occur in our relational lives. And, as someone who has experienced harm in my queer relationships, I search for these stories and I find another gap, another place where there is silence. The more I look at my own experiences of harm in queer relationships, and the stories that others have shared with me, it becomes clear to me that there is something confusing and insidious in the ways queers harm one another: We weaponize the very tools that are supposed to liberate and heal us. We invoke the language of boundaries to neutralize our needs and avoid being accountable for the ways in which our boundaries can hurt and harm others. We use the theory of transformative justice in our academic and professional work, but when asked to repair harm, we run because we are woefully unequipped or uninterested in putting theory into practice. We proclaim that we just have to let the soft animal of our body love what it loves to avoid reckoning with the ways in which our desires—and the choices that we make based on our desires—are so often shaped by a complex mix of trauma and the ideologies of systemic oppression. And so we escape doing the hard and necessary work of self-reflection and healing.

To add insult to injury, we romanticize those who embody the values and forms of relationality we desire and then we dispose of one another when things get messy and the other can't live up to the fantasies we've created of the radical queer subject. As I sat on a patio having a glass of wine with my best friend, we talked about harm in queer relationships. "Queers have been treated as disposable by their families and by society for so long," Natalie says in response. "We carry this legacy with us. How dare we replicate that disposability with one another? We owe each other so much more than that."

If we're going to talk about the ways that queers heal one another, we must also talk about the ways in which we wound each other. This requires us to pinpoint both the oppressive and the so-called radical logics we use to opt out of our shared responsibility to one another. We must not let the trauma caused by the colonial capitalist cisheteropatriarchy, and the forms of harm and violence used by these oppressive forces, be replicated within our communities.

We are never fully sovereign if we choose to be in relation with others. Sovereignty is the myth of neoliberal individualism, and I can see how it has found its way into the radical queer communities I am part of. Because our autonomy has been taken from us, because our needs or boundaries never mattered before, because we never got to center our self-care, we have swung from one end of the pendulum to the other. Now, in the name of self-care, we must respect one another's boundaries without question—as though our boundaries are neutral and incapable of causing harm. Such logic ignores the fact that we are beholden to one another.

I choose to end this book with my own experience of queer interpersonal harm in the hopes that I can shed some slight on this murky but all too familiar terrain. In their memoir and self-help book *Be Not Afraid of Love: Lessons on Fear, Intimacy, and Connection*, Mimi Zhu shares their experience of being in an abusive queer relationship. During their healing journey, Zhu encountered "a world of hauntings." The ghosts of shame and blame, and of their past, pre-abuse self who was "untouched by pain," were absent presences in their life. Try as they might, they could not outrun these ghosts. Eventually, Zhu was able to see how "even as our ghosts linger, they are there to remind us how potent and necessary our healing is. . . . It is when we embrace ourselves fully, hauntings and all, that we can forgive ourselves enough to provide permission to heal."

The ghosts of harm and abuse, of blame and shame, haunt queer community. None of us are untouched by pain. But we can learn how to touch one another—physically, emotionally, psychically—with the care and dignity that we deserve. Touch does not have to make us sick. I believe that we can do so much better, that we owe ourselves and one another so much more. In revealing my queer wounds, I hope you feel less alone with yours. And that together, we can begin to heal.

☾

I wake up in the morning on the verge of tears. I pick up my phone from my bedside table and dial Natalie's number. She picks up to me sobbing, gasping for breath.

"How could they do this? I don't understand."

"I know, baby," she responds. "You just can't understand. It doesn't make any sense."

It has been twelve days since the person I was dating sent me an email ending our relationship. Twelve days of waking up in tears, the pain rippling through my body.

C and I started talking in January. We got to know each other better when they signed up for a peer-support container I was running for folks living with trauma who're committed to fostering the forms of intimacy they dream of. As we started to slide into each other's DMs more frequently, I realized that I was crushing on them.

C is nonbinary and masc of center, an activist, educator, and artist, covered in tattoos. I was attracted to them physically and intellectually. We swapped links to our art and our writing, talked about the books we were reading about abolition and transformative justice, and flirted by responding to the memes we shared on our stories.

After our sessions wrapped up, C DMed me. They shared that out of a desire to be more vulnerable, they wanted to share that they had a crush on me and were wondering if I'd want to have a virtual date with them. Perhaps we could each set up a picnic during sunset and FaceTime each other. My heart skipped a beat. It had been so long since someone had asked me out, as I was usually the one who took the initiative. That they'd done so in the name of vulnerability, with such a romantic first date proposal, only made me swoon more.

On our first date, we talk for hours, as two people with prominent Gemini placements will. We laugh over our shared love of trashy reality dating shows and the horrors of cishetero romance and about our mutual interest in education and abolition. By the time we've been talking for three hours, the summer sun has started to go down in Alberta, and I realize how late it is. When C asks me if I want to do this again, I enthusiastically say yes. When their birthday present for me arrives, two weeks into us dating, I cry. Inside of a wooden box is a handwritten note and ten objects: some moss from their terrarium; an essential oil they made; a quartz stone "to help this connection grow."

In between dates we send each other poems, and I read them words from Billy-Ray Belcourt's *This Wound Is a World*:

> Love, says cultural theorist Lauren Berlant, "always means non-sovereignty" but only if we think of love as what opens us up to that which feel like it can rupture the ground beneath our feet. Berlant insists that love requires that we violate our own attachments, that we give into instability, that we accept that turbulence is the condition of relationality as such. We might agree, then, that love is a process of becoming unbodied; at its wildest, it works up a poetics of the unbodied.

In return C sends me photos of some of their favorite poems, all with a tinge of the erotic: "I smell sex in my hair when I awaken" writes Tatiana de la Tierra in her poem "Dreaming of Lesbos." After an hour of texting poems back and forth I fall into bed and text my two best friends: "C and I just had a mini-date sending each other poems. This is all I've been wanting."

By the second week of dating, C is making me a playlist and I feel like all of my teenage dreams are coming true. They send me teasers, including "yr heart" by Hand Habits, and tells me that this song makes them think of me. After I listen, I text C back and ask if they'll share more about why—a vulnerable ask. C makes a joke about not wanting to be vulnerable before continuing to type, sharing with me how this song makes them think about how open my heart is and how it's helping them be vulnerable too. The final two lines of the chorus calling us into softness and acknowledging the fear of getting hurt. The song, and C's interpretation, remind me of how intimacy is always a wager, a risk. One that we're both committed to taking together. My Cancerian heart is in heaven. This is the hysterical intimacy I've been yearning for.

It becomes clear that we need to meet in person and see what it feels like to be in the same space together. It's decided that I will come to visit them. We get on the phone, book my flights and an Airbnb, and start to count down the days. A few days before I am set to leave, C sends me a voice note to say that they no longer feel like it is necessary for me to stay in an Airbnb and that they'd love for me to stay with them for the seven days. C has told me multiple times that they don't commit to something unless they are totally sure, and so I want to trust them. At the same time, the scared part of me knows that I need to have the Airbnb as a backup, so we decide that I'll keep it for the first three days of the trip, even if I don't end up using it. After ten hours of travel, I arrive at the Airbnb, shower, put my suitcase into C's car, and check out of my Airbnb.

We spend the next six days exploring each other's bodies. Big grins across our faces, heads buried into pillows, we can't believe just how much chemistry we have. Switch4Switch, Trans4Trans magic. C takes me on a surprise date to a weaving class—something I've mentioned wanting to learn how to do—and I watch with glee as they make friends with all of the older ladies in the studio. We go to all of the queer, feminist, BIPOC-owned bookstores I want to check out, and we find ourselves purchasing many of the same books. We both burst out laughing when one of the suitors in *The Bachelorette* asks, "Have you ever heard of inner child work?" and we rewatch that moment again and again, delighted. As we talk about our relationship, I find myself stumbling: "Our relationship, well I mean us dating" and they respond, "We are in a relationship. Don't you think? That's what dating is." Their proclamation on the nature of our intimacy makes me feel safe.

At night we make dinner together and settle in to watch *Too Hot to Handle,* their dog sitting in between us. I was told that she had a lot of trauma, that she'd probably bark at me for the duration of my stay, and to not take it personally when she avoided my presence at all costs. I came prepared and with no expectations. But she doesn't bark at me. Instead, she sleeps above my head every night for my weeklong stay, reaching her paw out to my hand when I'm not touching her, asking me for connection. I watch C sit in shock as this sweet, traumatized dog lets me pet her, kiss her, and rub her belly.

"I've literally never seen her do this with anyone," C remarks, as they record a video to send to their ex-partner and co–dog parent.

"I told you, I'm a Cancer. Traumatized animals love me," I respond, smiling back at them.

In bed at night, as I stroke her belly, C and I talk about how their beloved animal is there to set an example, to show up so that we can show up vulnerably with one another, to not freak out and run away from this thing that is feeling so good.

There are a few moments during my stay, when for reasons unbeknownst to us, this sweet pup would jump up and go hide under the couch. As two humans with an understanding of disorganized attachment, we wonder if her attachment system is overwhelmed by the feelings of safety she is experiencing, and she is going back to her old safety mapping by hiding. A few days into the trip, I talk to my therapist and tell her about my new friend. I can tell that my own disorganized attachment is activated.

"It's just so easy to be here with them. And the sexual chemistry is insane. It feels like the first time I'm getting to experience emotional connection and sexual chemistry in the same person. And it is freaking me out."

"C's dog is a great metaphor for how you're feeling. Inside of you is a scared, traumatized little one. All you want is to connect with people who care about you. And, at the same time, it's terrifying. Maybe you can look at this dog as a reminder to not go under the couch," she offers.

"Right. And if I do find myself under the couch, I just have to remember to not make decisions from that place."

"Exactly. Don't make decisions from under the couch. Wait until your nervous system is regulated and see how you're feeling then."

During our time together we have one conflict. C's partner comes over so that we can all meet and hang out. One of the things that helps me feel secure in nonmonogamy is knowing my metamours (the polyamory term for your partner's partners/dates) because then they're no longer these fantasy people in my head. The three of us prepare dinner together and transition into an evening of playing games. It's fun and overall, I enjoy myself. When C asks me how I'm feeling after our night together, I tell them as much. But I also share that I feel saddened by the fact that their partner didn't asked me any questions. And that it didn't feel great when the two of them had conversations about people in their life that I didn't know and made no effort to include me.

"I think it's okay for people to not always feel included," C tells me.

A bit taken back, I respond, "I mean, I feel like there are certain situations where it makes sense that you might not always be part of the conversation. But this was me meeting your long-term partner for the first time."

"That's just how me and my people are. Like I don't know how it's gonna go if you meet my friends. This will just happen every time. Are you saying that I need to be thinking about you and whether you're included every second that we're together?"

"Well, not at every second. But I also just really want my humans to feel included. It's something I am thinking about when I'm introducing people for the first time. Like, if I want to catch up with a friend, I'll make sure that I'm including the new person: 'Hey, so and so has a new roommate and they just moved in today.' That way they know what we're talking about."

"Oh, so you're going to tell me what it is I have to say? Like there's a script I need to follow? I think we're all adults here and if you want to be included in the conversation, you can jump in and ask a question."

I can feel C getting frustrated, and my anxious attachment just wants to defuse the situation. But I feel unsettled by the individualism present in their argument that it's okay for people to feel excluded and that it's on the person who's being excluded to insert themselves into the conversation. As a femme dating a masc of center person, I also can't help but reflect on how femmes are notoriously the ones who consciously think about group dynamics and make sure that everyone feels included.

"I don't understand why this is upsetting you so much," C tells me as I sit there wiping away the tears that won't stop falling.

"It's just that I grew up in a family that didn't ask me questions. My dad and my brother had all of these things in common that they talked about, and I was always left out of the conversation."

When I tell them this, they soften. "Thank you for sharing that with me. It helps me understand you better."

The truth is my reaction to the evening is not just about past trauma. I'm recognizing how C and I have very different ways of embodying our value of community. I feel like I want to address my concerns, but by this time we've been talking for three hours and I'm just grateful to get to a place where they're no longer frustrated.

C looks at me with my lips puffy and swollen from crying, and says, "I just want you to know how much I appreciate you. I've never been with someone who is this emotionally available. I'm so grateful for how you showed up and moved through this with me. I really, really like you."

Worried that I've fucked everything up, I am soothed by C's words. And I still find myself going to bed feeling tense about the lack of resolution or collaboration. I tell myself it's okay that we might have differing opinions about inclusion and that I can pin this concern and come back to it later when we navigate meeting another one of their humans.

When we wake up the next day, I can tell that C is distant. They tell me how they haven't done that much processing in a long time:

"It's like a muscle that hasn't been stretched, and it's sore." They need space to come back to themself. I call my best friends to process what happened, to help quell the voice inside of me that is saying, "That's it. You've fucked it up." That voice is speaking loudly over another that whispers, *Do you want to be with someone who doesn't care if people are excluded? Do you really feel okay about how that conversation went last night? This person totally dismissed how you were feeling.*

In the late afternoon, C draws me a bath. When I step into the bathroom, I see candles everywhere, and there's the smell of lavender and rose in the bathwater. By nighttime I'm sitting on C in bed, both of us in our underwear, reading them poems about astrology and intimacy. When I put the book down, C starts to kiss me. Both of us are wet immediately. They get off the bed to grab their bag of strap-ons and ask me to pick which dick I want to feel inside of me. I sit back on top of them, naked, and ride their cock.

After we've both come, we smile in that post-fucking stupor kind of way. C tells me again how special I am. How much they've enjoyed our time together. How excited they are for us to be dating. That voice inside of me that was so afraid is soothed by all of the intimacy we've just shared, and I no longer hear its whispered warnings. We fall asleep, their dog above my head, one last time.

A few days after I get home, I receive an email from C, ending our relationship. The reason for this abrupt ending: our pacing is wildly different and they feel like it won't ever be possible to get on the same page. They need slowness. C is careful to explain that slowness is not avoidance; it's their commitment to being in the world in a way that's anti-capitalist and trauma-informed. They explain that they can't be in a position to hurt and disappoint me again and again. Ending things now is the most loving thing they can do. They hope we can still be friends and are open to processing this all with me in a few weeks. For now, they won't look at any emails from me for a couple of days, and I shouldn't expect a response for a week. They sign off the email with "best."

I sit in shock, staring at C's email on my phone. On our last day together, we decided on dates for me to visit again, seven weeks later, at the end of September. I was already going to be in a nearby city, and so we agreed that it made sense for me to pop in for a few days and connect. On the Monday morning that I left, we fucked on C's couch, and buried between their legs, I felt them come hard against my face. As they kissed me goodbye, they said, "See you September." Later that day, as I waited for my flight home, I purchased my tickets. A part of me was anxious: "What if they change their mind?" But I wanted to lean into secure attachment. I wanted to trust what C had told me: that they don't commit to things they don't want to do.

We'd talked during my visit about our pacing. As someone with a lot of fire in my chart, I am quick to take action, quick to feel, and quick to process. I have also learned just how much I need slowness in my life. In two out of three partnerships where we lived together, we didn't move in until we'd been dating for two years. In the case of the third, we moved in after nine months, mostly out of circumstance: he needed to move out of his place, and I needed a new roommate. When I've looked at other queers in my life U-Hauling in a matter of months and sharing I love yous by date three, I feel terror rise up in me. I may be fast, but I am also slow.

Given my knowledge of C's need for slowness, I wasn't surprised when they texted the day after I left to ask for some space to process and integrate our time together. They told me that they'd like it if we only texted each other once a day until our date on Saturday. It could be at the start or end of the day. And no interaction on Instagram. When they asked me how I felt, I honestly didn't know how to respond. I had anticipated that C might need some space, but it felt like a dramatic shift—from being together every day, having sex and being deeply intimate, and texting each other every day throughout the day prior to the trip, to only talking once a day. A shift lacking in slowness. Still, I'm used to being with people who need space to process. My only ask was that we text at night, so as to not disrupt my writing in the morning.

Thursday morning I picked up my phone and there was a text from C. They wanted to talk about our September trip and share how they're feeling about it.

"Okay, thanks for letting me know. But I really wish you could've respected my boundary around not texting in the morning."

C apologizes and goes on to tell me that they felt the need to tell me now, just in case I needed to make any changes with my flight.

Confused, I texted back: "Well now it sounds like you don't want me to come in September."

They confirm that this is the case. It feels too fast for us to see each other again after five weeks apart. That they're shocked that I went ahead and bought my tickets when they'd asked me for some space.

"Well, you asked for space from texting. You didn't say that your need for space had anything to do with our next trip. Plus, I bought the tickets on Monday. I really don't think this is an appropriate way to have this convo. I'm gonna take some time to process and ask that we not text until our date on Saturday."

C agreed.

The next morning, I woke up and looked at their Instagram stories—a whole other kind of masochistic torture in the age of social media. They'd shared a post that read: "A person's emotional response to your need isn't about you. You could be the best communicator in the world asking for a basic need, yet people will always perceive you through the lens of their own experiences, perceptions, and emotional capacity. How people receive your needs isn't about you. Remember that." The next slide was a quote from Emma Zeck (who, unfortunately, also happens to be a TERF and anti-vaxxer, though I knew C must have not known this): "conscious love says: i see you for who you are—not who i wish or imagine you to be. i take actions and set boundaries according to my observations. i untether myself from fantasies, illusions, projects and do not pedestal or lower another. the essence of me is a commitment to staying in reality at all costs. i do not cause suffering. illusions and attachments do." The last story I saw before I closed my phone was a poster by @caring.is.radical with a snail and the words "Moving slow is still moving."

I couldn't help but feel that C was subtweeting at me. Even in a best-case scenario, they knew it was possible I would look at their stories and see those words. I burst into tears, reached for my phone, and called Varia. Ten minutes into talking with her, I got the email from C, ending our relationship.

☾

What do we owe each other? I have been thinking about this question in the wake of this breakup.

In the days after C's email, I reflected back on that quote about needs. At one point in time, I'd said something similar. So many of us grew up in families where our needs didn't matter, where our boundaries were ignored. We may also have experienced intense reactions in the moments where we tried to articulate our needs (my brother slamming doors, punching holes in walls; my dad gaslighting me and shutting down). In the best of cases, it can be really hard to receive another person's boundaries, to hear their needs, especially when those needs conflict with your own. I know all too well how your needs can be turned against you by those who do not like your boundaries, who over-responsibilize you for having needs to begin with—and so it makes sense to me that we do not take others' responses into account when stating our needs.

It may also be the case that another person's need triggers something inside of you. I used to get so activated by people needing space to process their feelings while we were in conflict because it triggered my past trauma from my father and brother pulling away from me during conflict and never coming back to resolve and repair. My triggered response is my responsibility and should never be used to make someone feel bad about their need. And at the same time, the reality is that our needs can and do impact those we're in relationships with.

I am unsettled by the ways in which placing the onus entirely on the human who is having their response can work to negate our responsibility to one another. To say that "people will always perceive you through the lens of their own experiences, perceptions, and emotional capacity" is lacking in nuance. To act as if our responses happen in a vacuum of past trauma or emotional incapacity is not only pathologizing, but also ignores our interdependence.

This way of thinking weaponizes the language of boundaries to justify being unaccountable. Folks on the radical left will say, "This is just my boundary. You don't have to like it. I'm not responsible for how my boundary makes you feel." End of story. In this way, boundaries can be used to minimize your responsibility to those you've chosen to be in connection with.

I worry about how a sentiment like "another person's response isn't your responsibility" erases the ways in which our reactions to another person's need aren't just about us. There is something very individualistic about this approach to boundaries and needs. To quote my brilliant bestie, once again: "That's some neoliberal, every man is an island, bullshit. It's anti-connection and anti-responsibility." Where is the space for you to have a need (and for that need to be valid) and for that need to have a negative impact on me? As much as some folks on the radical left would like to believe, boundaries do not negate our responsibility to each other. This isn't an either/or situation.

When I tell someone what I need, I think about the context of our relationship, the differentials of power and oppression that we hold, and how we have related with one another up until this point in time. Our needs shift and change over time. And if our boundaries are drastically shifting from what they looked like in the past, maybe we should talk about that. This requires a commitment to slowing down, to giving ourselves the time and space to look at our boundaries within the context of our relationship with another person. I know that I have seen my current humans through the lens of my past experiences and have erected boundaries with them that represent what I needed in the past but didn't get. But these boundaries do not actually reflect what it is that I need now. The reality is that this kind of collaboration takes more time; it is a slow process that requires us to get curious, ask questions, and brainstorm possibilities.

Sometimes people can express their needs in ways that are callous, unkind, and unthoughtful (and not because that person is callous, unkind, or unthoughtful, but likely because they are activated and are trying to protect themselves). In my relationships, there's a big difference between saying "I need space right now" and "I know my need for space right now might feel jarring. Is there anything you need to feel supported before I step away?" As someone with a lot of abandonment trauma, I've shared with partners and loved ones that it is helpful for me to receive some affirmation of our connection ("I love you/care about you") and a timeframe for reconnecting (instead of "we'll talk later," it's "let's talk in an hour"). In this way, expressing our needs to another becomes a kind of collaborative process, an act of care that acknowledges our interdependence and responsibility to and for each other.

I'm reminded of somatic practitioner Prentis Hemphill's words: "Boundaries are the distance at which I can love you and me simultaneously." Boundaries are not just an act of self-care but an act of love—love for ourselves and others. I want us to be able to express our needs in a way that acknowledges our interdependence. I want us to feel like it's okay to stand strong in our boundaries while holding space for impact. I want us to ask: How do we care for ourselves and each other during these moments? I want there to be space for both me and you when it comes to honoring our needs.

I also want us to acknowledge that blanket statements about boundaries are woefully inadequate because the contexts of our relationships matter. Oftentimes, our needs feel so urgent, like, *I must have this right now!!* (always a great sign that our nervous system is activated and we are not in our window of tolerance). The more and more I question the urgency impulse, with its ties to colonialism, white supremacy, and capitalism, the more I realize that there is space to slow down, pause, connect, and collaborate.

I'm deeply saddened by C's choice to end our relationship without having this conversation. To be told by them that they're slow, and our pacing is incompatible, implies that I am fast. When I responded to their email, I told C how "one of the ways I embody slowness is to be with discomfort and uncertainty long enough to see if something can shift. I know that we were both experiencing discomfort when you asked for space to integrate and process. And I knew that that discomfort would pass and that I was committed to being with it because this connection with you felt truly special to me."

We cannot evoke the language of slowness while failing to acknowledge our inconsistency. In the wake of this breakup, my friends would use the term *love bombing* with me to describe how C showed up fast and hard at the start of our connection. In an interview with *Cosmopolitan*, Ami Kaplan, a psychotherapist in New York City, explains that *love bombing* is bombarding someone with "intense displays of attention and affection." And it is characterized as a form of emotional abuse:

> Love bombing is largely an unconscious behavior. It's about really getting the other person. Then, when they feel like they really got the person and they feel secure in the relationship, the narcissist typically switches and becomes very difficult, abusive, or manipulative.

She adds that the same person who was just "super idealizing of their partner will switch to devaluing them."

In sharing this definition, I want to name that I am wary of the overuse of the term *narcissist* within therapy worlds—especially on social media—and the ways in which "narcissistic abuse" is used to pathologize those who suffer from narcissistic personality disorder. The irony here is that, months later, I'll learn that C has been telling people in their life (including friends in Los Angeles, where they know I'm building community) that I have either narcissistic personality disorder or borderline personality disorder.

Like others committed to transformative justice, I stay away from using totalizing terms like *abuser* because we are so much more than what we do. I'm also critical of what gets labeled as *intense* in a world in which we've been taught to shove our emotions down and any outward display of emotion can all too easily be deemed "too much." I also want to be clear: C did not abuse me. And their behavior does not check all of the boxes for love bombing. They did not, for example, expect me to respond quickly to texts; nor did they make grand proclamations that we'd be together forever or say that we were meant to be. But there are many characteristics of love bombing that I can see now, in hindsight.

C sent me the most romantic gift I'd ever received two weeks into dating: They spent weeks making me a playlist filled with songs about romance and love before we met. C told me I was the most emotionally available person they'd ever been with; that they'd been drawn to me after hearing me talk about how I show up in my interpersonal relationships (information they'd gotten from being in my peer-support group and reading my writing online). C sent me texts about the feels they were having for me and told me again and again just how amazing I was. At the time, I felt like C was truly seeing me: that I finally had found someone who wanted to show up and romance me, someone who wanted to meet me in the vulnerability that I bring to my relationships.

After a month of dating, we then spent a week living together, having sex every day, and sharing deep moments of intimacy. And it is there where things started to go awry. Though, if I'm being honest, I saw some warning signs before. Two days before I was set to leave to visit C, they messaged me and said that their partner was going to come and spend the night. As two chronically ill humans, we've both been incredibly COVID cautious, and I knew that C was even more cautious than me. Still, my nervous system reacted, and I got anxious.

We hadn't talked about seeing anyone inside and unmasked leading up to the trip, and I was afraid that their partner might get them sick and we'd have to cancel the whole trip. I tried to bring up my concerns with C and ask for more information about their partner's protocols so that I could assuage my concerns. Admittedly, I was activated and did not do a good job sharing how I was feeling. C got upset with me. "Am I expected to get your permission before I see anyone else inside and unmasked?" they asked me. "You know that I'm even more cautious than you, so why would you think I'd do something to jeopardize our time together?"

Looking back, I can see how my anxiety made them feel unseen. After C said that they needed to step away from that convo, then continued texting with me, I practically begged them to get on a FaceTime call because I knew that if we talked with voices and faces we'd be able to move through this. Eventually, they FaceTimed me. I apologized for projecting my fears onto them, and they asked me if there was anything I needed to feel supported. Though we had come to a good place, I left the conversation feeling uneasy. It had been such a long time since I'd shared my anxieties with someone, and when I did they got frustrated with me. I didn't want to invalidate frustration—all feelings are necessary. And yet all I could feel was that I'd somehow disappointed them; like the idealized version of me that they'd been holding had cracked and they were seeing all of the mess that was underneath.

I can't help but think of the quote that C shared on their stories: "conscious love says: i see you for who you are - not who i wish or imagine you to be . . . i untether myself from fantasies, illusions, projections and do not pedestal or lower another . . . i do not cause suffering. illusions and attachments do." When C shared this post, it was like they were saying, "I am practicing conscious love and you are the one who wants me to be someone that I'm not." The irony is that I'd never placed them on a pedestal. What I see in these words now is their inability to meet me in my messiness, my anxiety, my fears. They wanted to date me because of the ways that I talked about moving through the hard moments of relationality—but when forced to do that work with me, they opted out.

To say "i do not cause suffering. illusions and attachments do" is under-responsibility disguising itself as self-empowerment. Humans cause suffering all the time. We hurt each other. And one of the ways that we do this is by projecting fantasies onto another person and disposing of them when they fail to live up to our expectations. Yes, attachment can lead to suffering. But the cause of that suffering is the choices we make in our attachments. As two humans who told each other how triggering inconsistency is, I was shocked by how C could go from such regular contact with me to very little, from such excitement about this connection to such trepidation.

I know this pattern all too well. It's one of my greatest wounds. C knew this. Before I left for Chicago, C and I talked about our sex aftercare needs.

"For me, the biggest trigger is having sex with someone and them pulling away right after, ghosting me, or ending the relationship."

"I'm so sorry that's happened to you. I would never do that," C told me. (This is what I recall C saying at the time, but now I wonder if I've imagined it.)

My disclosure and C's proclamation do not mean that they couldn't end things with me after we shared sexual intimacy. That wouldn't be a reasonable boundary. But when someone discloses their trauma to us, and we end up repeating the pattern, we owe them more than an email breakup. At the very least, we can acknowledge just how hurtful our actions might be, given their past wounding. That C was unable to do that shows me just how activated they had been at the time. Their body was doing everything it could to protect them, including moving out of connection with me. We went from "I want you I want you I want you," to "now I'm done." An old wound was ripped open.

(

When I am wounded, there is a question that plagues me: Why? Why did they do this? Why did this happen? And tied to this question are others: What did I do to deserve this? How didn't I see this coming? How can I prevent this from happening again? I know that these questions come from a younger part of me. As an adolescent and even as a young adult, I couldn't understand why I'd been hurt time after time by so many boys and men. Answering this question will enable younger me to feel safe, in control. As if, in knowing why, we can prevent this harm from happening again.

There is another reason to ask this question. In her book *Emergent Strategy*, adrienne maree brown writes:

> To transform the conditions of the "wrongdoing," we have to ask ourselves and each other "Why?" Even—especially—when we are scared of the answer. It's easy to decide that a person or group is shady, evil, psychopathic. The hard truth (hard because there's no quick fix) is that long-term injustice creates most evil behavior.

brown goes on to explain:

> in my mediations, "Why?" is often the game-changing, possibility-opening question. That's because the answers rehumanize those we feel are perpetrating against us. "Why?" often leads us to grief, abuse, trauma, often undiagnosed mental illnesses like depression or bipolar disorder, difference, socialization, childhood, scarcity, loneliness. Also, "Why?" makes it impossible to ignore that we might be capable of a similar transgression in similar circumstances. We don't want to see that.

Asking "Why?" in this case becomes a way of getting to the root cause of harm, of addressing the very conditions that enable harm to happen in the first place. We must ask ourselves this question.

When I called Natalie and asked her "How could C do this? I don't understand," I wasn't referring to C ending our relationship.

What hurt and confused me so much was how they chose to do it: via email, signing off with "best." They may have thought that it was the most loving thing to do, but their choice made me feel disposable. My favorite definition of love comes from the late bell hooks. In *All About Love*, hooks defines love as a verb, an action that we take: "When we are loving we openly and honestly express care, affection, responsibility, respect, commitment, and trust." In emailing me, C did not show me respect and negated their responsibility toward me. There was no affection in their email beyond "I hope we can be friends one day. I appreciate you, a lot." Talking to me with voices and faces was what our intimacy deserved, and it would've left my dignity intact.

I took my time responding to C's email. I knew that I was dysregulated and I wanted to make sure that my email named the harm I experienced, while also showing them the compassion and dignity that they—and I—deserved. At the end of my email, I asked for repair and told them what I would require to make that happen:

> *I need to know that you are committed to being curious, open to my feedback, and challenging your own conclusions. I also need you to show up ready to be accountable for the ways in which your actions have hurt me. This conversation should never have happened via email, and so I am asking you to not respond to what I have shared here via email, and to share those responses with me via a FaceTime call. If you are open to my requests, you can respond back and let me know. I do not have any timeline of when I need or expect a response from you. If you are not open to what I have asked for, which is what I need for repair, please do not respond to my email and respect my boundaries here. The door is always open for repair.*

An hour later, C responded. They apologized for hurting me. Said that they would reflect on my feedback. And that they weren't interested in connecting with me again. Three sentences. While it offered me some relief to read C's apology, an apology without changed behavior and repair is not an apology. In her blog post "The Four Parts of Accountability and How to Give A Genuine Apology," Mia Mingus, educator of transformative justice and disability justice, breaks down the components of a good apology. For Mingus, a good apology includes the following: "I'm sorry"; naming the hurt/harm caused ("breaking up with you via email wasn't kind of me"); naming the impact your actions had on the other person ("I can see why my actions made you feel disposable"); taking responsibility by naming your actions ("I can only imagine how painful that was for you because you told me about how many times you'd slept with people and then been ghosted"); and committing to not repeating the hurt/harm again.

In addition to the *what* of an apology is *how* we apologize, which includes making the apology as soon as possible, being genuine, being proactive, and letting go of control and the outcome. There are two pieces of the *how* that feel especially important to me. The first is to give the person and the conversation your full attention: "When you are apologizing to someone you care about, give them your full attention," Mingus shares. "This is not a time to rush, this is a time to go slow. This is a time to be thorough, not distracted. This is a moment to figure out what you and the other person need in order to be present." In writing a one-sentence apology and refusing any conversation with me, C made me feel that this apology was not worth their time or effort.

Tied to this piece is another element that was missing from C's apology: treating the apology as sacred. Mingus explains:

> Apologizing is part of accountability and accountability is a sacred practice of love. If you've hurt someone you care about, it is sacred work to tend to that hurt. You are caring for this person, the relationship you share, as well as your self. You are engaging in the sacred work of accountability, healing, and being in right relationship. This work is part of the broader legacy of transformative justice, love, and interdependence. Do not take it lightly and give it the respect it deserves.

If I have shared intimacy with someone, sexual or emotional, I see our connection as something sacred, regardless of the duration of the connection. When I mess up and I am given the opportunity to be accountable, I see that as a gift. Because when we refuse to be accountable, we not only harm the other person, but we harm ourselves too.

Causing harm can all too easily lead to shame in a culture that only understands accountability through the lens of punishment. Zhu, reflecting on the harm they caused when they "chaotically ventured into many short-term relationships without taking my lovers seriously," shares how "if we have caused harm, shame can create a hard protective shell around us that stops us from the difficult but necessary process it takes to reduce harm, atone for our mistakes, and make sure that we do not repeat the harm that was enacted." In refusing to be accountable to the harm we've caused, in choosing protection over connection, we block ourselves from the transformative possibility of healing from harm.

In a workshop I attended with Mingus, she said that transformative justice work is grief work—and this statement broke my heart with its truth. As someone who knows C's trauma history, and who believes that they do truly care deeply for people and want to show up ethically in their relationships, the most generous reading I have is that their nervous system was too dysregulated to show up in the ways that I know they want to: as someone who is accountable to harm.

I may never know what was happening for C in the days and weeks after our time together, and I am not interested in psychoanalyzing their behavior. And, in asking myself why, I can see that some scared part of them was telling them that they needed to move away from connection and toward protection, and so that was all they were capable of doing. This reality is heartbreaking. Not because I want to be with C. But because I know how much they wanted to be with someone who was emotionally available, romantic, vulnerable, and able to show up for the hard stuff. "Part of the reason I started crushing on you," C told me, "was because of how you talked about being in relationships with other people." I wish that they could have just said to me, "My nervous system is freaking out. How can we move through this together?"

Instead, C attributed the dissolution of our connection to a need for slowness, to a desire to live in a way that is anti-capitalist and trauma-informed—as though we do not share those same investments. The irony of invoking that language of anti-capitalist and trauma-informed while simultaneously disposing of someone you shared deep intimacy with is not lost on me. This is yet another example of queers weaponizing the very tools and language that are supposed to help us heal.

Being slow and trauma-informed is to collaborate, to ask questions, to get clarity instead of climbing the ladder of inference; it is to avoid reducing people and situations to black and white (fast or slow), and to seek out nuance. Being slow and trauma-informed isn't pulling away after having deep sexual intimacy with someone without asking them what they need—especially when that person has told you that they have a trauma history of men and masc of center folks doing that, and you have assured them you'd never do the same.

In asking "Why?" I see the ways in which toxic masculinity lives in C's actions. It's important to name that toxic masculinity lives within all of us regardless of our gender or lack thereof. As a femme, I feel reticent to talk about the presence of toxic masculinity within the trans masculine community because it is deeply complex and messy. Raised as girls and women, trans masculine folks know the experiences of being treated as objects for cishet male consumption. Being trans and nonbinary are also not privileged positions. But within my queer community, trans men and masculine of center folks are the most desired and the most proximate to power. We need to hold the tension that is part of existing at the intersections of power and oppression.

I have watched women and femmes treat one another as disposable, as competition, as threats. And, as someone who has been in relationships with people across the gender spectrum, I have never had a woman or femme abruptly end a relationship with me, have never been ghosted after sharing sexual intimacy. This isn't to say that it doesn't happen. I have spoken with other femmes in my life about the harm they've experienced from other women and femmes. I do worry, however, about replicating the line touted by men in the Men's Rights Movement and by incels, who claim that women can rape and cause harm in order to avoid acknowledging that harm happens disproportionately at the hands of cis men. As Aleo Pugh writes in "Re(Doing) Gender: Trans Men and the Reproduction of

Toxic Masculinity": "As transmasculine folks in particular, we need to be more critical about our positions and our culpability in reifying the gender hierarchy. While our male/masculine privilege may operate differently than cis men's, this does not negate its existence. Oftentimes, our replication of maleness/masculinity is nearly identical and equally as toxic."

What I know is that it's all too common for women and femmes to have sex with men and masc of center folks only to have them pull away abruptly afterward. Breaking up with me via email was the easy way out because it meant that C didn't have to witness my hurt or be accountable for it. To tell me that this was the most loving thing they could do placed them in the paternalistic position of knowing what is best for me. And saying that they didn't want to continually disappoint and hurt me was patronizing and robbed me of my agency. Furthermore, using the language of "anti-capitalist" and "trauma-informed" was the embodiment of the "rational" man talking down to the emotional and "irrational" woman.

In naming the presence of toxic masculinity in C's behavior toward me, I want to put what happened between the two of us into a larger social context: systemic oppression teaches us who deserves dignity and who doesn't. Our social context shapes our intimate relationships for better or worse (most often worse). When looking at harm and trauma, the focus is almost always on the individual and their closest relationships. But there are so many forces that shape how we show up in the world.

In *Polysecure,* Fern expands this narrow focus with the nested model of attachment of trauma, which includes the following layers: self, relationships, homes, local communities and culture, societal, and the global/collective. Our local communities and culture are the places we spend our time outside of our home (work, school, friends' houses, clubs, churches). Here we must take into consideration the cultural narratives that we have inherited from colonialism, racial capitalism, cisheteropatriarchy, transphobia, and other forms of oppression. At the level of societal forces are the social structures and systems (economic, legal, medical, political, religious) that dictate access to healthcare, legal rights and protections, education, food and drinking water. It is here that we must consider experiences of systemic oppression and structural violence. And finally, the global or collective covers our attachment with nature (earth, water, air, fire) and animals, the trauma of climate crisis and the impacts of natural disasters on our homes, communities, relationships, and ourselves, collective trauma and intergenerational trauma, and disconnection from spirit, from the sense of something bigger than ourselves.

Toxic masculinity hurts us all. It robs us of the magic of vulnerability and deep intimacy with one another. It teaches us to be hyper-individualistic and under-responsible. Under the hold of toxic masculinity, we believe that needing care is a weakness and that causing harm is something to ignore or to be ashamed of. We owe each other so much more than replicating the very dynamics that have harmed and traumatized us.

In her beautiful essay "Dreaming Accountability," Mia Mingus asks:

> What if we rushed towards our own accountability and understood it as a gift we can give ourselves and those hurting from our harm? What if we understood our accountability, not as some small insignificant act, but as an intentional drop in an ever-growing river of healing, care, and repair that had the potential to nourish, comfort, and build back trust on a larger scale, carving new paths of hope and faith through mountains of fear and unacknowledged pain for generations?

In acknowledging the root causes of harm, and the role that toxic masculinity played in C's treatment of me, I move toward the river that Mingus speaks of. In acknowledging the root causes of harm and stepping into accountability, we can unlearn, untether, transform, and heal.

☾

For weeks after the breakup with C, I wake up with lyrics from their playlist in my head, haunting me. I think of the pledge in Hand Habits' song "yr heart," to not harm or alarm the other. These words, which once made me swoon, now make me cry at the irony of having someone tell you that they trust you to not harm them, and then they harm you. I alternate between calling my two best friends, and they listen to me as I cry, and I reckon with this heartbreak.

I practice this meditation that I learned. Closing my eyes, I picture my adult self at the top of a winding staircase. There are twenty steps down, and at the bottom is my eleven-year-old self. One hand on my stomach, another over my heart, I count each step and focus on my breath. When I reach the bottom, I see my younger self curled up in bed in the fetal position, crying. I get into bed, and I wrap my arms around them and hold them as they cry. Then I see the spirit of my mom, lying down behind my adult self, holding me too. I listen to my younger self. "You don't just leave someone you care about," they repeat over and over. "Mom and dad loved each other so much. And then she died. When you find someone special, you can't turn your back on them." Every heartbreak occupies the past and the present. My heart is broken because C wasn't able to see all of the beauty in our connection. Because they weren't even able to be friends with me. They needed to cut ties with me totally. It feels impossible to understand. We owe each other, and ourselves, so much more than that.

Early on in getting to know one another, C told me that vulnerability is a portal—a gateway to deeper connection, intimacy, and possibility. Vulnerability is an embodied experience, made all too clear by its etymology. The word *vulnerable* comes from the Latin *vulnerābilis*, meaning wounding. Vulnerability, then, is our capacity to be wounded. The word *trauma* shares a similar root, coming from the word Greek τραῦμα, or wound. That there is a link between vulnerability and trauma does not surprise me. Our vulnerability, when not received well by others, or, when it is used against us, is a kind of trauma. And our trauma is a sign of our vulnerability. Trauma and vulnerability are open wounds.

Both literally and metaphorically, it is in our best interest to avoid being wounded. Wounds are uncomfortable at best and painful to life-threatening at worst. And yet, making ourselves impervious to wounding comes at a great cost. How can we truly be in connection with others when we keep them at a distance so that we may remain invulnerable (as though such a thing were even possible)? What I have learned is that my attempts to avoid being wounded haven't done much to prevent wounding from happening—because, annoyingly, I cannot control everyone and everything around me. To avoid being wounded, I would have to completely opt out of the social— and, even in my darkest moments, that's not something I have been willing to do.

I'd be lying if I said that keeping myself open to intimacy—and thus open to wounding—has been easy. Intimacy requires vulnerability. I return again and again to the words of Cree poet Billy-Ray Belcourt: "Love, says cultural theorist Lauren Berlant, 'always means non-sovereignty' but only if we think of love as what opens us up to that which feel like it can rupture the ground beneath our feet. Berlant insists that love requires that we violate our own attachments, that we give into instability, that we accept that turbulence is the condition of relationality as such." To be vulnerable, to love, to be intimate with another, is to open ourselves up to the possibility of being wounded.

At the same time, as the title of Belcourt's poetry collection attests, a wound can open up a whole new world. Vulnerability isn't just a wound. It is a kind of world building. As C told me: Vulnerability is a portal. Sometimes the portal takes us somewhere dark, forcing us to confront our fears, our traumas, our woundings. Other times, the portal shows us that the forms of intimacy we dream of are possible. In both cases, vulnerability is a portal to healing. I can see how, for C, being so vulnerable with me was all that they desired—and it opened up the portal to fear and trauma. Instead of being with the fear, and moving toward connection, their protector parts chose to move them toward protection, which meant cutting me out of their life entirely. Of course, I can never know if this is what happened for C. This is just my story—and I hold space to be wrong in my reading.

A few weeks after the breakup, C emails me to say that they've dropped out of a course we'd both signed up for. Seeing their name in my inbox feels like my heart has just been punched—especially since there's no mention of any repair. When I email them back, I tell them how confusing it is to hear from them after they've told me that they don't want to connect with me again. "You told me that you're friends with all of your exes. That you do repair work when you cause harm. And yet you're not interested in either of those things with me. It's so confusing and hurtful." When they write back, C tells me that they never meant forever when they said they didn't want to connect with me again. That they just needed space. They're sorry for the miscommunication. They're open to having a repair conversation.

We swap emails back and forth to discuss the terms. It becomes clear that we have two different aims. C wants to listen to me share about the harm they caused, and then to apologize. But I've already done that. I explain that what I need is to hear their reflections on how their actions were harmful. "I'm sorry," they write back, "but I can't give you what you're asking for. I just don't think that there's a right or wrong way to communicate information. I feel like you're asking for more than what is warranted here. We dated long distance, you came to visit, and I made the autonomous decision to break up with you. Break ups hurt, I know. And I can be here to witness that. But I can't offer anything else."

Their response clarified for me that we hold very different values around what it is that we owe those we've shared intimacy with. As someone invested in transformative justice, I too am wary of using the binaries of good/bad, right/wrong, as life is always so much more nuanced—and what is good for one person might be bad for another. I do, however, think that there are kind and caring ways to communicate, and that our communication should take the whole context of the relationship, and our power dynamics, into play. To glibly reduce our intimacy to "we dated, met each other, and broke up," shows me that our connection did not mean as much to them as it did to me (or, perhaps it did mean a lot to them and they just can't acknowledge it). Duration of relationship is so often used as a defense: "Oh, we only dated for x period of time." But what was the depth of the intimacy we shared? Short-term connections can be just as meaningful as those we spend years of our lives with. I want us to engage with one another in ways that honor our intimacy with one another.

I still hope that one day, C will reach out to do the hard work of repair, and I'll learn what was happening for them in the days and weeks after our time together. And I know that holding too tightly to such a hope will only cause me more pain. I need to let myself detach. A month after the breakup, I go over to Natalie's house. It's a full moon in Pisces, a perfect time to release the pain of this experience. And so we build a fire. In my lap are mementos of my time with C: one of their bandanas with their scent on it; a T-shirt of theirs that I wore during the trip; art we made together on the last day of my trip, with the words "vulnerability is a portal" written all over it; the letter they wrote me and the wooden box filled with the objects that made me cry. As a deeply sentimental person, one who has depended on old photographs of my mother as forms of memory, it hurts to say goodbye to this ephemera.

I think of the late José Esteban Muñoz, who wrote about queerness's "vexed relationship to evidence" in his book *Cruising Utopia*:

> Historically, evidence of queerness has been used to penalize and discipline queer desires, connections, and acts. When the historian of queer experience attempts to document a queer past, there is often a gatekeeper, representing a straight present, who will labor to invalidate the historical fact of queer lives—present, past, and future. Queerness is rarely complemented by evidence, or at least by traditional understandings of the term.

Muñoz turns to ephemera "as trace, the remains, the things that are left hanging, in the air like a rumor," focusing on that which is embodied in gestures that take place in queer dance. His words help me remember that even as I say goodbye to this evidence of our relationship, the relationship will forever live on in my body. To quote Belcourt once again: "the body is an assemblage, a mass of everyone who's ever moved us, for better or for worse."

I sit and stare at the fire for a while, objects clutched in my lap. Eventually, I stand and begin to place these items into the flames. I hold up C's shirt and turn toward Nat. On the front are the words "being emotionally manipulative isn't very punk rock of you," and our laughter is tinged by sadness. As I let go of each object, I honor what I've learned through this relationship: the magic of T4T, Switch4Switch sex; what it felt like to be matched in my vulnerability, even if it was short-lived; that I deserve to be romanced; clarity around what it is that we owe to each other; a deepening of my commitment to those that I share intimacy with—and the knowledge that this is one of my greatest strengths.

"The way you chose to end things with me was so hurtful. You treated me like I was disposable, like I didn't deserve your presence in the dissolution of this connection. I want you to know that, despite this pain, I have so much compassion for you. I hope that you can one day see what happened here with clear eyes and an open heart. That you can change your behavior. And that you can find your way to the kinds of deep intimacy and vulnerability that you told me you wanted. You deserve all of those things and more. We both deserve so much more."

I look up at Natalie, tears in my eyes. "It's just a bummer," I say.

Relationships ending—whether they're romantic, sexual, platonic, familial, communal—can be heartbreaking. But what breaks my heart the most is when we turn our backs on connection in order to protect ourselves. When we blow up the relationships we've been desiring and wanting for so long because we're terrified of getting our needs met—for then we'll have to grieve all of the times in our lives where we didn't receive the love and care that we deserved. As a teenager, I blew up the good relationships I had because they didn't mirror what I was used to, what was normalized at home: scraps of affection, punishment, coldness, manipulation, gaslighting, abuse. I am still scared of intimacy—I probably always will be—and I will no longer let my fear drive me away from those I know I can have loving relationships with.

"Yeah, it is a bummer," Natalie responds.

And then we both laugh.

There is still so much pain moving through me.

"They punched your heart, and then punched it again and again," Varia said to me one day when we were on the phone.

I was telling her about this new person I'm talking to—and how sad I was that I couldn't fully embody my usual state of excitement at getting to know someone. My heart feels more guarded than I'm used to. "You're tender, babe." Yes, oh so tender. And still, I keep myself open to what this new connection might be. Like adrienne maree brown, I want to dream beyond the wounds. I want my vulnerability to be a portal that guides me toward the kinds of intimacy that I know I deserve. Among the pain and the tenderness, the laughter and the tears, I can feel acceptance emerging. It is in that space that these queer wounds can begin to heal.

☾

It's the second week of September. It's been one month since C ended things. It's been five years since I started working with my therapist—which means it's been five years since I got sick and stayed sick. Five years since I let a man put his hand around my throat for the first time since my ex did so without my consent. Five years since I spent months in a state of dissociation, crying in the streets, and looking up plane tickets to Chicago, where Nate, the man who touched my neck, had moved in the days after we met. I had to go and find him. He had to know that we were meant to be together. My attachment system was in a state of complete and utter panic.

In the month after my relationship with C ended, I was such a mess. I worried that I was reverting back to that summer five years ago. I honestly hadn't been in such pain since. While so many things felt the same (*I want you I want you I want you until I don't anymore*; both of them living in Chicago; me unable to go a day without crying), I could see how different these experiences were, too. I wasn't fighting for someone who couldn't be with me. And I wasn't dissociating from my pain. I didn't need to anymore. I could be present with my tears, with my heartache, and with all of the trauma that C's actions brought to the surface: A.J., the boys of my youth, Ashley, Nate. Old wounds had been reopened.

If we follow a capitalist linear understanding of time, then we would see this moment as taking two steps back. But time isn't linear. It's cyclical. And so too is healing from trauma. I often think about my healing as a video game. I start on level one: stabilization. I advance to level two: reprocessing. Then I make it to level three: integration. And then I start all over, with the tools that I gained from the first round. At the start, it might feel like we're back at square one. That the past is repeating itself. I remind myself that I'm not the same person I was five years ago with Nate, or fifteen years ago with Ashley, or twenty-three years ago with A.J. It might be the same wound, but new skin has grown. The impact of their touch has lessened; it's less of a gash and more of a bruise.

This is not a reparative reading of harm. While I find much solace in knowing that I can alchemize this pain into my own healing, I also wish that the pain hadn't happened. Frankly, I'm tired. I'm ready for the person whose touch won't make me sick. And, at the same time, I know that the possibility of harm is always lurking in the dark corners of intimacy. There's so much we can do to mitigate the harm we cause others, while also accepting that we are imperfect, messy, hysterical beings who can and will fuck up as we reach for the forms of love, care, desire, and intimacy that we've been longing for. It's not the absence of rupture that makes intimacy and secure attachment possible; it's when we choose to stick around and do the work of repair. If there's anything we owe to ourselves and each other, it's the chance to heal the wounds we've caused and the wounds that we carry. I want us all to be so lucky.

ACKNOWLEDGMENTS

I believe that every book is a conversation and a collaboration—an assemblage of everyone who's ever moved us, for better or for worse (to borrow the words of Billy-Ray Belcourt). *Touch Me, I'm Sick* exists because of so many humans: those I know IRL, those I've connected with online, and those I've never met before but whose work and words have shaped and transformed me and helped me feel less alone. This is my attempt to thank you all for being my co-conspirators.

The book that is now in your hands first began in 2015 as my PhD dissertation at the University of Toronto. Under the guidance of my supervisor, the late Mari Ruti, I learned that it was much cooler to express complex ideas in a way that was accessible, rather than obtuse. This permission to say it plainly was a profound gift that transformed my writing. To my committee members, Dana Seitler (who stepped in as my supervisor at the last minute), Denise Cruz (who stayed on even after moving to NYU), and Naomi Morgenstern (who joined right as I was finishing), thank you for accepting my weirdo interdisciplinary project with open arms. And especial thanks to Dana, who told me about the Mudhoney song "Touch Me I'm Sick," and gave me the title for this book.

I'm so grateful for my friends who also did the crazy thing called a PhD, who read drafts of chapters, joined me for regular zoom cowriting hangs when I moved away, and who read my entire dissertation for my mock defense: Katherine Shwetz, Cristina D'Amico, André Babyn, Adie Todd, Joel Faber, Jess Thorpe, and Morgan Bimm.

While this book began in an academic context, it truly wouldn't have existed without the humans in my life that I've been grateful to love and be loved by. To my best friends, my three of cups, Natalie and Varia: you taught me that loving, supportive intimacy was not only possible but attainable. Our relationships, fueled by shared commitments to transforming how we think about and practice intimacy, have enabled me to flourish in ways that I'd never dreamed possible. You've truly set such a high bar for how best to love me. In these pages, I hope that I've managed to capture even just a fraction of the impact you've had on me. I can't wait to spend the rest of our lives growing, healing, collaborating, and building a better world together. Thank you for continually choosing to do life with me.

Thank you to my thought partner and dear friend Rio Romero for holding my hand, literally and metaphorically, through the publishing process. In moments where I have doubted myself, my writing, and whether this book matters, you have been one of my fiercest defenders and the ultimate hype person. I'm so lucky to have you by my side and can't wait to see the T4T magic we co-create together.

I'm also deeply indebted to my friend, fellow femme weirdo academic Raechel Anne Jolie, for spending a summer working with me as my writing coach and editor. When I found your book *Rust Belt Femme* and decided that I needed to be your friend, I never imagined that I'd get to collaborate with you in this way. You helped me figure out how to make the transition from academic text to memoir. Your brilliant brain—with its insightful questions, astute feedback, and ability to talk with me as I word vomited—as well as your endlessly kind and revolutionary heart, made this book infinitely better.

To my agent, Lauren Hall at Folio: thank you for being so excited about my voice, and for ensuring me that the last thing you wanted was to make me/this book fit into a box. To my editor, Rachael Marks, you see me and celebrate me for who I am as a writer. Thank you for bringing your passion and your precision to this project. What a magical gift! To Molly Woodward, Abby Luthin, and Susan Lumenello: Wow! Thank you for your detailed editorial work. And

I'm immensely grateful to Beacon's Frankie Karnedy, Caitlin Meyer, Becca Johnson, and Beth Collins for all of the work you did behind the scenes to bring this book to life. You've been a dream team!

To my somatic therapist, Amy: the work we've done together over the past seven years has quite literally changed my life. With your support, I truly feel like I've returned home to myself. Thank you for guiding me through the work of trauma healing, and for never being afraid to bring the witchy magic into our sessions together.

I also want to thank the 229 people who backed the Kickstarter I created in 2021. Your support enabled me to take time off from being a human hustling on the internet so that I could focus all my attention on writing. You took part in the practice of mutual aid and community care. Your support literally created the world in which this book has now come to life. I hope you can feel your spirit within these pages.

I'd like to take a moment to honor the lineages that have shaped my thinking and my practice—as a writer, teacher, and human being. To those working in the field of somatics, whom I have learned from formally and informally through their writing and work in the world, some of whom I'm lucky enough to now call friends: Kai Cheng Thom, Nkem Ndefo, Staci K. Haines, Deb Dana, Prentis Hemphill, Janina Fisher, Peter Levine, Arielle Schwartz, Stephen Porges, Richard Schwartz, Kekuni Minton, and Karine Bell.

Those working in disability justice have also been such crucial teachers for me as I learned what it meant to be a chronically ill, disabled human. In particular, I want to thank Leah Lakshmi Piepzna-Samarasinha, Patty Berne, Alison Kafer, and Mia Mingus. Unlearning the ways in which internalized ableism lives within me has enabled me to recognize that access needs don't just benefit those of us who're disabled; they benefit everyone. We all deserve care that enables us to not just survive but thrive.

And finally, my gratitude to the abolitionists and those working in transformative justice. Finding those committed to TJ and police and prison abolition has given me the language I needed to express my deep desire to transform the conditions that enable harm and abuse to happen in the first place. I believe that there are no "bad" or "good" people—just people trying to survive. Thank you to Kai Cheng Thom, Mia Mingus, Leah Lakshmi Piepzna-Samarasinha, adrienne maree brown, and Rania El Mugammar for believing that we all have the capacity for transformation.

May we always strive toward a radical vision for the world that is interdependent, loving, pleasurable, and just.

NOTES

TOUCH ME, I'M SICK

6   *I'm a literature student critical of the medical-industrial complex*: Mordecai Ettinger offered this definition of the MEC in a class I took with him: "The medical industrial complex is a profit-driven system comprised of interlocking institutions, corporations, and knowledge disciplines which manage, define, research, and control healthcare, health-related services, their provision, and social beliefs regarding health, wellness, and whose body is 'normal' or 'fit.'"

6   *This phrase is inspired by Maggie Nelson's reference to "the many gendered mothers of my heart"*: The Argonauts, 57.

6   *She notes how she is borrowing it*: Ward, "A Kentucky of Mothers."

7   *In the introduction to Dora*: Freud, Dora, x.

7   *Additionally, Dora has been "a source of heavy trials for her parents"*: Freud, Dora, 16.

7   *The following year, however, Dora's sick again*: Freud, Dora, 16.

7   *Dora displays all the characteristics of hysteria*: Freud, Dora, 18.

7   *A conflict of affects*: Affect is a synonym for feelings and also how we are moved emotionally by others: how others affect us.

7   *"This was surely just the situation to call up"*: Freud, Dora, 21.

8   *Dora feels it as "preponderantly or exclusively unpleasant."*: Freud, Dora, 22.

8   *Upon interpreting her aphonia*: Freud, Dora, 23.

8   *In a footnote, Freud describes this translation of affect*: Dora, 33.

8   *The flight into illness is, as Freud explains*: Dora, 36.

8   *"In the epidemic of hysteria, women were both accepting their inherent 'sickness'"*: Ehrenreich and English, Complaints and Disorders, 89–90.

9   *"How does one speak when one is weighed down"*: Cruz, Disquieting, 10.

9   *Systemic oppression "added to experiences of trauma"*: Cruz, Disquieting, 11.

9   *This speechlessness is "often driven into the body"*: Cruz, *Disquieting*, 11.

9   *Silence becomes a mode of resistance, "the refusal to conform"*: Cruz, *Disquieting*, 11.

9   *Remembering that Dora's symptoms began at a much earlier age*: Cesare Romano and others have put forth the hypothesis that Dora's father is the one who sexually abused her when she was five or six years old. Romano writes: "If, furthermore, it were true that, in accordance with my hypothesis, Dora was a victim of sexual abuse inflicted by her father during her early childhood—when she was five or six years old, thus exactly when [her father] contracted tuberculosis—and that the abuse implied oral contacts, Dora's reaction of violent nausea and disgust to a contemporary of her father's, Herr K., taking hold of her and kissing her on the mouth, would no longer be so incomprehensible. If this were the case, we would be dealing with a trauma that acts in two phases. . . . That is, the trauma experienced with Herr K. would not have had an effect in itself, but rather in its rendering traumatic the recollection of an analogous sexual episode with the father which had occurred during Dora's early childhood. This sexual episode, though, can only be presumed." Romano, *Freud and the Dora Case*, 21. See also Abhel-Rappe and Hengehold for similar hypotheses.

10   *Breuer and Freud explain that the "nature of the trauma precluded a reaction"*: Freud and Breuer, *Studies on Hysteria*, 13.

10   *"At the bottom of every case of hysteria there are one or more occurrences of premature sexual experience"*: Freud, "The Aetiology of Hysteria," 3rd ed., 204.

10   *Judith Herman explains that Freud was "increasingly troubled"*: Herman, *Trauma and Recovery*, 14.

11   *Obsolete meaning: An absence of ease; to feel uneasiness or discomfort*: Oxford English Dictionary, "disease," accessed September 2020, http://www.oed.com/view/Entry/54151

11   *It is not the case that all stories of chronic illness*: See Bessel van der Kolk's *The Body Keeps the Score*, Gabor Maté's *When the Body Says No*, and the work of Peter Levine, Deb Dana, and Stephen Porges.

12   *"As I read more about the history of invisible illness"*: Berkowitz, *Tender Points*, 39.

12   *"I know the true name of this disease"*: Berkowitz, *Tender Points*, 29.

12   *"Hysterics suffer for the most part from reminiscences"*: Freud and Breuer, *Studies on Hysteria*, 11.

14   *The term slut "is typically applied by females to other females"*: Tanenbaum, *Slut!*, 11–12.

15   *"When I imagine there having been an internet"*: Febos, *Girlhood*, 83.

15 *In 2016, the Centers for Disease Control and Prevention*: Sally C. Cur-
    tin et al., "Increase in Suicide in the United States, 1999–2014," Na-
    tional Center for Health Statistics, CDC, NCHS Data Brief No. 241,
    April 2016, https://www.cdc.gov/nchs/products/databriefs/db241.htm.

15 *While I felt so alone at the time*: Tanenbaum, *Slut!*, xiv.

15 *"You kicked my ass last night and that makes me want"*: Spencer,
    "Lucy DeCoutere on the Trauma of the Jian Ghomeshi Trial."

15 *I am not surprised to learn*: Tanenbaum, *Slut!*, 9.

16 *"Trauma survivors all too often develop"*: Fisher, *Healing the Frag-
    mented Selves of Trauma Survivors*, 30.

16 *"All of these behaviors"*: Fisher, *Healing the Fragmented Selves*, 30.

16 *"It would be rare in the mental health treatment world"*: Fisher, *Heal-
    ing the Fragmented Selves*, 42.

17 Fisher is not surprised that *"trauma and self-destructive behavior go
    hand in hand"*: Fisher, *Healing the Fragmented Selves*, 129.

17 *At the age of nineteen, I started a relationship with Ashley*: In the
    time since we were together, Ashley has come out as a trans woman. I
    am using she/her pronouns to honor the person that she is, and I also
    want to hold space for the power dynamics that existed at that time
    between the two of us.

19 *Her T-shirt was called "vile" and "disturbing"*: Kate Dries, "Designer
    of Menstruating Vagina Shirt 'Trolled the Mainstream Media,'" *Jezebel*,
    October 8, 2013, https://www.jezebel.com/designer-of-menstruating
    -vagina-shirt-trolled-the-main-1442571646.

20 *"Women's emotions are constantly labeled"*: Sisley, "Petra Collins
    Takes On Mental Health in New Show."

20 *There is Dora's "excessively repulsive fantasy"*: Freud, *Dora*, 45, 48, 124.

20 *In Three Essays on the Theory of Sexuality*: Freud, *Three Essays on
    the Theory of Sexuality*, 31.

20 *Within the hysteric exists an "exaggerated sexual craving"*: Freud,
    Three Essays on the Theory of Sexuality, 31.

20 *In his two-volume treatise published in 1904*: Hall, *Adolescence*, xiv–1.

21 *Hall tethers excess to sexuality*: Hall, *Adolescence*, 285, 497.

21 *"Simultaneous existence of contradictory tendencies, attitudes or feel-
    ings"*: Laplanche and Pontalis, *The Language of Psychoanalysis*, 26.

21 *"In Freud's vision we are, above all, ambivalent animals"*: Phillips,
    "Against Self-Criticism."

21 *"Thoughts in the unconscious live very comfortably side by side"*:
    Freud, *Dora*, 54.

22 *"I do not want to tell you how to feel"*: Ambivalently Yours, "Artist
    Statement," last modified December 6, 2022, ambivalentlyyours.com
    /artiststatement.

22   *Ambivalently Yours teamed up with Clea Felien and Damali Abrams the Glitter Priestess to explore "how the enthusiasm, language and rituals of girl culture"*: Thatiana Oliveira, "Three Visual Art Alumni Collaborate in Minneapolis," *Visual Ark* (blog), May 20, 2017, visualark .vcfa.edu/2017/05/20/three-visual-art-alumni-collaborate-in-minneapolis/.

23   *"The autonomous self and the relational self are shown to be interdependent"*: Brison, *Aftermath*, xi.

23–4 *"When the 'I' seeks to give an account of itself"*: Butler, *Giving an Account of Oneself*, 8.

24   *"Sick Woman Theory maintains that the body"*: Hedva, *Sick Woman Theory*, Section 5.

24   *"The status of untouchable is a very unreal and lonely one"*: Lorde, *The Cancer Journals*, 29.

24   *"You can die of that specialness"*: Lorde, *The Cancer Journals*, 29.

24   *Lorde thus "began quickly to yearn for the warmth"*: Lorde, *The Cancer Journals*, 29.

24   *In his national bestseller*: Maté, *When the Body Says No*, 43.

28   *"It does keep everyone at arm's length"*: Lorde, *The Cancer Journals*, 29.

28   *"The life histories of people with ALS"*: Maté, *When the Body Says No*, 43.

29   *In one such hallucination, or what Breuer called an "absence"*: Freud and Breuer, *Studies in Hysteria*, 46.

31   *"The sympathies of the girl herself"*: Freud, *Dora*, 13.

31   *Astrologer Chani Nicholas writes*: Nicholas, *You Were Born for This*, 75.

31–2 *"Intentional and informed giving and receiving of abundance"*: kamra sadia hakim, *care manual: dreaming care into being*, n.p.

32   *For the Care Collective, authors of* The Care Manifesto: The Care Collective, *The Care Manifesto*, 5–6.

32   *"The word care in English comes from the Old English* caru*"*: The Care Collective, *The Care Manifesto*, 27.

32   *"But what is care?"*: Bellacasa, *Matters of Care*, 1.

32   *We've been taught that care should produce a "warm pleasant affection"*: Bellacasa, *Matters of Care*, 2.

32   *"On average across 66 countries representing two-thirds of the world's population"*: Dowling, *The Care Crisis*, 19.

32   *Dowling goes on to note how "the ratio varies by region"*: Dowling, *The Care Crisis*, 24–25.

33   *"Disability rights works to bring disabled people to the table"*: Piepzna-Samarasinha, *Care Work*, 15.

33   *"Our focus is less on civil rights legislation as the only solution to ableism"*: Piepzna-Samarasinha, *Care Work*, 23.

33   *For Puar, the problem with rights discourses is that they "produce human beings"*: Puar, *The Right to Maim*, 15.

34   *Puar puts forth the concept of debility*: Puar, *The Right to Maim*, xviii.

34   *Disablement has a before and an after, whereas debility "comprehends those bodies"*: Puar, *The Right to Maim*, xiv.

34   *The Centers for Disease Control and Prevention (CDC) defines endemic*: "Principles of Epidemiology," Centers for Disease Control, last modified May 18, 2012, https://www.cdc.gov/csels/dsepd/ss1978 /lesson1/section11.html.

35   *"We will not all be disabled"*: Puar, *The Right to Maim*, xiv.

35   *Debility draws attention to how "while some bodies may not be recognized"*: Puar, *The Right to Maim*, xv.

35   *"Rich people of the government mak[e] decisions about the provision"*: Spade, *Mutual Aid*, 21.

35   *For Spade, "mutual aid projects mobilize lots of people"*: Spade, *Mutual Aid*, 28–29.

36   *"All forms of care between all categories of human and non-human"*: The Care Collective, *The Care Manifesto*, 40.

36   *They are quick to clarify, "In advocating for promiscuous care"*: The Care Collective, *The Care Manifesto*, 41.

36   *In* Emergent Strategy: brown, *Emergent Strategy*, 87, 21, 82.

36   *This commitment takes shape in "a series of small repetitive motions"*: brown, *Emergent Strategy*, 93.

36   *"Interdependence is not about the equality of offers in real time"*: brown, *Emergent Strategy*, 95.

36   *"The radical notion that providing care is work"*: Piepzna-Samarasinha, *Care Work*, 141.

36   *"In disabled communities, we talk about the idea that we can still offer"*: Piepzna-Samarasinha, *Care Work*, 146–47.

37   *"If interdependency is in our DNA, what does it mean when we fall"*: "what happens when we can't live interdependency all the time?" *Radical Access Mapping Project* (blog), November 9, 2015, radical accessiblecommunities.wordpress.com/2015/11/09/what-happens -when-it-feels-like-we-cant-live-interdependency-all-the-time/.

37   *One possible response to the final question*: brown, *Emergent Strategy*, 69.

AMBIVALENT DESIRES, UGLY SEX

39   *I've made this confession before*: Kristen Roupenian has since published "Cat Person" in her short story collection, *You Know You Want This*, and so I'll be using the citations from her book.

40   *"A very depressing drama about the Holocaust"*: Kristen Roupenian, "Cat Person," *You Know That You Want This*, 82.

40   *"Probably it would be like that bad kiss"*: Roupenian, "Cat Person," 85.

40   *"When Robert was naked"*: Roupenian, "Cat Person," 91.

41   "Hi im not interested in you stop textng me": Roupenian, "Cat Person," 96.

41   *"I just wanted to say you looked really pretty" and "I really miss you"*: Roupenian, "Cat Person," 99.

41   *In his open letter to Margot*: Smith, "Dear Cat-Person Girl."

42   *This claim also promotes the false belief*: A 2013 study by the World Health Organization (*Global and regional estimates of violence against women: Prevalence and health effects of intimate partner violence and non-partner sexual violence*, 2013) noted that 70 percent of the women who've experienced physical and/or sexual violence were the victims of intimate-partner violence (IPV). Devries et al., in "The Global Prevalence of Intimate Partner Violence Against Women," 1527–28, support these findings, claiming that the most common form of violence that women experience is from intimate partners.

42   *"And the same holds true for her choice to have three drinks"*: Thankfully, Robyn Pennacchia responded for women everywhere when she wrote back to Kyle Smith. The most brilliant part of Pennacchia's response is the revelation that Smith once wrote a novel "about a man who drinks a lot and has sex with a lot of women, and who, for some reason, has a lot of refrigerator issues." Pennacchia asks: "Are you concerned for him, Kyle? Are you worried about his life choices? Why did you not, instead, choose to write a story about a human person who makes literally all of the right life choices and had everything turn out great?" ("Dear National Review Guy Who Wrote an Open Letter").

42   *"But the thought of what it would take to stop what she had set in motion"*: Roupenian, "Cat Person," 88.

42   *"Coercion is rarely absolute"*: Rodríguez, "Queer Sociality and Other Sexual Fantasies," 340.

42   *Rodríguez goes on to point out that "most of the sexual contracts"*: Rodríguez, "Queer Sociality and Other Sexual Fantasies," 340.

43   *"During fleeting casual sexual encounters"*: Febos, *Girlhood*, 243.

43   *There are other reasons we engage in empty consent: "the need to protect our bodies"*: Febos, *Girlhood*, 230, 238, 245.

44   *Rather, I'm drawn to ugliness*: Nina Athanassoglou-Kallmyer offers a great summary of this history in her contribution to Rodrigues and Przybylo, *On the Politics of Ugliness*, "Ugly," 31–49.

44   *"Ugliness or unsightliness is much more"*: Rodrigues and Przybylo, *On the Politics of Ugliness*, 1.

44   *"Her female characters are so fucking ugly"*: Calloway, *what purpose did i serve in your life*, n.p. In *what purpose did i serve in your life*, Calloway takes photos of herself and overlays them with words of criticism. This section of the book is unpaginated. Another

anonymous comment reads, "This sounds really catty . . . but why does everyone keep referring to her as some 'great beauty?' She doesn't really have any 'it-factor' . . . she's just totally DTF."

44   *Ugliness, then, is "attributed to those bodies that deviate"*: Ferens and Sikora, *Ugly Bodies*, iv; "*[I]t is about behaviors that depart from the social norms"*: Rodrigues and Przybylo, *On the Politics of Ugliness*, 8.

45   *The ugly is thus not only an aesthetic category*: See Sianne Ngai's seminal text *Ugly Feelings*.

45   *"Reveal the ease or disease with which one body might incorporate another"*: Siebers, *Disability Aesthetics*, 1.

45   *"Our visceral responses to dirt, the grotesque, plainness, and/ or monstrosity"*: Rodrigues and Przybylo, *On the Politics of Ugliness*, 5.

45   *Katie Roiphe uses the term* bad sex *to refer to the blurry line between*: See Roiphe, *The Morning After*. I do want to flag that I don't love Roiphe's argument that we should just accept bad sex. Katherine Angel argues, "Instead of resigning ourselves to the inevitability of bad sex, and even romanticizing it as merely youthful misadventure, we should subject it to sustained scrutiny. Bad sex emerges from gender norms in which women cannot be equal agents of sexual pursuit, and in which men are entitled to gratification at all costs." Angel, *Tomorrow Sex Will Be Good Again*, 27. I really appreciate Angel's critiques of Roiphe's post-feminist hot take.

45–6   *"Joyless, exploitative encounters that reflect a persistently sexist culture"*: Traister, "Why Sex That's Consensual Can Still Be Bad. And Why We're Not Talking About It."

46   *"With what exceeds and undoes the subject's fantasmatic sovereignty"*: Berlant and Edelman, *Sex, or the Unbearable*, 2.

48   *"What pornography both portrays and endeavors to perpetuate"*: Kipnis, "She-Male Fantasies and the Aesthetics of Pornography," 124–25.

48   "Anti-pornography feminism," she writes, "shares a highly questionable alliance": Kipnis, *Dirty Looks*, 124.

48   *"The movement's attacks on sexual exploitation and violence"*: Ellen Willis, "Lust Horizons" in *No More Nice Girls*, 204.

49   *"A radical theory of sex must identify, describe, explain"*: Gayle Rubin, "Thinking Sex," in *Deviations*, 145.

49   *"Biological phenomenon or as an aspect of individual psychology"*: Rubin, "Thinking Sex," 147.

49   *"Sex negativity, the fallacy of misplaced scale"*: Rubin, "Thinking Sex," 148.

49   *"Presumed guilty until proven innocent"*: Rubin, "Thinking Sex," 148.

49   *"Transsexuals, transvestites, fetishists"*: Rubin, "Thinking Sex," 148.

49   *Desires outside of the "charmed circle" of reproductive heterosexuality*: See pages 157–63 in Rubin's "Thinking Sex" for a discussion

of obscenity laws, age-of-consent laws, and other legal prohibitions regarding sexual acts, as well as pages 175–76 for more on sex laws pertaining to S/M practices.

49   *"The legal apparatus of sex is staggering"*: Rubin, "Thinking Sex," 163.

49   *"A great deal of antiporn propaganda implies"*: Rubin, "Thinking Sex," 169.

50   *"This discourse on sexuality is less a sexology than a demonology"*: Rubin, "Thinking Sex," 172.

50   *Rubin highlights how the logic at play*: See *The Philosophy of Pornography*, 89–104. In particular: "Diagnoses of Transformation: 'Pornification,' Digital Media, and the Diversification of the Pornographic" by Susanna Paasonen, and Susan J. Brison's "'The Price We Pay'? Pornography and Harm," in which Brison defines pornography along the same lines as Dworkin and MacKinnon as "violent degrading misogynistic hate speech" (91). For a much longer accounting of the sex/porn wars, check out Srinivasan, *The Right to Sex*.

50   *This attention to injury and harm*: For more on the ethical and philosophical concerns surrounding Black women's participation in BDSM practices and its historical roots, see Cruz, *The Color of Kink*, 34–40.

50   *"Performances of black female sexual aggression"*: Cruz, *The Color of Kink*, 3.

50   *"A practice that explicitly uses race to script"*: Cruz, *The Color of Kink*, 33.

50   *"Black women's history of racial-sexual violence"*: Cruz, *The Color of Kink*, 20.

51   *Examples of "BDSM's therapeutic possibility"*: Cruz, *The Color of Kink*, 63.

51   *Pushing back against the politics of respectability*: Cruz, *The Color of Kink*, 65, 72.

51   *"How do we begin to make sense of willful sexual fantasies"*: Rodríguez, *Sexual Futures, Queer Gestures, and Other Latina Longings*, 26.

51   *"Activate abjection as a resource for a reclamation"*: Rodríguez, *Sexual Futures, Queer Gestures, and Other Latina Longings*, 21.

51   *"To deny our fantasies because they are too twisted"*: Rodríguez, *Sexual Futures, Queer Gestures, and Other Latina Longings*, 185.

52   *I am curious about the ways in which many feminists are fixated*: If you want to learn more about how third-wave feminism and postfeminism have taken up this mantle under the guise of sexual empowerment, see Angel, *Tomorrow Sex Will Be Good Again*, and Maggie Nelson's chapter "The Ballad of Sexual Optimism" in *On Freedom*.

52   *"Does the need to act out fantasies of debasing oneself"*: Willis, *Lust Horizons*, 207.

52   *At the same time, I too "don't believe our sexual desires"*: Willis, *Lust Horizons*, 207.

53   *"Consenting partners have a right to their sexual proclivities"*: Willis, *Lust Horizons*, 208.

54   *As Lisa Carver of* Vice *magazine notes*: Carver, "Marie Calloway on Her New Novel and Being Called 'Jailbait.'"

55   *The comments range from "slut"—which is superimposed over a photo of Calloway*: Calloway, *what purpose*, 151, 149.

55   *"Blah blah blah. It's a case of internet oversharing-turned-emotionally-hurtful"*: Nolan, "Girl, Microfamed."

55   *"Seeing that women have been historically and contemporarily excluded"*: Petro, "In Defense of Marie Calloway."

55   *An anonymous contributor to the now defunct literature blog*: "anonymous contribution to the 'subgenre' of 'literary' 'essay' known as 'how i feel about marie calloway,'" *HTMLGIANT*.

56   *Hazel Cills refers to "adrien brody" as a "dispassionate account"*: Cills, "Marie Calloway's 'Adrien Brody.'"; *"calm, clinical . . . utterly pared down and horrifyingly bald"*: Marche, "The New Bad Kids of Fiction."

56   *"Joins a new chapter in the literature of disaffection"*: Orange, "Men Respond to Marie."

56   *"Suggestion of mournful detachment [which is] characterized by affectlessness"*: Spiers, "But Is It Good?"

56–57 *"Flat, declarative, and personal. It's the language of Livejournal updates"*: Molotkow, "Marie Calloway, Degrading Sex, and Books About It."

57   *The man is twice her age*: Calloway, *what purpose*, 103.

57   *"Seemed to uphold human dignity and the sacredness"*: Calloway, *what purpose*, 103–4.

57   *"Sexually excited, because he was betraying those values"*: Calloway, *what purpose*, 104.

57   *Adrien Brody's admission and his justification*: Calloway, *what purpose*, 104.

57–58 *"Couldn't pass up the chance to sleep with [her] intellectual idol"*: Calloway, *what purpose*, 104.

58   *"I think that you can tell a lot about a person"*: Calloway, *what purpose*, 107.

58   *"It was all pictures of modelesque brunette women"*: Calloway, *what purpose*, 108.

58   *"I've never been able to figure out why"*: Calloway, *what purpose*, 112.

58   *A page later she explains that she feels frustrated*: Calloway, *what purpose*, 113.

58   "I'm totally powerless in the face of men": Calloway, *what purpose*, 138.

58   *Her feelings of annoyance continue after the act has taken place*: Calloway, *what purpose*, 115.

59   *"Have this intelligent conversation with me"*: Calloway, *what purpose*, 115.

59   *"An elaborate strategy of purification"*: Calloway, *what purpose*, 139.

59   *"She works under an assumed name"*: Calloway, *what purpose*, 139.

60   *"Looking searchingly at something; a searching gaze"*: OED *Online*, 2nd ed. (Oxford: Oxford University Press, 2020), under "scrutiny," oed.com/view/Entry/173778.

60   *"I opened my eyes and looked into his and smiled"*: Calloway, *what purpose*, 115.

60   *While Marie describes ugly sex via flat affect*: Calloway, *what purpose*, 139.

61   *It is true that I have found far more representations of ugly sex*: Some others in the cishet ugly sex canon: *How Should a Person Be?* by Sheila Heti; *Acts of Service* by Lillian Fishman (though the two women in the book do have sex with each other, in the presence of the man they're both fucking); *Good Girl* by Anna Fitzpatrick.

61   *"While it's well-known that straight sex is full of fake female orgasms"*: Febos, *Body Work*, 61.

61   *Despite the fact that "all of us queers know that not all of our sex is healthy"*: Febos, *Body Work*, 62.

62   *Torrey Peters's novel* Detransition, Baby *is one of the few places*: Peters, *Detransition, Baby*. The novel switches back and forth between using the name Ames when referring to the character in the present moment, and Amy when looking at scenes before she detransitioned.

62   *"The question, for Reese"*: Peters, *Detransition, Baby*, 5.

62   *"Was similar to her others"*: Peters, *Detransition, Baby*, 6.

62   *"Do we really need these tonight?"*: Peters, *Detransition, Baby*, 7.

62   *"Why she put up with him: He got it."*: Peters, *Detransition, Baby*, 7.

63   *"But she wouldn't say that she liked him"*: Peters, *Detransition, Baby*, 48.

63   *"Had long since discovered that most talk"*: Peters, *Detransition, Baby*, 53.

63   *"On a fetish site with the word 'tranny' in the name"*: Peters, *Detransition, Baby*, 49.

63   *"It's a mark of prudish inexperience to think"*: Peters, *Detransition, Baby*, 49.

63   *She doesn't care that Stanley refers to her genitals as "purely decorative"*: Peters, *Detransition, Baby*, 53.

63   *"You don't get to choose who you fuck"*: Peters, *Detransition, Baby*, 51.

63   *"Sexual self-objectification may mean one thing"*: Srinivasan, "The Right to Sex," in *The Right to Sex*, 81–82.

63   *"I transitioned for gossip and compliments"*: Andera Long Chu, "On Liking Women," *N+1* (Winter 2018), nplusonemag.com/issue -30/essays/on-liking-women.

64   *"Our most passionate convictions about sex"*: Willis, *Lust Horizons*, 201.

64   *"This declaration, as Chu is well aware"*: Srinivasan, "The Right to Sex," 89.

64   *"Reese spent a lifetime observing cis women"*: Peters, *Detransition, Baby*, 59.

64   *"Liberal feminists—especially the trans-hating variety"*: Peters, *Detransition, Baby*, 61.

64   *"She'd be over here, getting knocked around"*: Peters, *Detransition, Baby*, 61.

65   *"I will not call a male 'she'"*: Chu, "On Liking Women."

65   *In the car ride over to Glamour Boutique*: Peters, *Detransition, Baby*, 138.

65   *"The stories were dangerous"*: Peters, *Detransition, Baby*, 138.

66   *"The femininity forced upon the males"*: Peters, *Detransition, Baby*, 138.

66   *"Just think she hated femininity and equated it with humiliation"*: Peters, *Detransition, Baby*, 138.

66   *"Weddings are so kinky"*: Peters, *Detransition, Baby*, 139.

66   *"Fantasies of domestic bliss are likewise"*: Rodríguez, *Sexual Futures*, 179.

66   *Amy remembers "the day at the Glamour Boutique as erotically charged"*: Peters, *Detransition, Baby*, 150.

66–67   *The sex that she has with Patrick is "a distant faraway sex"*: Peters, *Detransition, Baby*, 151.

67   *And it is in this "faraway place" that "she could enjoy herself"*: Peters, *Detransition, Baby*, 151.

67   *"The word 'dissociate' sounded pathologizing to her at first"*: Peters, *Detransition, Baby*, 128–1.

67   *And so she "grew to dread and avoid sex with specifically"*: Peters, *Detransition, Baby*, 129.

67   *"Felt like some kind of healing, some kind of redemption"*: Peters, *Detransition, Baby*, 152.

67   *"Manifestations of struggles between parts"*: Fisher, *Healing the Fragmented Selves of Trauma Survivors*, 12.

68   *"You have one mind, out of which different thoughts"*: Schwartz, *No Bad Parts*, 7.

68   *"Remembering a time when you faced a dilemma"*: Schwartz, *No Bad Parts*, 8.

69   *Fisher explains that our brain is divided into two halves*: Fisher, *Transforming the Living Legacy of Trauma*, 73.

69   *In between the left and right sides is the corpus callosum*: "From research comparing the brains of traumatized children and teens with those of non-traumatized young people, we know that trauma seems to be associated with a smaller than-average corpus callosum—meaning that it is underdeveloped, interfering with the ability of the left and right brains to communicate and collaborate with each other." Fisher, *Healing the Fragmented Selves of Trauma Survivors*, 23.

69   *Under chronic stress and trauma, a "survival-related splitting occurs"*: Fisher, *Healing the Fragmented Selves*, 75.

71   *"The disorganized attachment style"*: Fern, *Polysecure*, 43.

75   *"I [didn't] know what I should do: two states of mind in me"*: Sappho and Carson, *If not, winter: fragments of Sappho*, 52.

75   *"Eros seemed to Sappho at once an experience"*: Carson, *Eros the Bittersweet*, 3.

75   *"An ambivalent being, at once friend and enemy"*: Carson, *Eros the Bittersweet*, 5.

75   *"All our desires are contradictory"*: Carson, *Eros the Bittersweet*, 11; Weil, *The Simone Weil Reader*, 364.

75   *"Pleasure and pain at once register upon the lover"*: Carson, *Eros the Bittersweet*, 11.

75–76 *"I consented because of skin hunger"*: *Skin hunger* is a term that arose from the horrific studies conducted by American psychologist Harry Harlow in the years of the Second World War. Harlow separated infant rhesus macaques from their birth mothers and replaced them with two surrogates: one made out of wire and wood and another covered in cloth. What surprised Harlow was that the baby monkeys overwhelmingly chose the embrace of the cloth mother even when the wire mother was the only one holding a bottle of milk. From this study, Harlow concluded that we need affection as much as—if not more than—we need nourishment. If we are deprived of touch, we become hungry for it.

76   *"You survive by finding beauty in impossible and bleak situations"*: "Alok on Unruly Beauty/245," *For the Wild* (podcast).

76   *My ugly sexual encounters also served as a stepping stone*: José Esteban Muñoz, *Cruising Utopia: The Then and There of Queer Futurity*, 2009.

76   *"To allow ourselves to be unafraid of the contaminations of ambivalence"*: Nelson, *On Freedom*, 85.

77   *"As the (generational) effects of global capitalism"*: Mia Mingus, "Moving Toward the Ugly."

HYSTERIA'S GHOSTS

80   *Selfie has been defined*: Oxford English Dictionary, "selfie," accessed September 2020, www.oed.com/view/Entry/173778.

80   *"[A] selfie is a photographic object that initiates the transmission"*: Senft and Baym, "What Does the Selfie Say?," 1589.

80   *"At the heart of selfie production and selfie viewership"*: Nicole Erin Morse, *Selfie Aesthetics*, vii.

80   *These relational definitions run counter to the cultural anxiety*: See Keen, *The Internet Is Not the Answer*; McCain et. al, "Personality and Selfies," 126–33; Walker, "The Good, the Bad, and the Unexpected Consequences of Selfie Obsession"; and Weiser, "#Me: Narcissism and Its Facets as Predictors of Selfie-Posting Frequency," 477–81.

80   *These same detractors are quick to decry selfies*: For readings on the move from self-portraits to selfies, see Levin, "The Selfie in the Age of Digital Recursiveness"; Murray, "Notes to Self," 490–516; Rettberg, *Seeing Ourselves Through Technology*; Suler, "From Self-Portraits to Selfies," 175–80.

80   *"The stories we tell about selfies reinforce"*: Morse, *Selfie Aesthetics*, ix.

81   *"The prophecy was not that Narcissus would love himself"*: Dombeck, *The Selfishness of Others*, 111–112.

81   *Forums like Instagram—in which the selfie*: Wunker, *Notes from a Feminist Killjoy*, 17.

81   *"Who will see this? How many people will like it?"*: Morse, *Selfie Aesthetics*, xi, 1.

82   *Sickness selfies draw attention to*: Khakpour, *Sick*, 211.

82   *I also see these images participating in*: Field, "The Archive of Absence."

82   *Speculative archives, Morse argues, "produce new histories"*: Morse, *Selfie Aesthetics*, 116.

82   *"In a normal immune response, the body creates antibodies"*: O'Rourke, "The Mysteries of Chronic Illness."

83   *Among some of the more commonly known diseases*: AARDA, *The Cost Burden of Autoimmune Disease*.

83   *"The National Institutes of Health (NIH) funded autoimmune research"*: Moore, *Body Horror*, 196.

83   *"The medical system is also strategic to women's oppression"*: Ehrenreich and English, *Complaints and Disorders*, 31.

83   *"While autoimmune diseases impact twenty percent of the population"*: AARDA, *The Cost Burden of Autoimmune Disease*.

83   *"Women are twice as likely to have autoimmune diseases"*: Dusenbery, "Regarding the Pain of Women."

83   *"More than half of all American women"*: Dusenbery, *Doing Harm*, 20.

84   *"Men wait an average of 49 minutes before receiving an analgesic"*: Fassler, "How Doctors Take Women's Pain Less Seriously."

84   *"Rachel's physical scars are healing"*: Fassler, "How Doctors Take Women's Pain Less Seriously."

84   *"Observation indicated that the subject was seen laughing"*: Wang, "'Subject Was Seen Laughing': A P.I. Insurance Surveillance Report."

85   *"Describes the many forms of government documents"*: Samuels, *Fantasies of Identification*, 122.

85   *"The overmastering fantasy of modern disability"*: Samuels, *Fantasies of Identification*, 121.

85   *By 1690, three thousand women*: Didi-Huberman, *Invention of Hysteria*, 13.

85–86 *For Charcot, the Salpêtrière was "a kind of living pathological museum"*: Charcot, "Leçons sur les maladies du système nerveux," 3–4.

86   *But as Didi-Huberman notes*: Didi-Huberman, *Invention of Hysteria*, xi.

86   *"Hysteria was an inherited disease of the nervous system"*: Showalter, "Hysteria, Feminism, and Gender," 33.

86   *Didi-Huberman explains that Charcot's goal was to codify*: Didi-Huberman, *Invention of Hysteria*, 51.

86   *"The Salpêtrière itself featured prominently in the newspaper articles"*: Marshall, *Performing Neurology*, 32.

87   *"Men did not enter the Salpêtrière as patients"*: Didi-Huberman, *Invention of Hysteria*, 80.

87   *They believed that there was much to gain from*: Bourneville and Regnard, *Iconographie photographique de la Salpêtrière*, iii.

87   *"Tall, well-developed (neck a bit thick, ample breasts, underarms and pubis covered with hair)"*: Bourneville and Regnard, *Iconographie photographique de la Salpêtrière*, 125.

87   *She was a "living work of art"*: Didi-Huberman, *Invention of Hysteria*, 122.

87   *It is noted in the* Iconographie *that Augustine's "poses or passionate attitudes"*: Bourneville and Regnard, *Iconographie photographique de la Salpêtrière*, 736; Didi-Huberman, *Invention of Hysteria*, 117.

88   *"The sort of dramaturgical cutting of her symptoms into acts"*: Didi-Huberman, *Invention of Hysteria*, 117.

88   *"Correspond mainly to two events of her existence"*: Désiré Magloire Bourneville, and Paul Regnard, *Etudes cliniques Iconographie Photographique de la Salpêtrière*, 736.

88 *And this was, obviously, quite a traumatizing event*: Bourneville and Regnard, *Iconographie photographique de la Salpêtrière*, 126.

88 *"C . . . , after making her all sorts of dazzling promises"*: Bourneville and Regnard, *Iconographie photographique de la Salpêtrière*, 126.

88 *The following day Augustine falls ill*: Bourneville and Regnard, *Iconographie photographique de la Salpêtrière*, 126–27.

88 *"The green eyes of a cat looking at her"*: Bourneville and Regnard, *Iconographie photographique de la Salpêtrière*, 127.

89 *In a rather disturbing transcription*: Bourneville and Regnard, *Iconographie photographique de la Salpêtrière*, 146–48.

89 *"Had actually sat in on Charcot's classes"*: Bourneville and Regnard, *Iconographie photographique de la Salpêtrière*, 192.

89 *"Understood perfectly that childhood trauma explains"*: Walusinski, Poirier, and Déchy, "Augustine," 226–27.

89 *As I read the translation of this scene*: Didi-Huberman, *Invention of Hysteria*, 158.

90 *"In these moments [of pain], it can be hard to find myself attractive"*: Margeaux Feldman (@softcore_trauma), "It's been a while since I've shared a bathtub selfie."

91 *"You go and lie in the sulphurous water"*: Palmer, *Sanatorium*, 20.

91 *Floating, for Palmer, "eases physical pain"*: Palmer, *Sanatorium*, 12, 47.

91 *"[C]overed a multitude of conditions, including what would now be diagnosed"*: Bradley, "Why Is 18th-Century Bath Considered the Model for Modern Day Spas?"

91 *"At the other end of the scale from the luxurious spas"*: Royal College of Physicians of Edinburgh, "Bathing by prescription: A Brief History of Treatment by Water."

92 *"In the early nineteenth century, physicians designed"*: Sarah Zhang, "Showering Has a Dark, Violent History," *The Atlantic*, December 11, 2018, theatlantic.com/health/archive/2018/12/dark-history-of -showering/577636/.

92 *"The plunge bath was formerly and sometimes is now substituted"*: *Journal of the American Medical Association* (1867), quoted in Braslow, *Mental Ills and Bodily Cures*, 38–39.

92 *Hydrotherapy became a "form of therapeutic discipline"*: Braslow, *Mental Ills and Bodily Cures*, 34.

92 *"Baths play an important part in the treatment of hysteria"*: Rosenthal and Putzel, *A Clinical Treatise on the Diseases of the Nervous System*, 52.

92 *"Treatment [that] involved aiming a powerful jet of water"*: Horwitz, "Medical Vibrators for Treatment of Female Hysteria."

92 *"Feeling extreme relief from hysteria"*: Horwitz, "Medical Vibrators for Treatment of Female Hysteria."

93   *"Convulsions, lethargy, and an episodic presentation of the rigid"*:
      Goldstein, *Hysteria Complicated by Ecstasy*, 12.

93   *"Episodes of the* transport des sens, *a migration of sensory capabil-
      ity"*: Goldstein, *Hysteria Complicated by Ecstasy*, 13.

93   *Nanette would receive three diagnoses from Despine*: "Derived from
      the ancient Greek for 'seizure,' and occupying a place in the annals
      of medicine that dates back to Greek antiquity, catalepsy was re-
      garded in the early nineteenth century as an exceptionally rare pa-
      thology. Its major symptoms were a sudden loss of both sensibility
      and voluntary muscular movement." Goldstein, *Hysteria Compli-
      cated by Ecstasy*, 47.

93   *"An evil person, a rural policeman* (garde champêtre)*"*: Goldstein,
      Hysteria Complicated by Ecstasy, 13.

93   "Attentat à la pudeur—*both a vernacular term and a technical legal
      one"*: Goldstein, *Hysteria Complicated by Ecstasy*, 83.

93   *"She sees him coming, hurls reproaches at him"*: Goldstein, *Hysteria
      Complicated by Ecstasy*, 106–07.

93   *Despite Nanette repeating this scene, in every detail*: Goldstein, *Hys-
      teria Complicated by Ecstasy*, 107.

94   *"Peclet so terrified the girl that her agitated mental state"*: Goldstein,
      Hysteria Complicated by Ecstasy, 86.

94   *"The adults in her life had failed her"*: Goldstein, *Hysteria Compli-
      cated by Ecstasy*, 125.

94   *"As Nanette embarked on the career of a nervous patient"*: Goldstein,
      Hysteria Complicated by Ecstasy, 56.

94   *Nanette "immediately protested his act of bad faith"*: Goldstein, *Hys-
      teria Complicated by Ecstasy*, 16.

95   *"Gained a measure of mastery over the Scottish shower"*: Goldstein,
      Hysteria Complicated by Ecstasy, 16.

95   *"In 2017 I received an Arts Council England grant to complete re-
      search"*: Palmer, "Wellness Is a Seductive Lie—and It Is Changing
      How We Treat Illness."

96   *"Unlike the sanatorium, NHS rehab is not glamorous"*: Palmer,
      "Wellness Is a Seductive Lie."

96   *Poor women's relationship to sickness was to blame themselves*:
      Ehrenreich and English, *Complaints and Disorders*, 51.

96   *"Upper- and upper-middle-class women were 'sick'"*: Ehrenreich and
      English, *Complaints and Disorders*, 45.

97   *"Water is both common and in the commons"*: After Globalism Writ-
      ing Group, "Water as Protagonist," 16.

97   *"Water stands as the symbol and vehicle for inequality"*: After Glo-
      balism Writing Group, "Water as Protagonist," 15–16.

97   *"Water is the foundation, the magical liquid that sustains"*: After
      Globalism Writing Group, "Water as Protagonist," 16.
98   *"Nothing I feel is more deadly than the isolation"*: Ratcliffe, "Sick:
      An Interview with Porochista Khakpour."
98   *"When we recognize the leakiness of pain"*: Alyson Patsavas, "Recov-
      ering a Cripistemology of Pain," 214.
98   *"I am so full of sickness"*: Palmer, *Sanatorium*, 26.

FEMME4FEMME INTIMACY

101   *"What we Taurus north node people want is to merge"*: Washuta,
      White Magic, 55.
101   *"The first step toward self-acceptance for Taurus north node people"*:
      Washuta, *White Magic*, 55.
101   *"The North Node in Taurus is helping you achieve"*: Astrology Owl,
      "North Node (NN) in Taurus, Chiron in Taurus."
102   *"Your bruises include moments where you find yourself searching"*:
      I cannot for the life of me figure out where I read this. Most likely
      Chani's newsletter.
103   *In her* Radical Love Letters *series*: Jolie, "dangerous, life-giving, &
      impossible to withhold."
104   *"It behooves [sic] us to pause when we are told that protecting hu-
      man life"*: Jolie, "dangerous, life-giving, & impossible to withhold."
104   *"Can we keep each other safe and also keep joy alive?"*: Jolie, "dan-
      gerous, life-giving, & impossible to withhold."
104   *The irony of the internalized misogyny inherent in this misreading*:
      RM Barton explains how, "Without a butch, a femme woman's queer-
      ness is often overlooked. Other queer women may fail to read her as
      sufficiently queer, and—even worse—straight men may think she's in-
      terested in *them*. Thus, femmes may feel like they have to continually
      and aggressively assert their queerness to be acknowledged by other
      queer people or understood by straights." Barton, "On Femininity and
      Being a Fierce, Autonomous, Radical, Queer Femme."
105   *"Femme: a person who has one of a million kinds of queer"*: Piepzna-
      Samarasinha, "A Modest Proposal for a Fair Trade Emotional Labor
      Economy," 136.
105   "Forget femme invisibility; the thing most femmes I know are im-
      pacted by": Piepzna-Samarasinha, "A Modest Proposal for a Fair
      Trade Emotional Labor Economy," 137.
105   *I want to name that as a white nonbinary femme*: Human Rights
      Campaign, *An Epidemic of Violence*, 2021. While the number of
      trans people murdered has slowly decreased (thirty in 2023 and
      thirty-two in 2024, as I sit here at the start of 2025, days after

Trump's inauguration and his declaration that there are only two genders, I fear that these numbers will be on the rise again.

106   *"Weak, less than, not as smart or competent"*: Piepzna-Samarasinha,
"A Modest Proposal for a Fair Trade Emotional Labor Economy," 137.

106   *"A gender experience that is never tied to biological sex"*: Rose and
Camilleri, *Brazen Femme*, 12.

111   *Drawing on split-brain theory and the structural dissociation model*:
Janina Fisher renamed van der Hart et al.'s "apparently normal part
of the personality" to "Going On With Normal Life Self": "In avoid-
ing the words, 'apparently normal,' my goal is to emphasize the positive evolutionary function of parts of us driven to survive or persevere
and to challenge clients' tendencies to see their ability to function as a
'false self' and their trauma-related responses as the 'true self.'" Fisher,
Healing the Fragmented Selves of Trauma Survivors, 25.

111   *These parts are called fight, flight, freeze, attach-cry*: Fisher and van
der Hart et al. use "cry for help" but my therapist uses "attach-cry,"
which is what I'll use throughout.

112   *"To get up each morning and face death"*: Fisher, *Healing the Fragmented Selves*, 66.

112   *"Unsafe behaviors historically labeled 'self-destructive'"*: Fisher, *Healing the Fragmented Selves*, 13.

113   *"When we disown needs that can't be met"*: Fisher, *Healing the Fragmented Selves*, 66.

113   *"The discussion of safety is another topic"*: Fisher, *Healing the Fragmented Selves*, 122.

113   *"The research ultimately concluded that unresolved trauma"*: Kain
and Terrell, *Nurturing Resilience*, 49.

113   *"Epigenetically, disorganized attachment can be passed on"*: Kain and
Terrell, *Nurturing Resilience*, 50.

114   *"Because closeness and safety are intertwined when we are dependent"*: Fisher, *Healing the Fragmented Selves*, 133.

114–15 *"Reflects the relationship between a proximity-seeking attach part"*:
Fisher, *Healing the Fragmented Selves*, 133.

115   *I loved how they describe "being-femme"*: Fournier, "In Your Face."

118   *"Regulation is the term used to describe our ability to manage"*: Kain
and Terrell, *Nurturing Resilience*, 20.

118   *"Allow us to develop the early ability to self-regulate"*: Kain and Terrell, *Nurturing Resilience*, 22.

119   *The faux window requires the use of what Kain and Terrell call*: Kain
and Terrell, *Nurturing Resilience*, 90–91.

119   *"The most common error made by professionals and lay people"*:
Fisher, *Healing the Fragmented Selves*, 128–29.

121   *"Children don't get traumatized because they get hurt"*: *The Wisdom of Trauma*, directed by Maurizio Benazzo and Zaya Benazzo.

121   *"Interoception is the process by which we notice"*: Kain and Terrell, *Nurturing Resilience*, 26.

122   *"Whether an external event or person is pleasurable"*: Kain and Terrell, *Nurturing Resilience*, 27.

122   *"It's not shocking to me that difficulty with interoception"*: Kain and Terrell, *Nurturing Resilience*, 56.

122   *"Clients who lack a 'safety map' are primarily tuned"*: Kain and Terrell, *Nurturing Resilience*, 33.

123   *Our ability to distinguish between threat and danger*: Kain and Terrell, *Nurturing Resilience*, 33.

126   *"I understand femme connections as politically significant friendships"*: Schwartz, *Soft Femme*, 2.

126   *It is through these femmeships that I learned*: *Femmeship* is a term I first heard from Andi Schwartz, who cites Karina Hagelin as the femme who introduced her to the term.

126   *"A healthy sense of self and seeing themselves"*: Fern, *Polysecure*, 19–21.

127   *"Dopamine, produced by the hypothalamus"*: Wu, "Love, Actually."

127   *"Kids who are securely attached to their adult caregivers"*: Nagoski, *Come as You Are*, 116.

131   *I've read so many scholars' writings on queer temporality*: I'm going to resist the academic urge to give you a literature review here. Instead, I'll point you to some of the more canonical works that you can choose to explore, or not: Judith Halberstam's *In a Queer Time and Place: Transgender Bodies, Subcultural Lives*; Lee Edelman's *No Future: Queer Theory and the Death Drive*; Kathryn Bond Stockton's *The Queer Child, or Growing Sideways in the Twentieth Century*; José Esteban Muñoz's *Cruising Utopia: The Then and There of Queer Futurity*; Heather Love's *Feeling Backward: Loss and the Politics of Queer History*; and the special issue of *GLQ: Queer Temporalities*.

132   *"The body is an assemblage, a mass of everyone"*: Billy-Ray Belcourt, *This Wound Is a World*, 59.

132   *"The idea that survivorhood is a thing to 'fix' or 'cure'"*: Piepzna-Samarasinha, "Not Over It, Not Fixed, and Living a Life Worth Living," 226.

132   *"To imagine survivor futures where we are* thriving": Piepzna-Samarasinha, "Not Over It, Not Fixed, and Living a Life Worth Living," 232.

133   *"Long after internal attachment bonds have been established"*: Fisher, *Healing the Fragmented Selves*, 257.

SOFT MAGIC

139   *"What would you say, by the way, if I told you"*: Sigmund Freud to Wilhem Fliess, January 17, 1897, in *The Complete Letters of Sigmund Freud to Wilhem Fliess.*

140   *"I google spells to take the PTSD out of me"*: Washuta, *White Magic*, 12.

140   *"Every day, the universe reminds me"*: Washuta, *White Magic*, 8.

141   *Philosopher Silvia Federici explains that one of the most threatening aspects*: See Federici, *Caliban and the Witch*, and Federici, *Witches, Witch-Hunting and Women.*

141   *"The power to boldly and unapologetically embrace nature"*: Herstik, "Material Girl, Mystical World: The Hoodwitch."

141   *"You don't need to be fixed, my queens"*: Hedva, "Sick Woman Theory," Section 4.

141   *"What would it feel like to imagine we are destroying capitalism"*: Elizabeth, "Trash-Magic," 25.

142   *"A general orientation to the world that foregrounds vulnerability"*: Schwartz, "The Cultural Politics of Softness."

142   *"Softness is not 'showing up' as a temporary, band-aid solution"*: Schwartz, "The Cultural Politics of Softness."

142   *"Embodiment," writes Haines, "encourages us to keep growing"*: Haines, *The Politics of Trauma*, 10.

142   *"What do you want? What do you value?"*: Haines, *The Politics of Trauma*, 164.

146   *"For me, at this point in my life"*: Barthes, *Mourning Diary*, 133.

147   *"Diane Wolkstein argues as much when she writes"*: Wolkstein and Kramer, *Inanna*, 158.

147   *"Since I, thy daughter, was young, I have not known the play"*: Wolkstein and Kramer, *Inanna*, 158.

147   *"This underground goddess, whose realm is dry and dark"*: Wolkstein and Kramer, *Inanna*, 158.

148   *"Without realizing it, I fought to keep my two worlds separated"*: van der Hart, Nijenhuis, and Steele, *The Haunted Self*, 13.

149   *"The parts of self that have been given the worst jobs"*: Nicholas, "A Note from Chani on Venus Retrograde."

151   *"Anchoring is when we intentionally develop a root system"*: Mack, "Trauma and Tarot."

152   *For Bennett, objects have the power to act upon us*: Bennett, *Vibrant Matter*, 6.

152   *"How matter that is considered insensate, immobile, deathly"*: Chen, *Animacies*, 2.

152   *"Rewrite conditions of intimacy, engendering different communalisms"*: Chen, *Animacies*, 3.

161   *Story follows state, after all:* The words *story follows state* come from the work of Deb Dana who works in the field of Polyvagal Theory.

QUEER WOUNDS; OR WHAT WE OWE EACH OTHER

163   *"We will all mess up and make terrible mistakes"*: Mingus, "The Four Parts of Accountability & How to Give a Genuine Apology."

163   *"We will all hurt people we love and care about at some point"*: Mingus, "The Four Parts of Accountability & How to Give a Genuine Apology."

163   *And yet, not very many of these stories are out there*: A few notable exceptions are Melissa Febos's *Abandon Me* and Carmen Maria Machado's *In the Dream House*. These stories also exist in the pages of books about transformative justice, including the anthologies *The Revolution Starts at Home* and *Beyond Survival*, and Kai Cheng Thom's *I Hope We Choose Love*.

163   *"This is in part because there are so many fewer descriptions"*: Febos, *Body Work*, 61.

163   *Despite the fact that "all of us queers know that not all of our sex is healthy"*: Febos, *Body Work*, 62.

164   *"Queerness and abuse are both subjects that are typically thought"*: Levine, "Why Carmen Maria Machado Wrote a Memoir of Queer Domestic Abuse."

164   *"I enter into the archive that domestic abuse between partners"*: Machado, *In the Dream House*, 5.

164   *The organization Spring Up defines disagreement*: Spring Up, *Transformative Justice Workbook*, 5.

165   *Abuse "is the misuse of power to cross someone else's boundaries"*: Thom, "My Ex-Roommate Says I'm Abusive for Leaving My Dirty Dishes in the Sink. Do I Owe Them Accountability?"

165   *"Behaviors (physical, emotional, economic, sexual, and many more) intended to"*: brown, *We Will Not Cancel Us*, 27.

165   *"The suffering, loss, pain, and impact that can occur"*: brown, *We Will Not Cancel Us*, 28.

165   *"Harm is when the actions of a person (or people)"*: Spring Up, *Transformative Justice Workbook*, 5.

165   *"We are tracking for safety, adapting to belong"*: Haines, *The Politics of Trauma*, 133.

165   *"Safety gets created when your agency"*: Haines, *The Politics of Trauma*, 136.

165   *"Secure and vulnerable, authentic and without fear"*: Haines, *The Politics of Trauma*, 136.

166   *"Those who were able to avoid further rejection"*: "Rejection," *Good Therapy*.

166   *"We need to be part of the pack"*: Haines, *The Politics of Trauma*, 141.

166   *"When faced with shame, the brain reacts"*: Davis, "The Neuroscience of Shame."

166   *"Can result in permanently dysregulated autonomic functioning"*: Bradshaw, *Healing the Shame That Binds You*, quoted in Davis, "The Neuroscience of Shame."

167   *"As a community, we have a tendency to respond only to harm"*: Thom, *"I Hope We Choose Love*, 59.

167   *I'm grateful for the writing on queer intimate partner violence*: Namely, *The Revolution Starts at Home*; *Beyond Survival*; and *Queering Sexual Violence*.

168   *We proclaim that we just have to let the soft animal of our body*: The line "you only have to let the soft animal of your body love what it loves" comes from Mary Oliver's poem "Wild Geese."

168   *Sovereignty is the myth of neoliberal individualism*: Neoliberalism is a political stance that is invested in privatization (e.g., of healthcare), free market capitalism, and decreased government spending. Because of its investment in capitalism, neoliberalism is highly individualistic, meaning that it promotes a "pull yourself up by the bootstraps" mentality, placing the onus of success onto the individual. Neoliberalism does not promote community care or interdependence.

169   *The ghosts of shame and blame, and of their past*: Zhu, *Be Not Afraid of Love*, 105–06.

169   *"Even as our ghosts linger, they are there to remind us how potent"*: Zhu, *Be Not Afraid of Love*, 105–06.

170   *"Love, says cultural theorist Lauren Berlant, 'always means non-sovereignty'"*: Belcourt, *This Wound Is a World*, 58.

170   *"I smell sex in my hair when I awaken"*: de la Tierra, "Dreaming of Lesbos."

177   *They'd shared a post that read*: @theeqschool, posted on terricole, Instagram, December 15, 2023, https://www.instagram.com/terricole/p/C05RjGvotc6/.

178   *"I couldn't help but feel that C was subtweeting at me"*: A subtweet is a post (originating on Twitter, but that can be found on all social media platforms) that is directed at a particular person without directly mentioning them. Subtweets are usually a form of mockery or criticism, a passive-aggressive way of telling someone how you feel.

179   *As much as some folks on the radical left would like to believe*: In a conversation with my editor and friend Raechel Anne Jolie, she shared with me her observation that so many folks in anarchist and communist scenes aren't engaged in conversations about boundaries that recognize the nuances of boundary work within safe and supportive relationships. I see this reflected in online radical left spaces, on Instagram and other social media venues, particularly among those who identify as feminists, as queer, and as committed to mental health education and transformative justice.

180 *"Boundaries are the distance at which I can love you and me simultaneously"*: Prentis Hemphill (@prentishemphill), "A reminder," Instagram, April 5, 2021, http://instagram.com/p/CNSzFO1A21C/.

181 *Love bombing is bombarding someone*: Field, "What Is Love Bombing?"

181 *"Love bombing is largely an unconscious behavior"*: Kaplan, "Everything You Need to Know About Love Bombing and Why It's So Dangerous."

184 *"To transform the conditions of the 'wrongdoing,' we have to ask"*: brown, *Emergent Strategy*, 148.

184 *"In my mediations, 'Why?' is often the game-changing"*: brown, *Emergent Strategy*, 148.

185 *"When we are loving we openly and honestly express care"*: hooks, *All About Love*, 14.

185 *While it offered me some relief to read C's apology*: For more on apologies and accountability, see Mia Mingus's blog post "The Four Parts of Accountability & How to Give a Genuine Apology." For Mingus, an apology is one of the four parts of accountability (alongside self-reflection, changed behavior, and repair). I believe that our apologies must include these four elements in order to truly be apologies.

186 *For Mingus, a good apology includes the following*: Mingus, "The Four Parts of Accountability & How to Give a Genuine Apology."

186 *"Apologizing is part of accountability and accountability is a sacred practice"*: Mingus, "The Four Parts of Accountability & How to Give a Genuine Apology."

187 *Zhu, reflecting on the harm they caused*: Zhu, *Be Not Afraid of Love*, 111, 113.

189 *"As transmasculine folks in particular, we need to be"*: Pugh, "Re(Doing) Gender."

190 *"What if we rushed towards our own accountability"*: Mingus, "Dreaming Accountability."

194 *"Queerness is rarely complemented by evidence"*: Muñoz, *Cruising Utopia*, 65.

194 *"As trace, the remains, the things that are left hanging"*: Muñoz, *Cruising Utopia*, 65. Here Muñoz focuses on the queer ball scene. For an introduction into this world, watch the film *Paris Is Burning*. For

more contemporary examples, see the television series *Pose* and the ballroom competition show *Legendary*.

194   *"The body is an assemblage, a mass of everyone"*: Belcourt, *This Wound Is a World*, 59.

195   *Like adrienne maree brown, I want to dream beyond:* brown, "Dream Beyond the Wounds."

BIBLIOGRAPHY

AARDA. *The Cost Burden of Autoimmune Disease: The Latest Front in the War on Healthcare Spending*, 2011. http://www.diabetesed.net/page /_files/autoimmune-diseases.pdf.

After Globalism Writing Group. "Water as Protagonist." *Social Text* 134, vol. 36, no. 1 (2018): 15–23.

Alok. "Alok on Unruly Beauty/245." *For the Wild* podcast, hosted by Ayana Young, August 4, 2021. http://forthewild.world/listen/alok-on-unruly -beauty-245.

Angel, Katherine. *Tomorrow Sex Will Be Good Again: Women and Desire in the Age of Consent*. New York: Verso, 2021.

Anonymous. "anonymous contribution to the 'subgenre' of 'literary' 'essay' known as 'how i feel about marie calloway.'" *HTMLGIANT*, May 1, 2012. http://htmlgiant.com/reviews/anonymous-contribution-to-the -subgenre-of-literary-essay-known-as-how-i-feel-about-marie-calloway/.

Astrology Owl. "North Node (NN) in Taurus, Chiron in Taurus." January 5, 2021. http://astrologyowl.com/north-node-nn-in-taurus-chiron -in-taurus/.

Athanassoglou-Kallmyer, Nina. "Ugly." In *On the Politics of Ugliness*, edited by Sara Rodrigues and Ela Przybylo. New York: Palgrave Macmillan, 2018.

Barthes, Roland. *Mourning Diary*. New York: Farrar, Straus and Giroux, 2012.

Barton, R. M. "On Femininity and Being a Fierce, Autonomous, Radical, Queer Femme." *Wussy Magazine*, February 19, 2024. https://www .wussymag.com/all/on-femininity-and-being-a-fierce-autonomous-radical -queer-femme.

Belcourt, Billy-Ray. *This Wound Is a World*. Minneapolis: University of Minnesota Press, 2019.

Bellacasa, María Puig de la. *Matters of Care: Speculative Ethics in More Than Human Worlds*. Minnesota: University of Minnesota Press, 2017.

Benazzo, Maurizio and Zaya, dir. *The Wisdom of Trauma*. Science and Nonduality, 2021.

Bennett, Jane. *Vibrant Matter: A Political Ecology of Things*. Durham, NC: Duke University Press, 2010.

Berkowitz, Amy. *Tender Points*. Oakland, CA: Timeless Infinite Light, 2015.

Berlant, Lauren. *Cruel Optimism*. Durham, NC: Duke University Press, 2011.

———. *On the Inconvenience of Other People*. Durham, NC: Duke University Press, 2022.

Berlant, Lauren, and Lee Edelman. *Sex, or the Unbearable*. Durham, NC: Duke University Press, 2014.

Bourneville, Désiré Magloire, and Paul Regnard. *Etudes Cliniques Iconographie Photographique de la Salpêtrière*, vol. 1. Paris, 1877. https://www.archive.org/details/b21912865_0001/page/n5.

———. *Iconographie Photographique de la Salpêtrière*, vol. 2. Paris, 1878. https://www.archive.org/details/iconographiepho00regngoog.

Bradley, Ian. "Why Is 18th-Century Bath Considered the Model for Modern Day Spas?" *Lithub*, January 22, 2021. http://lithub.com/why-is-18th-century-bath-considered-the-model-for-modern-day-spas/.

Bradshaw, John. *Healing the Shame That Binds You*. Deerfield Beach, FL: HCI Books, 1988.

Braslow, Joel. *Mental Ills and Bodily Cures: Psychiatric Treatment in the First Half of the Twentieth Century*. Los Angeles: University of California Press, 1997.

Breiding, M. J., J. Chen, and M. C. Black. *Intimate Partner Violence in the United States*. National Center for Injury Prevention and Control, Centers for Disease Control and Prevention, 2014.

Brison, Susan. *Aftermath: Violence and the Remaking of a Self*. Princeton, NJ: Princeton University Press, 2002.

———. "'The Price We Pay'? Pornography and Harm." In *The Philosophy of Pornography*, 2014.

brown, adrienne maree. "Dream Beyond the Wounds." *Ding*. Accessed November 25, 2024. http://dingdingding.org/issue-2/dream-beyond-the-wounds/.

———. *Emergent Strategy: Shaping Change, Changing Worlds*. Chico, CA: AK Press, 2017.

———. *We Will Not Cancel Us: And Other Dreams of Transformative Justice*. Chica, CA: AK Press, 2020.

Brownmiller, Susan. *Against Our Will: Men, Women and Rape*. New York: Simon and Schuster, 1986.

Butler, Judith. *Giving an Account of Oneself.* New York: Fordham University Press, 2005.

Calloway, Marie. *what purpose did i serve in your life.* New York: Tyrant Books, 2013.

The Care Collective, *The Care Manifesto.* London: Verso Book, 2020.

Carson, Anne. *Eros the Bittersweet: An Essay.* Dallas: Dalkey Archive, 2022.

Carver, Lisa. "Marie Calloway on Her New Novel and Being Called 'Jailbait.'" *Vice,* June 26, 2013. http://vice.com/en/article/wdpw59/marie-calloway/.

Center for Disease Control. "Lesson 1: Introduction to Epidemiology, Section 11: Epidemic Disease Occurrence." CDC Archive, last reviewed May 18, 2012 (archived document). https://archive.cdc.gov/www_cdc_gov/csels/dsepd/ss1978/lesson1/section11.html.

Charcot, Jean-Martin. "Leçons sur les maladies du système nerveux." *Oeuvres completes.* Lectures in nine volumes collected and published by Bourneville, Babinski, Bernard, Féré, Guinon, Marie, Gilles de la Tourette, Brissaud, Sevestre. Paris, 1886–1893.

Chen, Ching-In, Jai Dulani, and Leah Lakshmi Piepzna-Samarasinha, eds. *The Revolution Starts at Home: Confronting Intimate Violence Within Activist Communities.* Chico, CA: AK Press, 2016.

Chen, Mel Y. *Animacies: Biopolitics, Racial Mattering, and Queer Affect.* Durham, NC: Duke University Press, 2012.

Chu, Andera Long. "On Liking Women." *N+1* (Winter 2018). http://nplusonemag.com/issue-30/essays/on-liking-women.

Cills, Hazel. "Marie Calloway's 'Adrien Brody.' Coming of Age: Millennials' Most Earth-Shaking Sexual Moments." *Rolling Stone,* March 31, 2014. http://www.rollingstone.com/culture/culture-lists/coming-of-age-millennials-most-earth-shaking-sexual-moments-22239/.

Coleman, Lindsay, and Jacob M. Held, eds. *Contemporary Perspectives.* Lanham, MD: Rowman and Littlefield, 2014.

Cruz, Ariane. *The Color of Kink: Black Women, BDSM, and Pornography.* New York: New York University Press, 2016.

Cruz, Cynthia. *Disquieting: Essays on Silence.* Toronto: Book*hug Press, 2019.

Dana, Deb. *The Polyvagal Theory in Therapy: Engaging the Rhythm of Regulation.* New York: W. W. Norton and Co., 2018.

Davis, Shiley. "The Neuroscience of Shame," CPTSD Foundation, April 11, 2019, http://cptsdfoundation.org/2019/04/11/the-neuroscience-of-shame/.

de la Tierra, Tatiana. "Dreaming of Lesbos," Poetry Foundation, http://poetryfoundation.org/poems/147272/dreaming-of-lesbos.

Devries, K. M., et al. "The Global Prevalence of Intimate Partner Violence Against Women." *Science* 340, no. 6140 (2013): 1527–28.

Didi-Huberman, Georges. *Invention of Hysteria: Charcot and the Photographic Iconography of the Salpêtrière*. Translated by Alisa Hartz. Cambridge, MA: MIT Press, 2003.

Dixon, Ejeris, and Leah Lakshmi Piepzna-Samarasinha, eds. *Beyond Survival: Strategies and Stories from the Transformative Justice Movement*. Chico, CA: AK Press, 2020.

Dombeck, Kristen. *The Selfishness of Others: An Essay on the Fear of Narcissism*. New York: Farrar, Straus, and Giroux, 2016.

Dowling, Emma. *The Care Crisis*. London: Verso Books, 2021.

Dusenbery, Maya. *Doing Harm: The Truth About How Bad Medicine and Lazy Science Leave Women Dismissed, Misdiagnosed, and Sick*. New York: Harper Collins, 2018.

———. "Regarding the Pain of Women." *Lithub*, March 29, 2018. lithub.com/regarding-the-pain-of-women.

Dworkin, Andrea. *Pornography: Men Possessing Women*. New York: Penguin, 1979.

Ehrenreich, Barbara, and Deirdre English. *Complaints and Disorders: The Sexual Politics of Sickness*. New York: Feminist Press at the City University of New York, 2011.

———. *Witches, Midwives, and Nurses: A History of Women Healers*. New York: Feminist Press at the City University of New York, 2010.

Elizabeth, Maranda. "Trash-Magic: Signs and Rituals for the Unwanted." In *Becoming Dangerous: Witchy Femmes, Queer Conjurers, and Magical Rebels*, edited by Katie West and Jasmine Elliott. Newburyport, MA: Red Wheel/Weiser, 2019.

Fassler, Joe. "How Doctors Take Women's Pain Less Seriously." *The Atlantic*, October 15, 2015. http://www.theatlantic.com/health/archive/2015/10/emergency-room-wait-time-sexism/410515.

Febos, Melissa. *Abandon Me*. New York: Bloomsbury USA, 2018.

———. *Body Work*. New York: Catapult, 2022.

———. *Girlhood*. New York: Bloomsbury Publishing, 2021.

Federici, Silvia. *Caliban and the Witch: Women, the Body and Primitive Accumulation*. Brooklyn, NY: Autonomedia, 2004.

———. *Witches, Witch-Hunting and Women*. Brooklyn, NY: Autonomedia, 2018.

Feldman, Margeaux. *Soft Magic*. Tangled Arts + Disability, Toronto, 2021. https://cripritual.com/feldman/.

Ferens, Dominika and Tomasz Sikora, eds. "Ugly Bodies: Queer Perspectives on Illness, Disability, and Aging." Special issue. *InterAlia: A Journal of Queer Studies* 11a (2016).

Fern, Jessica. *Polysecure: Attachment, Trauma and Consensual Nonmonogamy*. Vancouver Island: Thorntree Press, 2020.

Field, Allyson Nadia. "The Archive of Absence: Speculative Film History and Early African American Cinema." Paper presented at Humanities Day, University of Chicago, October 15, 2006.

Field, Barbara. "What Is Love Bombing?" *Verywell Mind*, April 13, 2022. http://verywellmind.com/what-is-love-bombing-5223611.

Fisher, Janina. *Healing the Fragmented Selves of Trauma Survivors: Overcoming Internal Self-Alienation*. New York: Routledge, 2017.

———. *Transforming the Living Legacy of Trauma*. Eau Claire, WI: PESI Publishing, 2021.

Fournier, Lauren. "In Your Face." *Canadian Art*, June 17, 2019. http://canadianart.ca/features/in-your-face.

Freud, Sigmund. "The Aetiology of Hysteria." *Standard Edition of the Complete Psychological Works*, Vol. 3. Translated by James Strachey. London: Hogarth Press, 1962.

———. *An Autobiographical Study*. Edited by James Strachey. New York: W. W. Norton and Co., 1963.

———. *The Complete Letters of Sigmund Freud to Wilhelm Fliess, 1887–1904*. Edited by Jeffrey Moussaieff Masson. Cambridge, MA: Belknap Press of Harvard University Press, 1985.

———. *Dora: An Analysis of a Case of Hysteria*. Introduction by Philip Rieff. Chicago: Touchstone Press, 1997.

———. *Three Essays on the Theory of Sexuality*. Translated by James Strachey. New York: Basic Books, 2000.

———. *Beyond the Pleasure Principle and Other Writings*. Translated by John Reddick. New York: Penguin Books, 2003.

Freud, Sigmund, and Joseph Breuer. *Studies in Hysteria*. Translated by Nicola Luckhurst. New York: Penguin Books, 2004.

Goldstein, Jan. *Hysteria Complicated by Ecstasy: The Case of Nanette Leroux*. Princeton, NJ: Princeton University Press, 2009.

Haines, Staci K. *The Politics of Trauma: Somatics, Healing, and Social Justice*. Berkeley, CA: North Atlantic Books, 2019.

hakim, kamra sadia. *care manual: dreaming care into being*. Detroit: Flower Press, 2022.

Hall, G. Stanley. *Adolescence: Its Psychology and Its Relations to Physiology, Anthropology, Sociology, Sex, Crime, Religion and Education*, Vol. 1. New York: D. Appleton and Company, 1907.

Hamilton, Anita. "American Apparel's 'Period Power' T-Shirt Lays Bare the Labia and Tackles a Taboo." *Time*, October 8, 2013. http://newsfeed.time.com/2013/10/08/american-apparels-period-power-t-shirt-lays-bare-the-labia-and-tackles-a-taboo/.

Hamraie, Aimi, Cassandra Hartblay, and Jarah Moesch. *#CripRitual*, 2022. https://cripritual.com/about-the-exhibition/.

Hand Habits. "yr heart." Track 1 on *yr heart*. Saddle Creek. Released 2017.

Hedva, Johanna. "Sick Woman Theory." *Mask Magazine*, January 19, 2016. http://www.maskmagazine.com/not-again/struggle/sick-woman-theory.

Herman, Judith. *Trauma and Recovery: The Aftermath of Violence—from Domestic Abuse to Political Terror*. New York: Basic Books, 2015.

Herstik, Gabriela. "Material Girl, Mystical World: The Hoodwitch." *The Numinous*, April 26, 2016. http://the-numinous.com/2016/04/26/the-hoodwitch.

hooks, bell. *All About Love*. New York: Harper, 1999.

Horwitz, Rainey. "Medical Vibrators for Treatment of Female Hysteria." *Embryo Project Encyclopedia*, February 29, 2020. http://embryo.asu.edu/pages/medical-vibrators-treatment-female-hysteria.

Human Rights Campaign Foundation. *An Epidemic of Violence: Fatal Violence Against Transgender and Gender Non-Conforming People in the United States in 2021*. HRC.org, 2021. https://reports.hrc.org/an-epidemic-of-violence-fatal-violence-against-transgender-and-gender-non-conforming-people-in-the-united-states-in-2021.

Hustvedt, Asti. *Medical Muses: Hysteria in Nineteenth-Century Paris*. London: Bloomsbury, 2011.

Jolie, Raechel Anne. "dangerous, life-giving, & impossible to withhold: radical love letter #43." *Substack*, August 12, 2020. https://raechelannejolie.substack.com/p/dangerous-life-giving-and-impossible.

Kain, Kathy L., and Stephen J. Terrell. *Nurturing Resilience: Helping Clients Move Forward from Developmental Trauma—An Integrative Somatic Approach*. Berkeley, CA: North Atlantic Books, 2018.

Kaplan, Ami. "Everything You Need to Know About Love Bombing and Why It's So Dangerous." *Cosmopolitan*, September 15, 2022. http://cosmopolitan.com/sex-love/a26988344/love-bombing-signs-definition/.

Keen, Andrew. *The Internet Is Not the Answer*. New York: Atlantic Monthly Press, 2015.

Khakpour, Porochista. *Sick: A Memoir*. New York: Harper Perennial, 2018.

Kipnis, Laura. "She-Male Fantasies and the Aesthetics of Pornography." In *Dirty Looks: Women, Pornography, Power*, edited by Pamela Church Gibson and Roma Gibson. London: British Film Institute, 1994.

Laplanche, Jean, and Jean-Bertrand Pontalis. *The Language of Psychoanalysis*. Boca Raton, FL: Routledge, 2018.

Levin, Adam. "The Selfie in the Age of Digital Recursiveness." *InVisible Culture* 20 (2014). https://doi.org/10.47761/494a02f6.f3a5894d.

Levin, Joanna. "Lady MacBeth and the Daemonologie of Hysteria." *ELH* 69, no. 1 (2002): 21–55.

Levine, Nick. "Why Carmen Maria Machado Wrote a Memoir of Queer Domestic Abuse." *AnOther Magazine*, January 8, 2020. http://another

mag.com/design-living/12174/carmen-maria-machado-in-the-dream
-house-memoir-interview.

Levine, Peter A. *Waking the Tiger: Healing Trauma*. Berkeley, CA: North
Atlantic Books, 1997.

Lorde, Audre. *The Cancer Journals*. San Francisco: Aunt Lute Books, 1997.

Lorentzen, Christian. "Sheila Heti, Ben Lerner, Tao Lin: How 'Auto' Is 'Aut-
ofiction'?" *Vulture*, May 11, 2018. http://www.vulture.com/2018/05
/how-auto-is-autofiction.html.

Machado, Carmen Maria. *In the Dream House: A Memoir*. Minneapolis:
Graywolf Press, 2019.

Mack, Lindsay. *Trauma and the Tarot*. Soul Tarot School. http://www.soul
tarotschool.com.

Manguso, Sarah. *The Two Kinds of Decay: A Memoir*. New York: Picador,
2009.

Marche, Stephen. "The New Bad Kids of Fiction." *Esquire*, June 10, 2013.
http://www.esquire.com/entertainment/books/a23000/marie-calloway
-tao-lin/.

Marshall, Jonathan W. *Performing Neurology: The Dramaturgy of Dr. Jean-
Martin Charcot*. New York: Palgrave Macmillan, 2016.

Maté, Gabor. *When the Body Says No: The Cost of Hidden Stress*. Toronto:
Vintage Canada, 2003.

McCain, Jessica L., Zachary G. Borg, Ariel H. Rothenberg, Kristina M.
Churillo, Paul Weiler, and W. Keith Campbell. "Personality and Selfies: Narcissism and the Dark Triad." *Computers in Human Behavior*
64 (2016): 126–33.

Mingus, Mia. "Dreaming Accountability." *Leaving Evidence* (blog), May 5,
2019. http://www.leavingevidence.wordpress.com/2019/05/05
/dreaming-accountability-dreaming-a-returning-to-ourselves-and
-each-other.

———. "Moving Toward the Ugly: A Politic Beyond Desirability." *Leaving
Evidence* (blog), August 22, 2011. http://www.leavingevidence.word
press.com/2011/08/22/moving-toward-the-ugly-a-politic-beyond
-desirability/.

———. "The Four Parts of Accountability & How to Give a Genuine
Apology," *Leaving Evidence* (blog), December 18, 2019. http://www
.leavingevidence.wordpress.com/2019/12/18/how-to-give-a-good
-apology-part-1-the-four-parts-of-accountability/.

Molotkow, Alexandra. "Marie Calloway, Degrading Sex, and Books About
It." *Hazlitt*, June 11, 2013. http://www.hazlitt.net/feature/marie
-calloway-degrading-sex-and-books-about-it.

Moore, Anne Elizabeth. *Body Horror: Capitalism, Fear, Misogyny, Jokes*.
Chicago: Curbside Splendor Publishing, 2017.

Morse, Nicole Erin. *Selfie Aesthetics: Seeing Trans Feminist Futures in Self-Representational Art*. Durham, NC: Duke University Press, 2022.

Muñoz, José Esteban. *Cruising Utopia: The Then and There of Queer Futurity*. Durham, NC: Duke University Press, 2009.

Murray, Derek Conrad. "Notes to Self: The Visual Culture of Selfies in the Age of Social Media." *Consumption Markets and Culture* 18, no. 6 (2015): 490–516.

Nagoski, Emily. *Come as You Are: The Surprising New Science That Will Transform Your Sex Life*. New York: Simon and Schuster, 2015.

National Center for Transgender Equality. "Murders of Transgender People in 2020 Surpasses Total for Last Year in Just Seven Months." TransEquality.org, August 7, 2020. http://www.transequality.org/blog /murders-of-transgender-people-in-2020-surpasses-total-for-last-year -in-just-seven-months.

Nelson, Maggie. *The Argonauts*. Minneapolis: Graywolf Press, 2015.

———. *On Freedom: Four Songs of Care and Constraint*. New York: McClelland and Stewart, 2021.

Ngai, Sianne. *Ugly Feelings*. Cambridge, MA: Harvard University Press, 2005.

Nicholas, Chani. "A Note from Chani on Venus Retrograde." *Chani* (newsletter), January 4, 2023. http://chaninicholas.com/a-note-from-chani -on-venus-retrograde/.

———. *You Were Born for This*. San Francisco: HarperOne, 2020.

Nolan, Hamilton. "Girl, Microfamed." *Gawker*, December 21, 2011. http:// www.gawker.com/5870033/girl-microfamed.

Orange, Michelle. "Men Respond to Marie: The Titillating, Frustrating Debut by Online Lit's *Enfant Terrible*." *Slate*, June 7, 2013. http://www .slate.com/culture/2013/06/marie-calloway-what-purpose-did-i -serve-in-your-life-is-a-titillating-frustrating-debut.html.

O'Rourke, Meghan. "The Mysteries of Chronic Illness." Speech, Harvard University, Cambridge, MA, December 17, 2014. http://youtube.com /watch?v=rEGTvgaPQhg&t=11s.

———. "What's Wrong with Me?" *New Yorker*, August 26, 2013. http:// www.newyorker.com/magazine/2013/08/26/whats-wrong-with-me.

Paasonen, Susanna. "Diagnoses of Transformation: 'Pornification,' Digital Media, and the Diversification of the Pornographic." In *The Philosophy of Pornography: Contemporary Perspectives*, edited by Lindsay Coleman and Jacob M. Held. Lanham, MD: Rowman and Littlefield, 2014.

Palmer, Abi. *Sanatorium*. London: Penned in the Margins, 2020.

———. "Wellness Is a Seductive Lie—and It Is Changing How We Treat Illness," *The Guardian*, June 22, 2020, http://theguardian.com/books /2020/jun/22/wellness-is-a-seductive-lie-abi-palmer-sanatorium.

Patsavas, Alyson. "Recovering a Cripistemology of Pain: Leaky Bodies, Connective Tissue, and Feeling Discourse." *Journal of Literary and Cultural Disability Studies* 8, no. 2 (2014): 203–18.

Patterson, Jennifer. *Queering Sexual Violence: Radical Voices from Within the Anti-Violence Movement.* New York: Riverdale Avenue Books, 2016.

Pennacchia, Robyn. "Dear National Review Guy Who Wrote an Open Letter to the 'Cat Person' Girl. . . ." *Wonkette*, December 14, 2017. http://www.wonkette.com/dear-national-review-guy-who-wrote-an-open-letter-to-the-cat-person-girl.

Peters, Torrey. *Detransition, Baby.* New York: Penguin Random House, 2021.

Petro, Melissa. "In Defense of Marie Calloway." *xoJane*, February 29, 2012.

Phillips, Adam. "Against Self-Criticism." *London Review of Books*, March 5, 2015. http://www.lrb.co.uk/v37/n05/adam-phillips/against-self-criticism.

———. *Becoming Freud: The Making of a Psychoanalyst.* New Haven, CT: Yale University Press, 2014.

Piepzna-Samarasinha, Leah Lakshmi. *Care Work: Dreaming Disability Justice.* Vancouver: Arsenal Pulp Press, 2018.

Porges, Stephen. "The Polyvagal Theory: New Insights into Adaptive Reactions of the Autonomic Nervous System." *Cleveland Journal of Medicine* 76, no. 2 (2009): 86–90.

Puar, Jasbir K. *The Right to Maim.* Durham, NC: Duke University Press, 2017.

Pugh, Aleo. "Re(Doing) Gender: Trans Men and the Reproduction of Toxic Masculinity," *Urge*, February 21, 2017, http://urge.org/redoing-gender-trans-men-and-the-reproduction-of-toxic-masculinity/.

Radical Access Mapping Project. "What Happens When We Can't Live Interdependency All the Time?" November 9, 2015. http://www.radicalaccessiblecommunities.wordpress.com/2015/11/09/what-happens-when-it-feels-like-we-cant-live-interdependency-all-the-time/.

Ratcliffe, Jane. "Sick: An Interview with Porochista Khakpour." *Tin House*, June 4, 2018. http://tinhouse.com/sick-an-interview-with-porochista-khakpour.

"Rejection." *Good Therapy*, March 7, 2019. http://www.goodtherapy.org/learn-about-therapy/issues/rejection.

Rettberg, Jill W. *Seeing Ourselves Through Technology: How We Use Selfies, Blogs, and Wearable Devices to See and Shape Ourselves.* New York: Palgrave MacMillan, 2014.

Rodrigues, Sara, and Ela Przybylo, eds. *On the Politics of Ugliness.* New York: Palgrave Macmillan, 2018.

Rodríguez, Juana María. "Queer Sociality and Other Sexual Fantasies." *GLQ: A Journal of Lesbian and Gay Studies* 17, no. 2–3 (2011): 331–48.

————. *Sexual Futures, Queer Gestures, and Other Latina Longings*. New York: New York University Press, 2014.

Roiphe, Katie. *The Morning After: Sex, Fear, and Feminism on Campus*. Boston: Little, Brown, 1994.

Romano, Cesare. *Freud and the Dora Case: A Promise Betrayed*. London: Karnac Books, 2015.

Rose, Chloë Brushwood, and Anna Camilleri, eds. *Brazen Femme: Queering Femininity*. Vancouver: Arsenal Pulp Press, 2003.

Roupenian, Kristen. *You Know You Want This: "Cat Person" and Other Stories*. New York: Scout Press, 2019.

Royal College of Physicians of Edinburgh. "Bathing by Prescription: A Brief History of Treatment by Water," September 16, 2015. https://www.rcpe.ac.uk/heritage/heritage-blog/bathing-prescription-brief-history-treatment-water.

Rubin, Gayle. "Thinking Sex: Notes for a Radical Theory of the Politics of Sexuality." In *Deviations: A Gayle Rubin Reader*. Durham, NC: Duke University Press, 2011.

Samuels, Ellen. *Fantasies of Identification: Disability, Gender, Race*. New York: New York University Press, 2014.

Sappho and Anne Carson. *If not, winter: fragments of Sappho*. New York: Vintage Books, 2002.

Schwartz, Andi. "The Cultural Politics of Softness." *GUTS: A Canadian Feminist Magazine*, December 27, 2018. http://gutsmagazine.ca/the-cultural-politics-of-softness/.

————. *Soft Femme III: Femmeship* (zine). Toronto. 2021.

Schwartz, Richard C. *No Bad Parts: Healing Trauma and Restoring Wholeness with the Internal Family Systems Model*. Boulder, CO: Sounds True, 2021.

Senft, Theresa M., and Nancy K. Baym. "What Does the Selfie Say? Investigating a Global Phenomenon." *International Journal of Communication* 9, no. 22 (2015): 1588–1606.

Showalter, Elaine. "Hysteria, Feminism, and Gender." In *Hysteria Beyond Freud*, edited by Sander L. Gilman et al. Berkeley: University of California Press, 1993.

Schulman, Sarah. *Conflict Is Not Abuse: Overstating Harm, Community Responsibility, and the Duty of Repair*. Vancouver: Arsenal Pulp Press, 2016.

Siebers, Tobin. *Disability Aesthetics*. Ann Arbor: University of Michigan Press, 2010.

Sisley, Dominique. "Petra Collins Takes On Mental Health in New Show." *Dazed Magazine*, April 7, 2016. http://www.dazeddigital.com/photography/article/30666/1/petra-collins-takes-on-mental-health-in-new-show.

Smith, Kyle. "Dear Cat-Person Girl." *National Review*, December 13, 2017. http://www.nationalreview.com/2017/12/pervasive-culture-sex -drunkeness-regret/.

Spade, Dean. *Mutual Aid: Building Solidarity During this Crisis (and the Next)*. London: Verso Books, 2020.

Spencer, Ruth. "Lucy DeCoutere on the Trauma of the Jian Ghomeshi Trial: 'After Everything I Went Through, Jian Is Free.'" *The Guardian*, March 25, 2016. http://www.theguardian.com/world/2016/mar/25 /jian-ghomeshi-trial-lucy-de-coutere-interview.

Spiers, Elizabeth. "But Is It Good? The Problem with Marie Calloway's Affectless Realism." *Flavourwire*, June 18, 2013. http://www.flavorwire .com/398643/but-is-it-good-the-problem-with-marie-calloways -affectless-realism.

Srinivasan, Amia. *The Right to Sex: Feminism in the Twenty-First Century*. New York: Farrar, Straus and Giroux, 2021.

Suler, John. "From Self-Portraits to Selfies." *International Journal of Applied Psychoanalytic Studies* 12, no. 2 (2015): 175–80.

Tanenbaum, Leora. *Slut!* New York: Harper Perennial, 2020.

Tembeck, Tamar. "Selfies of Ill Health: Online Autopathographic Photography and the Dramaturgy of the Everyday." *Social Media and Society* 1 (January–March 2016): 1–11.

Thom, Kai Cheng. *I Hope We Choose Love: A Trans Girl's Notes from the End of the World*. Vancouver, BC: Arsenal Pulp Press, 2019.

———. "My Ex-Roommate Says I'm Abusive for Leaving My Dirty Dishes in the Sink. Do I Owe Them Accountability?" *Xtra Magazine*, March 15, 2022, http://xtramagazine.com/love-sex/relationships/roommate -conflict-219744A.

Traister, Rebecca. "Why Sex That's Consensual Can Still Be Bad. And Why We're Not Talking About It." *The Cut*, October 20, 2015. http://www .thecut.com/2015/10/why-consensual-sex-can-still-be-bad.html.

van der Hart, Onno, Ellert R. S. Nijenhuis, and Kathy Steele. *The Haunted Self: Structural Dissociation and the Treatment of Chronic Traumatization*. London: W. W. Norton, 2006.

van der Kolk, Bessel. *The Body Keeps the Score: Brain, Mind, and Body in the Healing of Trauma*. New York: Penguin Books, 2014.

Walker, Melissa. "The Good, the Bad, and the Unexpected Consequences of Selfie Obsession." *Teen Vogue*, August 6, 2013. http://www.teenvogue .com/story/selfie-obsession.

Walusinski, Oliver, Jacques Poirier, and Hubert Déchy. "Augustine." *European Neurology* 69 (2013): 226–28.

Wang, Esmé Weijun. "'Subject Was Seen Laughing': A P.I. Insurance Surveillance Report," *The Toast*, October 27, 2015. http://www.the-toast .net/2015/10/27/insurance-surveillance-report/.

———. *The Collected Schizophrenias: Essays*. Minneapolis: Graywolf Press, 2019.

Ward, Dana. "A Kentucky of Mothers." *PEN America*, January 22, 2014.

Washuta, Elissa. *White Magic: Essays*. Portland, OR: Tin House, 2021.

Weil, Simone. *The Simone Weil Reader*. G. A. Panichas, ed. New York: Dorset Press, 1981.

Weiser, E. B. "#Me: Narcissism and Its Facets as Predictors of Selfie-Posting Frequency." *Personality and Individual Differences* 86 (2015): 477–81.

Willis, Ellen. "Lust Horizons: Is the Women's Movement Pro-Sex?" In *No More Nice Girls: Countercultural Essays*. Minneapolis: University of Minnesota Press, 2012.

Wolkstein, Diane, and Samuel Kramer. *Inanna: Queen of Heaven and Earth: Her Hymns and Stories*. New York: Harper Collins, 1983.

World Health Organization et al. *Global and Regional Estimates of Violence Against Women: Prevalence and Health Effects of Intimate Partner Violence and Non-Partner Sexual Violence*, 2013. https://www.who .int/publications/i/item/9789241564625.

Wu, Katherine. "Love, Actually: The Science Behind Lust, Attraction, and Companionship." *Science in the News*, February 14, 2017.

Wunker, Erin. *Notes from a Feminist Killjoy: Essays on Everyday Life*. Toronto: Book*hug, 2016.

Zhu, Mimi. *Be Not Afraid of Love: Lessons on Fear, Intimacy, and Connection*. London: Penguin Random House, 2022.

ABOUT THE AUTHOR

Margeaux Feldman is a writer, a public educator, and an artist. They hold an MFA in creative writing from CalArts and a PhD in English literature and sexual diversity studies from the University of Toronto. Margeaux's essays have been published in the *Sonora Review*, *GUTS: A Canadian Feminist Magazine*, *PRISM*, *Rabble*, and *The Ex-Puritan*, amongst others. They also created the online community Softcore Trauma, where they share memes and writing that testifies to their experiences living with trauma and chronic illness. They currently live in Los Angeles with their two elderly cats. You can learn more about them on their website www.margeaux feldman.com and read new writing from them in their newsletter *CARESCAPES* at www.carescapes.substack.com.